374
57

REPORT NO. 6

WELFARE AND STRIKES

The Use of Public Funds to Support Strikers

by

ARMAND J. THIEBLOT, JR.

and

RONALD M. COWIN

Foreword by HERBERT R. NORTHRUP

HD
6508
T44

Published by

INDUSTRIAL RESEARCH UNIT
Wharton School of Finance and Commerce
University of Pennsylvania

Distributed by

University of Pennsylvania Press
Philadelphia, Pennsylvania 19104

195994

Foreword

In 1968, the Industrial Research Unit inaugurated its Labor Relations and Public Policy monographs as a means of examining issues and stimulating discussions in the complex and controversial areas of collective bargaining and the regulation of labor-management disputes. The first four studies in the series dealt with aspects of the National Labor Relations Act and its administration. The fifth report contained papers read at the fiftieth anniversary conference of the Industrial Research Unit, at which many aspects of labor relations and public policy were discussed. This monograph—Report No. 6 in the series—breaks new ground. It is the first empirical analysis of the impact of government payments to strikers on the American collective bargaining system and on the settlements of disputes under that system.

Organized labor's drive to achieve greater bargaining power, through such mechanisms as coalition bargaining, union mergers, and the development of stronger, unified national and international federations, has created a number of problems for union officials. One of the most significant is the cost of a massive walkout. In order to sustain their drive for larger bargaining units, union officials must promise the rank and file great gains, a factor which can give rise to stronger management resistance and to higher strike incidence. Since strikes on these issues are likely to last a considerable period and involve a large number of persons, the cost of maintaining them can be enormous.

To accomplish their strike objectives, union leaders must be able to protect members from severe economic pain during prolonged labor-management disputes. Various tactics have been developed by organized labor to achieve this goal while at the same time attempting to minimize the financial impact of strikes on union treasuries. One such tactic is the selective strike strategy, where, for example, a union strikes only the key plants of a large firm instead of the entire operation. Another tactic, which has become increasingly important to unions in recent years, is to incorporate public and private welfare funds (from such programs as Food Stamps, Aid to Families with Dependent Children, General Assistance, and Unemployment Insurance) into the union's strike assistance program. The General Electric strike of 1969-1970 (involving almost 150,000 workers), where it is estimated that about $25 million in public welfare was distributed to strikers, and the General Motors strike of 1970 (involving nearly 330,000 workers), where an estimated $30 million in public aid was dispensed to strikers, provide dramatic examples. Such strategy involving the use of public funds to subsidize union strike efforts is the subject of this book by Dr. Armand J. Thieblot and Mr. Ronald M. Cowin.

Considerable interest regarding the payment of public aid to strikers did not begin developing until the copper industry strike of 1967-1968. This strike, involving a coalition of unions against an entire industry, lasted nearly nine months. During it, striking copper miners in communities of Arizona, Montana, Nevada, New Mexico, and Utah were reported using various forms of welfare to sustain their walkout. By the end of the 1969-1970 General Electric strike, where the public strike assistance mentioned above was used, this interest had developed into great concern. By then it was obvious that if strikes become injurious only to one party (management) because the other party (labor) is being subsidized by the government, a strike will not serve its purpose of inducing a reasonable settlement. In such situations, collective bargaining could cease and union dictation of terms and conditions of employment occur instead, with unreasonable and inflationary settlements the likely result. In addition, concern has been expressed that public policies which permit strikers to obtain welfare could have serious financial impacts on government and the taxpaying public and add additional burdens to our already troubled welfare system.

While the General Motors strike was occurring, an interesting case was being litigated. A strike by the Teamsters' Union against a division of the International Telephone and Telegraph Company (ITT) in Massachusetts causes the company to file a suit in federal district court demanding that this Commonwealth be enjoined from distributing welfare payments to strikers. Counsel for ITT argued that such payments were an unfair and illegal intrusion by a state in the area of collective bargaining which the federal government had preempted by the Taft-Hartley Act. ITT's case rested on the assumption that welfare payments to strikers encouraged the strikers to remain on strike and discouraged the union from compromising its demands, and, therefore, interfered with the federal policy of free collective bargaining. The district court dismissed the case.

The Court of Appeals, First Circuit, affirmed the lower court,* but in its opinion appeared quite troubled by its lack of information. It noted that ITT was making a novel claim which had not heretofore been considered either in welfare or labor law. The Court of Appeals opinion then set forth the empirical knowledge that it would have desired in order to rule on ITT's claim of injury by virtue of welfare payments to strikers:

> . . . how many states permit strikers to receive welfare; whether or not strikes tend to be of longer duration where welfare is received; and studies or expert testimony evaluating the impact of eligibility for benefits on the strikers' resolve; a comparison between strike benefits and welfare benefits; the impact of the requirement that welfare recipients accept suitable employment; how many strikers actually do receive welfare benefits; and a host of other factors. In addition, the state's legitimate interests must also be considered: its interests in minimizing hardships to the families of strikers who have no other resources than the weekly pay check, its concern in avoiding conditions that could lead to violence, its interest in forestalling economic stagnation in local communities, etc.

Nowhere was the evidence gathered which could answer these intriguing questions. This is precisely what this study attempts to do. Dr. Thieblot and Mr. Cowin, who commenced their research in late 1970, also endeavored to determine whether public money support to taxpayers is becoming a pervasive phenomenon or whether it is confined to major strikes or to particular areas. Their study included a careful analysis of literature, detailed interviews with company, union, and welfare officials, and several case studies in which interviews were sought with management and union participants and local welfare officials, and in which newspaper and other local sources of information were carefully studied. The conclusions, for which the authors are solely responsible, are based upon the empirical information reported in this carefully documented study.

*   *   *   *

This study is divided into three parts. Part One (Chapters I and II) is basically introductory. Chapter I summarizes the

---

* *ITT Division* v. *Minter*, 435 F.2d 989 (1st Cir., 1970); cert. denied, 420 U.S. 933 (1971).

nature of welfare programs which are now available to strikers; Chapter II explains the theory of how the American collective bargaining system is supposed to work and, particularly, what is the role of the strike in making collective bargaining an effective dispute settling and wage settling mechanism. Chapter II then examines theoretically what might be expected to occur if strikers receive tax supported funds.

Part Two (Chapters III-VI) deals with the empirical evidence: how tax supported payments to strikers first occurred and developed since the New Deal of the 1930's and a series of case studies which answer, with a wealth of factual material, the questions posed by the court in *ITT Division* v. *Minter,* and which as well point up other problems and issues.

The final part (Chapters VII, VIII, and IX) weighs the various arguments, including those presented in recent court cases, and presents the conclusions and recommendations of the authors. Appendix A presents a description of the most important of the public aid programs available to strikers, expanding on the discussion in Chapter I; Appendix B presents union documents.

*   *   *   *

It will be obvious to anyone reading this study that it could not have been written without the unstinting help of numerous company, union, and welfare officials, including those at both national and at local plant, union, and welfare agency levels. This we gratefully acknowledge. The authors would especially like to express their appreciation to their wives, Bernice and Diane, for the assistance and encouragement which they provided.

The typing was done by Mrs. Veronica M. Kent and the Misses Nancy Von and Rebecca Giles. The manuscript was edited and the index prepared by Mrs. Marie R. Keeney, and data construction was assisted by Miss Elsa Klemp and Mr. Michael Johns. Mrs. Margaret E. Doyle, Administrative Assistant of the Industrial Research Unit, handled the numerous administrative duties associated with the project. This study was financed by a fund for general Industrial Research Unit research donated by four industrial foundations and thirteen companies.

Dr. Armand J. Thieblot, Associate Professor of Management, College of Business and Public Administration, University of Maryland, did his undergraduate work at Princeton and received his MBA and Ph.D. degrees at the University of Pennsylvania. He is the author of *The Negro in the Banking Industry* and co-author of *Negro Employment in Finance.* Mr. Ronald M. Cowin received his undergradute degree at the University of Oregon, spent four years in the Marine Corps, where he reached the rank of Captain, and is scheduled to receive his MBA from Pennsylvania's Wharton School in May 1972.

HERBERT R. NORTHRUP, *Director*
Industrial Research Unit
Wharton School of Finance and Commerce
University of Pennsylvania

Philadelphia
April 1972

TABLE OF CONTENTS

Kimberly-Clark Corporation Strikes 152

  Munising, Michigan 152
  Niagara, Wisconsin 153

Leeds and Northrup Company Strike 156

  Strike Assistance Program 157
  Use of Welfare Assistance 158
  Union Viewpoint 167
  Management Viewpoint 169
  Welfare Agency Viewpoint 170
  Summary 172

California and Hawaiian Sugar Company Strike 173

New York Telephone Strike 175

Weyerhaeuser Company Northwest Pulp and Paper-
  board Strike 177

Concluding Remarks 177

PART THREE   ANALYSIS, CONCLUSIONS, AND REC-
  OMMENDATIONS

VII. COST ESTIMATES AND POSSIBLE BENEFITS 189

  Cost-Benefit Comparisons 189

    Dollar Costs 190
    Indirect Costs 194
    Total of Direct and Indirect Cost 196
    Imputed Costs 197
    Cost Summary 198
    Benefits 199

  Benefits and Costs Compared 201

VIII. DO STRIKERS HAVE A "RIGHT" TO WELFARE? 202

  The Moral "Right" to Welfare—The Pro-Arguments
    Considered 202

    Taxpayers' Rights 203
    Starving Children 204
    Company Subsidies 205
    Industrial Peace 206

LIST OF TABLES

LIST OF FIGURES

PART ONE

Introduction

Description of Welfare Programs Available to Striking Workers and the Impact of Welfare in Terms of the Nature of Collective Bargaining

CHAPTER I

Tax Supported Programs
Available for Strikers

Supporting strikers on a widespread basis with public welfare funds is a relatively recent phenomenon. Although instances of public support for strikers are occasionally found as long ago as the New Deal and such funds were used in the steel industry strike in 1959-60, these were isolated instances. It remained for the strikes of the late 1960's and early 1970's to establish the current trend of increasing use of public welfare in strikes. Recent strikes against General Motors, Westinghouse, International Telephone and Telegraph, most other major strikes, and many minor ones have been characterized by welfare payments to strikers. As this trend continues, the direct costs involved in an increasing amount of public support to an increasing proportion of strikers will be substantial. In addition, the structure of welfare payments, the length and settlement terms of strikes, the relative bargaining power of the participants in labor disputes, and the level of inflation and taxes in the country as a whole are likely to be affected to a greater or lesser degree, even assuming that wage and price boards operate effectively.

How this situation came about, how it works in practice, and what have been, and promise to continue to be, the implications thereof are all discussed in subsequent chapters. But to understand what is involved both for the welfare programs which are being utilized as strike benefits and for the institution of collective bargaining which is being vitally affected, it is necessary to understand the nature and content of these programs, and how the collective bargaining system works. This chapter briefly summarizes the structure and costs of the welfare system and the welfare programs available to strikers;[1] Chapter II

---

[1] A fuller explanation of the Aid to Families with Dependent Children, Food Stamp, and Unemployment Compensation programs is found in Appendix A.

examines the nature of collective bargaining and the role of
the strike.

STRUCTURAL COMPLICATION IN THE
WELFARE SYSTEM

Social welfare payments, public assistance, and relief reflect a
heritage going back to Elizabethan England and in some degree
to ancient Rome. Most of the specific programs now being used
in this country find their antecedents in the activities of an individual or group espousing the cause of some neglected or un-
fortunate aspect of society and seeking publicly financed relief
for its miseries. These causes, at various stages of our country's
history, were typically undertaken first on the private, then the
local, then state, then national level, thus creating an administrative stratification which is still reflected today. Political and
administrative stratification has greatly complicated the structure of public assistance and social welfare programs.

Further complications arose from what was generally held
until the New Deal period of the 1930's to be a lack of constitutional mandate, either federal or state, to provide welfare.
Much of the social legislation of the 1930's, which continues to
be the basis of current programs, was drafted to circumvent
this difficulty. One effect was that, although the federal government felt it could compel state action in certain directions—
toward an unemployment insurance program, for example—it
could not compel specific action within the rather broad outlines
laid down. Thus, the programs vary greatly from state to state.
Somewhat later, when federal pressures associated with social
reforms were sufficient to insure that at least some programs
were adopted uniformly by the states, this problem was amelio-
rated but not completely relieved.

Finally, social welfare and public assistance programs have
become so pervasive that overlaps exist and administrative re-
sponsibilities are fuzzy at each level of government. At the
federal level, for example, many of the agencies consolidated
with the Department of Health, Education and Welfare continue to operate semiautonomously, and other major administrations, including the Department of Labor, the Department of
Agriculture, and the Department of Defense, oversee significant
programs. It is little wonder that in a system this complex a
concerted effort has succeeded in discovering the means of
providing strikers with access to some welfare programs.

Overall Cost of Social Welfare

The social welfare system is not only complex, it is also expensive. Discounting price changes, per capita social welfare expenditures in 1966 were 600 percent greater than in 1929, and more than twice as great as in fiscal year 1950. Between 1966 and 1971, total outlays doubled again, and totalled $170.7 billion in 1971. Table 1 shows this most recent rise, and the nature of spending in 1971. At that time, the total welfare system was 51.2 percent of all government expenditures.

TABLE 1. *Expenditures for Social Welfare*
Federal and State and Local Outlays
1971

Type of Program	Federal	State and Local	Total
		(in billions)	
Social insurance	$53.6	$12.5	$ 66.1
Social security	35.2	—	35.2
Medicare	7.9	—	7.9
Public employees' retirement	6.4	3.6	10.0
Unemployment insurance and employment services	1.6	5.1	6.7
Other	2.5	3.8	6.3
Public aid	13.1	8.7	21.8
Medical programs	5.3	5.3	10.6
Veterans' benefits	10.3	0.1	10.4
Education	6.5	49.1	55.6
Housing	0.8	0.1	0.9
Other programs	2.8	2.5	5.3
1971 Total	$92.4	$78.3	$170.7
1966 Total	$45.4	$42.6	$ 88.0

Source: *U.S. News & World Report*, January 3, 1972, p. 43.

Social welfare expenditures are requiring an increasing proportion of the gross national product. In each succeeding year except three since the end of World War II, a higher proportion of gross national product has been devoted to this purpose. In 1968, the percentage surpassed the 1936 depression peak, and in each year since then it has set a new record, despite the overall high level of prosperity. In 1971, social welfare expenditures were 16.9 percent of the gross national product.[2]

DEFINITIONS OF WELFARE

It is important to note that "welfare" as used in this book is a broader concept than "relief," as that term was used during the 1930's, and also includes more than is commonly implied when used by the popular press. Indeed, welfare is such a far-ranging concept that there are no official terms consistently used in the literature of the field to define it; the best understanding can probably be derived from the generic use to mean whatever forms of public assistance services are under current discussion. This book will often follow the generic understanding and use "welfare" interchangeably with "public assistance" in that way. There is, however, much to be learned from classifying welfare programs by function, funding, or administration. This can be done in numerous ways,[3] but a very useful one is a classification which categorizes programs as social insurance or public aid. These are the major paths followed in establishing welfare programs to meet their common goal of shielding classes of individuals from various economic risks or perils, or providing special benefits to designated groups.

---

[2] U.S. Department of Health, Education and Welfare, Social Security Administration, *Social Welfare Expenditures Under Public Programs in the United States, 1929-1966*, Office of Research and Statistics, Research Report No. 25, and *U.S. News and World Report*, June 7, 1970, p. 43.

[3] See, for example, U.S. Department of Health, Education and Welfare, Social Security Administration, *Statistical Supplement*, 1965, which differentiates the broad programs at the federal level, or California Legislature, Senate Social Welfare Subcommittee of General Research, *A Study of Welfare Expenditures*, California Legislature, Vol. XXI, No. 15 (Sacramento: Senate of the State of California, 1969), pp. 15-19, which provides a further (and different) breakdown of federal programs and reviews in detail the twenty-seven major welfare programs which are at least partially administered, supervised, or subject to review by some nine relevant California state agencies.

Social Insurance

Social insurance is a term which is applied to those welfare programs which provide income maintenance or other benefits as a shield against the economic hazards of old age, disability, loss of employment, death, and the costs of ill health. Some sort of contributory or prepayment arrangements are necessary, and so these benefits are deemed an earned right. No means tests are necessary to receive benefits, but the recipients may be called upon to demonstrate other qualifications, such as past employment or contributions, to be eligible.

Social insurance programs may be administered directly by the federal government, by the states under federal plans, or by state and local governments. Funding may be from any of the sources (and in certain state programs, from private insurance companies) but the federal share is greater than 80 percent of the total. The programs which are included as social insurance are shown in Figure 1.

Strikers have found convenient access to only two of the social insurance programs listed in Figure 1. Both of them will be discussed as "unemployment insurance" later in this chapter.

Public Aid

The second of the major categories of the welfare system is public aid. Included here are the welfare programs that provide money payments, goods, and services to needy persons and families. Because contributory or prepayment arrangements are not required by these programs, their benefits lack the connotations of being earned rights enjoyed by the social insurance programs. Public aid programs are available as a matter of administrative right to all who fall prey to the economic hazard against which the programs provide shields and who can meet the means or income tests and other statutory requirements for eligibility.

Public aid programs are conveniently broken into two subgroups: public assistance and other public aid. In the first of these are the categorical assistance programs—such as Aid to the Blind—aided by the federal government under the mandate provided by the Social Security Act of 1935, and General Assistance programs—sometimes called "relief"—which are financed entirely by state and local governments. In the "other public aid" category are a diversity of programs such as work relief,

FIGURE 1. *Public Welfare System*
Social Insurance Programs

Administered directly by
the federal government:

> "Social Security" (Old-age, survivors,
> disability, and health insurance—OASDHI)

> Railroad programs
> > retirement
> > *unemployment*
> > disability insurance

> Federal employee retirement systems

Administered under
federal-state laws:

> Public employee retirement, state and
> local systems

> *Unemployment insurance*

> Workmen's compensation
> > Hospital and medical benefits

> Temporary disability insurance
> > Hospital and medical benefits

Source: U.S. Department of Health, Education and Welfare, Social Security
Administration, *Social Welfare Expenditures Under Public Pro-*
grams in the United States, 1929-1966, Office of Research and Statistics, Research Report No. 25, Table I-1.

Note: Programs used extensively by strikers are italicized.

antipoverty, refugee assistance, food distribution, and others. All of the major programs included in either of these categories of public aid are shown in Figure 2.

PROGRAMS USED BY STRIKERS

Most of the programs which have been used by strikers are in the public aid category. As noted in Figure 2, these include AFDC, Medical Assistance, General Assistance, and Surplus Commodities and Food Stamps. We shall discuss each of these briefly in turn, and also unemployment compensation, which is part of the social insurance category. The three most important specific programs—Food Stamps, AFDC, and Unemployment Compensation—are given additional and more detailed coverage in Appendix A.

Aid to Families with Dependent Children (AFDC)

The AFDC program is the welfare program most in the public eye. It is the largest of the "categorical public aid" programs in terms of the amount of assistance payments rendered under it. It was a part of the original Social Security Act package, and is administered by the individual states under guidelines established by the Department of Health, Education and Welfare. Its basic purpose is to provide financial aid and medical assistance to children who lack financial support and care, and it also seeks to preserve family units and provide family rehabilitation when possible.

The history of the AFDC program, its administrative details, and statistics are included in Appendix A. One historical development, however, must be mentioned here, because it brought in the changes which have allowed striker participation in many states. In May 1961, in a move designed to ease administrative burdens and to promote stronger family relationships, Congress allowed the states to extend AFDC coverage to the children of unemployed parents, thus creating the AFDC-U program.[4] Strikers are not discussed in the enabling legislation of this program, but the courts have generally held that in the absence

---

[4] AFDC-U was established by Congress May 8, 1961. This original legislation provided for aid to dependent children who had been deprived of parental support because of the unemployment of a "parent." In 1968, Congress amended the statute and replaced the word "parent" with the word "father." Section 607, Subchapter IV, Title 42, Social Security Act.

FIGURE 2. *Public Welfare System*
Public Aid Programs

Public Assistance Programs:

Categorical assistance programs:

Old-Age Assistance (OAA)

*Aid to Families with Dependent
Children (AFDC)*

Aid to the Blind (AB)

Aid to the Permanently and Totally
Disabled (APTD)

Medical Assistance for the Aged ("Medicare")

Medical Assistance ("Medicaid")

General Assistance programs ("relief")

Other Public Aid:

Emergency and general relief programs:

Surplus Commodities
Food Stamps
Refugee Assistance

Economic opportunity programs:

Job Corps
Neighborhood Youth Corps
Work Experience

Source: U.S. Department of Health, Education and Welfare, Social Security
Administration, *Social Welfare Expenditures under Public Pro-
grams in the United States, 1929-1966*, Office of Research, Report
No. 25, Table I-1.

Note: Programs used extensively by strikers are italicized. Most of the
depression-era programs (now defunct) were public aid programs.
These included the Civilian Conservation Corps, Civil Works Administration, Works Projects Administration, National Youth Administration, Reconstruction Finance Corporation, Federal Emergency Relief Administration, and Farm Security Administration.

of any specific prohibitions strikers can be, or even must be, eligible for benefits.[5]

The adoption of the AFDC-U option opened the doors to strikers, since prior to it federal AFDC support was restricted to families with an absent, dead, or disabled father, and thus was beyond use by most strikers.[6] Recent court interpretations have reinforced this extension (pending congressional clarification) by denying those states which have adopted the AFDC-U program discretion regarding the granting or denying of benefits to children whose father is involved in a labor-management dispute. (The development of the legal questions involved here is included in Chapter VIII.)

Since 1961, twenty-two states and the District of Columbia have adopted the unemployed father option. However, certain means tests and other requirements must be met to qualify for participation. For example, a thirty-day waiting period must pass before a family with an unemployed father can qualify for aid; an AFDC-U recipient must register for work; and an AFDC-U applicant must meet the program's income and asset tests.

If the applicant meets all of these requirements, he may qualify for the benefits provided by the program. These vary with the state, the family size of the applicant, and a number of other factors (covered in Appendix A). In California, a typical state, total monthly benefits vary from $166 for a family with one child up to $404 with nine (or more if there are more children).[7] Program statistics reveal that, throughout the United States, average monthly payments per family in fiscal 1971 were $240.[8]

---

[5] Robert W. Clark III, "Welfare for Strikers: *ITT* v. *Minter*," *University of Chicago Law Review* (Fall 1971 forthcoming), pp. 88-91; *Francis and Wright et al.* v. *Davidson and Hobson*, Civil No. 71-853-K, U.S. District Court, District of Maryland, January 28, 1972, p. 52.

[6] Effective May 1, 1961, the AFDC program also provides payments to families for foster home care of dependent children (Section 608, Subchapter IV, Title 42, Social Security Act). Strikers are known to have received benefits under this provision.

[7] California State Department of Social Welfare, Form DFA 234 C (6/67).

[8] U.S. Department of Health, Education and Welfare, Social and Rehabilitation Service, *Public Assistance Statistics*, NCSS Report A-2, Table 8, issued monthly. Figures cited compiled from individual monthly reports, all subject to revision.

"Fringe benefits" are often available under this program. These can take the form of mortgage payment support, matching funds on home repairs, day care or nursing home services and, in those states which have adopted "Title XIX," complete medical assistance (discussed below). The costs of the AFDC program for assistance and administration are shared among all levels of government on a formula basis which usually is approximately four parts federal to three parts state to two parts local.

For an idea of the relative size of the program, consider that under AFDC in fiscal 1971, a monthly average of 9,557,000 persons were recipients of a total of $5.75 billion in direct payments, an increase of 39 percent from the previous year and up from $1.86 billion in 1966. Included here were a monthly average 730,000 recipients under the AFDC-U segment who received total payments of $413.3 million, up 74 percent from the previous year.[9] Strikers have made considerable use of this program, as our case studies will demonstrate, and show every indication of using it even more heavily in the future.

Medical Assistance

Medical Assistance (or Medicaid) is usually found in conjunction with other programs, notably AFDC. Created in 1965, Medicaid is now in effect in all states except Alaska and Arizona. The goal of the program was to encourage the individual states to establish a unified minimum package of medical aid for everyone receiving public assistance under federally aided programs. Financed under Title XIX of the Social Security Act, funding is similar to other federal-state programs. All three levels of government share assistance and administrative costs on a complex formula under which the federal government carries from 50 to 83 percent of total costs.[10]

As is usual, the federal governments set only the minimum aid standards and eligibility requirements, leaving wide discretion to the states. For example, a state may include the families of unemployed fathers even if it does not have an AFDC-U program. About a third of the states make Medicaid available on

---

[9] From Appendix A, Table A-7.

[10] U.S. Department of Health, Education and Welfare, Social and Rehabilitation Service, *Characteristics of State Assistance Programs Under Title XIX of the Social Security Act*, Public Assistance Series No. 49 (1970 ed.).

a means test of the parents alone regardless of the number of parents in the house or of their employment status. For these as others, a milder eligibility standard may be used if the state has adopted the special provisions for "medically indigent" as well as "categorically indigent" persons. Both in states which have these optional provisions and in those having AFDC-U programs, strikers and their families could qualify for Medicaid, and aspects of this program are therefore clearly germane to the striker situation.

Medicaid is almost entirely a vendor-payment program whose usage is based on services demanded. Therefore, no specific amount or even range of benefits can be ascribed to a particular case. Nevertheless, a striker or some other individual who knows he will be eligible for only a limited period of time for the discretionary benefits available would be foolish not to use them, for they can be extensive. For example, in the forty-eight states and the District of Columbia which have Medicaid, thirty provide essentially unlimited dental care, and thirty-three allow payments to optometrists. Thirty will pay for eyeglasses, and some of those will even permit contact lenses.[11] Elective surgery, unlimited outpatient services, diagnostic work, prescribed drugs, chiropractic services, and other items whose use might be considered optional under normal circumstances are also available to a greater or lesser degree to program recipients under the state plans.

Although it is impossible to pinpoint the benefits of which an individual striker might avail himself and his family, it is possible to find statistics concerning usage by members of AFDC families. Because AFDC is the program through which strikers would most likely become eligible for Medicaid, the figures should be comparable.[12] Average monthly bills paid per recipient in this category were $47.25 in August of 1970, $51.55 in November of 1970, $59.70 in February of 1971, and $53.70 in

---

[11] Various restrictions exist in the different states on these services and goods, but the numbers noted are for those states where, in the opinion of the authors, those services or goods could be reasonably expected; the summary is based on programs in effect January 1, 1970.

[12] In view of the argument that strikers know they will be temporarily welfare recipients, and therefore may perhaps use more elective medical services such as dental care or eyeglasses, these figures may be somewhat low.

May of 1971 [13] and therefore, the monthly benefit for a family
of four all of whom used Medicaid would average more than
$200, based on these 1970-1971 figures.

However, not all AFDC recipients use Medicaid every month.
During fiscal 1970, about 10.7 million members of AFDC families used the program, at a cost to the taxpayer of $1.6 billion.[14]
This averages to $50 per month per family of four and indi-
cates that in any particular month only one recipient in four
is utilizing Medicaid. We shall subsequently use this $50 figure
in estimating total striker benefits from this program, even
though the indications are that both Medicaid costs and striker
use of the program are accelerating upward.

General Assistance

Although the Social Security Act of 1935 provided public assistance support for several different categories of needy persons
(and included also provisions for emergency relief) there remained a number of persons not covered by the federal um-
brella. For the care of these persons, most states have retained
General Assistance or relief programs administered by the counties. Because most specific types of indigents have been provided for by tailored programs, the remaining elements are
unstructured and highly individualized, requiring flexible programs. There are no federal requirements for general relief
programs and counties within each state use them as they see
fit, limited only by the provisions of the state welfare codes.

Residency requirements, means tests, work requirements, and
other factors determining eligibility are often at county discretion. In many states, assistance may be granted in cash or kind
to provide groceries, rent, etc. Each person's needs are considered individually, and the total amount of relief is at the county's
discretion. In these cases, the general relief program is usually
funded entirely from county funds.

Because of these varying conditions, striker eligibility differs
from county to county. At least thirty states, however, including the majority of the highly industrialized ones, grant gen-

---

[13] U.S. Department of Health, Education and Welfare, Social and Rehabilitation Service, *Medical Assistance (Medicaid) Financed Under Title XIX
of the Social Security Act,* May 1971, NCSS Report B-1 (October 1971),
Table 6.

[14] U.S. Department of Health, Education and Welfare, Social and Rehabilitation Service, *Medicaid, Fiscal Year 1970,* NCSS Report B-5, various tables.

eral assistance benefits to strikers.[15] The use of this program has been found to be greatest in covering the thirty-day waiting period mandatory under the AFDC-U program and in those states where strikers have been held to be ineligible for other forms of welfare. Because the costs of general assistance fall directly on them, most counties are anxious to shift recipients over to other welfare programs as rapidly as possible.

Few general statistics on this program are available, but as an example, during fiscal 1971, eighteen cities distributed a total of $415 million to a monthly average of about one-half million persons.[16] Administrative expenses in this program tend to be higher than for most others, and can be as much as 30 percent of assistance payments.[17]

The Food Stamp Program

Food stamps were introduced experimentally in 1961 and made permanent in 1964. Their use remains a county option as an alternative to surplus food distribution, and although some counties still have not adopted them, their use is so widespread that we shall ignore the surplus commodity program in their favor.

The basic purposes of the Food Stamp program include strengthening the agricultural economy and finding better uses for surplus foods, as well as providing improved levels of nutrition for low-income households. It is administered in accordance with a national plan under the Department of Agriculture by the welfare departments of participating states and some regional administrations of its own. Certain means tests must be met in order to qualify, but there is no waiting period. Tests to be met for participation are not normally as severe as those for AFDC.

In participating communities, persons whose incomes are below a prescribed limit can buy, for a small amount, a special script worth a larger amount when presented at the local food store or supermarket. The amount paid for the stamps depends on the family size and economic status of the purchaser.[18] Food

[15] Clark, *op. cit.*, p. 97.

[16] U.S. Department of Health, Education and Welfare, *Public Assistance, op. cit.*, Table 13, individual months.

[17] Calculated from California Legislature, *op. cit.*, p. 43.

[18] *Federal Register*, "Food Stamp Program," Vol. XXXVI, No. 146, Part II, July 29, 1971.

stamps may be received in addition to AFDC or other welfare payments, and may also be received by families which have considerable income. For example, a family with four children may still be eligible if nonexempt income is less than $493 a month. Benefits to a household of the same size vary from $9 to $148 a month depending on income level.

Strikers are now specifically included for coverage in the Food Stamp program, and the use of this program has been the most widespread form of public support in strikes. The cost of food stamps, except administrative, is borne entirely by the federal government.

The details of this program are found in Appendix A. During fiscal year 1971, almost 9.5 million persons participated—three times as many as two years earlier—and the total federal subsidy to food stamp purchasers was $1.5 billion. This amount was almost three times as great as one year earlier,[19] and more than seven times larger than the expenditures for food stamps and surplus commodities combined in 1966.

Unemployment Insurance

Unemployment insurance provides cash benefits to regularly employed members of the labor force who involuntarily become unemployed but who are able and willing to accept suitable jobs. Like other social insurance programs, unemployment insurance is funded by means other than general revenues. Specific provisions vary from state to state, but the covered employees rarely contribute to the fund from which benefits are drawn. Because of this and because state administration allows payments to strikers in some cases, unemployment insurance qualifies as a program providing public aid to strikers.

The details of the development of unemployment insurance, its administration, eligibility requirements, coverage, and benefits are found in Appendix A. For here, it is sufficient to note that about 80 percent of total wage and salary employment (exclusive of the railroad workers, federal civilian workers, and members of the armed forces who are included under separate federal programs) are covered by state plans. These provide benefits of up to one-half the weekly wage to a maximum ranging from $50 a week to $123 weekly, depending on the state.

---

[19] Total food purchased with coupons exceeded $2.7 billion, but this figure includes the purchase price of the stamps. U.S. Department of Agriculture, Food and Nutrition Service, Food Stamp Program, *Statistical Summary of Operations,* June 1970 and 1971.

As an indication of the size of the unemployment insurance program overall, total disbursements from the funds during fiscal year 1971 were slightly more than $5.2 billion. Of this total, the railroad program accounted for about $45 million.[20]

States pay unemployment insurance to those who can demonstrate past employment establishing attachment to the labor force and actions during the claim period establishing a current attachment. Usually, this means some minimum amount of employment during a one-year base period and a willingness and ability to register for suitable work available. There are some other circumstances which disqualify a worker for unemployment insurance. For example, all states disqualify workers who leave work without good cause or are discharged for misconduct. All jurisdictions also disqualify workers involved in a labor dispute or strike except for the railroad system. However, the degree of disqualification varies considerably from state to state. Some reduce or eliminate benefit rights, some lengthen the waiting period before an individual can begin to receive benefits.[21]

Although most unemployment compensation laws disqualify strikers for the duration of a labor dispute, two states impose the disqualification for only a specified time. There are thus three cases in which strikers actively on strike may receive unemployment compensation: strikers under the railroad law are instantly eligible to receive benefits; strikers in Rhode Island may receive benefits (of up to $91 weekly) after a statutory one-week waiting period and a six-week disqualification period; and strikers in New York State may receive benefits (of up to $85 weekly) after a one-week waiting period and a seven-week disqualification.

In addition, strikers in fourteen other states may become eligible for unemployment insurance if their work stoppage is termed a lockout,[22] and in yet others, benefits may go to persons idled

---

[20] *Monthly Labor Review*, Vol. 94, Table 10.

[21] U.S. Department of Labor, Bureau of Unemployment Security, *Comparison of State Unemployment Insurance Laws*, No. U-141, August 1967.

[22] The difference between a strike and a lockout is more a matter of semantics than anything else, and at times the definitional distinction between the two in unemployment compensation laws leads to deliberate misuse or misapplication. After a 155 day strike at Westinghouse in 1956, the state unemployment compensation director in Pennsylvania termed the stoppage a "lockout," and thus the strikers were eligible for compensation. Westinghouse took the matter to the courts and won a reversal. See, *Westinghouse Electric Corp.* v. *Unemployment Compensation Bd. of Review*, 144 A.2d 852, 187 Pa. Super. 416 (1958).

by a strike, even if they have a direct interest in the dispute or if their idleness was caused by their own refusal to cross picket lines.[23]

The existence of these lockout provisions in the unemployment compensation laws of several heavily industrial states has led to the rise of selective strikes, which may be deliberately designed to collect benefits. In the 1970 General Motors strike, for example, two groups of employees received unemployment compensation. One comprised the New York State employees of the company, who were paid approximately $5.25 million in unemployment insurance while the strike continued. The other included a number of General Motors employees in other states who were ordered by their union to remain on the job in order to produce parts for General Motors' competitors and thus add to the pressure on the company; they were eventually laid off because disruptions in the system caused by the strike kept the company from operating those plants. These employees, who clearly stood to gain from concessions won by the strike, and who were paid strike benefits by their union, filed for an estimated $36 million in strike benefits on the grounds that they had been "locked out." [24]

Organized labor is unflagging in its efforts to make unemployment insurance available to strikers in more states. Under the special provisions which apply to railroad workers this is currently the case, and it is perhaps because of the dismal experience of the American railroads and of companies in New York and in Rhode Island being required to finance the strikes against themselves that no more jurisdictions have made payments available to strikers under the general programs. The rest continue to follow the logic of President Nixon who, in his July 8, 1969 message to Congress, summarized unemployment for workers on strike as follows:

> The unemployment tax we require employers to pay was never intended to supplement strike funds to be used against them.

---

[23] This is true, for example, under the federal program for railroad employees. Between 1953 and 1971, American railroads paid out a total of $53,766,002 in unemployment compensation to strikers and to others who refused to cross picket lines. Figures compiled by Board and provided by National Railway Labor Conference, February 26, 1972.

[24] George B. Morris, Jr., "Controls or Collective Bargaining—Restraints and Realities," address before The Conference Board, New York, June 3, 1971, pp. 14-15. Mr. Morris, a vice president of General Motors, noted that some of the payments to those affected were being challenged.

A worker who chooses to exercise his right to strike is not voluntarily unemployed.

In two States, workers on strike are paid unemployment insurance benefits after a certain period. This is not the purpose of the unemployment insurance system.

I propose a requirement that this practice of paying unemployment insurance benefits to workers directly engaged in a strike be discontinued.[25]

Other Social Welfare

Other social welfare, as its name implies, is a residual of welfare programs not covered in the above listings. Some of these programs are far from miscellaneous. Health and medical programs expended more than $7 billion in fiscal 1966, veterans' programs more than $6 billion, and educational programs more than $32 billion. Fellowships and traineeships accounted for almost $600 million, and about $500 million was spent on school lunches. Another $2 billion was dispensed in other ways. Current total expenditures are almost twice as great.

Although these are massive programs, only the School Lunch program has found much use by strikers insofar as our researchers have been able to discover it, and that use is primarily as an ancillary benefit available to striker recipients of other types of welfare. Striker use of the School Lunch program will be discussed where appropriate in the later chapters.

SUMMARY

It is not difficult to see that, although categorization of the various welfare programs helps to differentiate them, many areas of potential confusion continue to exist. In this book, the terms "public support" and "welfare" will be used interchangeably as a general term for whatever of the categories mentioned above have found actual or potential use by strikers. The major differentiations which we shall follow are those between publicly financed or administered programs and private ones (such as union strike benefits or the Salvation Army). We shall also differentiate between public programs activated by the strike situation and those which may have been in effect prior to the

---

[25] U.S. House of Representatives, 91st Congress, First Session, *Hearings on H.R. 12625*, 1969, p. 12. (Emphasis in original.)

strike and have no reason for discontinuance during it (such as public education or rent-subsidized housing).

The programs specifically examined above are but a few of those which make up the publicly financed assistance system of the country. They are, however, the major programs of interest in strike situations. Food stamps are available to practically all strikers who apply for them. Aid to Families with Dependent Children is limited to those jurisdictions which have adopted an unemployed father program. This program is very significant for strikers because of its high benefits. It has a one-month waiting period, but during that month it is possible that a striker might be able to use the General Assistance program for relief. The means tests and other requirements of all of these programs are not very severe. If AFDC-U and general assistance were available in all states, we would estimate that between 25 and 50 percent of all persons on strike could qualify if they applied. Unemployment compensation is available to railroad workers with no waiting period and to those who live in New York and Rhode Island, but only after seven to eight weeks. Strikers in other states may receive unemployment benefits if their employer is charged with a lockout or if their fellow workers in other plants caused the plant stoppage and they are not deemed direct participants, even though they directly profit from the results. If certified for any assistance program requiring a means test, strikers may also be eligible for Medicaid and other fringe benefits. All of these benefits are tax free.

It is an interesting question to consider how it came about that in times of great prosperity, hundreds of thousands of highly paid, independent-thinking American workmen have come to accept "being on welfare" not only with equanimity but even some glee in discovering a new tool against their employers during labor disputes. This certainly represents a break with the traditions of the American working man of the last generation and may well pose a grave threat both to the welfare system and, as we shall see, to free collective bargaining. The next chapter will explore the fragile structure of collective bargaining and evaluate the degree to which the rise of public striker support threatens its precarious balances of power. In Chapter III, we shall return to the union-sponsored development of welfare as a strike fund item.

CHAPTER II

Collective Bargaining Theory and the Role of the Strike

The admittedly imperfect collective bargaining system in the United States exists as a result of years of experimentation as to how to determine wages, hours, and working conditions in a manner that will achieve the most satisfactory economic and social results. Numerous controversies have arisen here and in other democratic countries as to what is the best or fairest method of deciding basic industrial relations questions.[26] If any answer has emerged, it is that no objective criteria are, or can be, developed to determine the employment relationship to the satisfaction of everyone.

THE EMPLOYMENT RELATIONSHIP

The employment relationship is an economic one. What is economically desirable or even necessary for the good of the business may be quite different from what would be personally pleasant or satisfactory to workers or the unions. Sometimes, the very existence of the union as a force may make it economically unsound for the employer or corporate manager to operate as he deems most desirable. Additionally, economic conditions change, and economic science is not exact. No one can promise without fear of error that a certain wage will be "proper" to balance income and employment, or wages and profits in a given industry. Moreover, what is "fair" in one particular instance is "unfair" in another. Thus, there is no objective, exact answer to disputes over wages, working condi-

---

[26] This analysis is based on Herbert R. Northrup, *Compulsory Arbitration and Government Intervention in Labor Disputes* (Washington: Labor Policy Association, Inc., 1966), pp. 180-185, by permission of the publisher.

tions, and other terms of employment, either on the basis of economics or on the basis of equity. "Too high" wages do accelerate or cause unemployment, "too low" ones do impede living standards and purchasing power. Between extremes in any given situation, there is likely to be a wide latitude of equally possible opportunities, no one of which can be determined to be the "proper" wage.

The facts of economics which make it nearly impossible to determine a "proper" wage, and the facts of equity which make it equally difficult to determine what is "fair" to all concerned, make it all the more important to protect the premise upon which our industrial society is built—that is, the freedom to work or withdraw labor, either singly or in concert. Such freedom has never been considered a totally unrestricted one. Nor does it mean a return to eighteenth-century society. But to protect it requires balance and, above all, more governmental restraint than interference.

Balancing Liberties—and Strength

The rise of great combinations of capital in this and other countries through the corporate form spurred demands for curbing business freedom. In effect, the unrestricted freedom of business was felt to impinge upon the freedom of others. From this developed such regulation as the Interstate Commerce Act, the Sherman Antitrust Act, the Securities Exchange Act, and numerous other federal and state enactments. Then, in the 1930's, came the enactment of laws designed to spur the growth of labor combinations in an attempt to build up the power of labor through unions so that bargaining power in the market place would be equated and reasonably "fair" wages and conditions of work would result. The net effect was also to create a whole set of new problems, and more and more governmental regulation of labor combinations. As in the case of freedom for business combinations, freedom for labor combinations was found to impinge on the freedom of others. The Wagner Act was followed by the Taft-Hartley and Landrum-Griffin laws.

Although these laws regulated union and employer tactics and certain strikes relating to these tactics, they sought to preserve the basic right to withhold labor—the right to strike. (The main exception was the emergency procedures of the Taft-Hartley Act. This moved into the arena of strike control most gingerly, and like its Railway Labor Act counterpart, only as a postponement technique.) The laws regulating tactics and the weapons of conflict continue to stress the philosophy that "great restraint should be exercised in interfering with the freedom of the seller and the buyer of labor to participate in determining the conditions of sale. These freedoms can be preserved only under conditions of equitable joint determination of the terms of sale, namely through bona fide collective bargaining. Otherwise they are shrunken or lost to the degree that the terms are fixed unilaterally or imposed from the outside." [27]

To permit general wage fixing by government fiat is also to surrender consumer sovereignty. For if wages are fixed, so must prices be determined and resources allocated by the price fixers, not by consumer dictates. That such arrangements are not likely to be compatible with a free society is amply demonstrated by contemporary events in this and in other countries.[28]

Therefore, it is difficult in ordinary times to disagree with the succinct summary of Professor John Perry Horlacher:

> Essentially economic disagreements between labor and management are best resolved by the arbitrament of economic facts and forces. To the extent that the disagreements are noneconomic and involve the parties' rights, prerogatives, status, emotions and fetishes—the whole complex of imponderables in their relationship—they are best settled by mutual accommodation. Management and labor ought not to be forced by political pressures or political action to relinquish their sovereignty, their right and power to decide themselves how mutual concerns shall be adjusted between them.[29]

This, however, assumes that the system is working to the general satisfaction of the public. Obviously this has not been occurring in recent times for the results have contributed substantially to the inflationary pressures and international imbalances which, in 1971, resulted in government intervention, a

---

[27] John Perry Horlacher, "A Political Science View of National Emergency Disputes," *The Annals*, Vol. CCCXXXIII (January 1961), p. 86.

[28] For an illuminating study of how the combination of economic *and* political power in the single hand of government destroys freedom, see Calvin B. Hoover, *The Economy Liberty and the State* (New York: Doubleday & Co., Anchor Books, 1961).

[29] Horlacher, *loc cit.*

wage-price freeze, and a stabilization program. One aspect was, of course, the desire to curb the discretion of unions and managements to determine the terms and conditions of employment at least until their determinations were more in line with the public interest. Nevertheless, the aim of this stabilization program—as that of similar ones in the past—has been a return to free collective bargaining as rapidly as possible, and even under the current restraints, no general move has been made to set aside the right to strike.

The Function of the Strike

In a famous article which drew on his experience as chairman of the World War II National War Labor Board, Professor George W. Taylor described the function of the strike or lockout in the collective bargaining system "as the motive power which induces a modification of extreme positions and then a meeting of minds. The acceptability of certain terms of employment is determined in relation to the losses of a work stoppage that can be avoided by an agreement. In collective bargaining, economic power provides the final arbitrament." [30]

During strikes, both sides suffer costs. To the union the costs during a strike include loss of wages to the union member, and losses to the union treasury because of dues not received and of strike benefits paid. In addition a strike involves a risk to union officials who can be defeated for office if the strike turns out badly for the members. To the company, losses include sales not made and customers lost, either temporarily or permanently and the costs of covering overhead while nonproductive. Of course, the costs of disagreement are often indeterminate because, among many other things, the length of a strike is unpredictable. But the anticipated cost of a strike is most important. Essentially each party in negotiations must weigh the cost of agreeing to the other's proposals against the cost of disagreeing with them. Hence, if one assumes that economic factors are compelling—that is, that such matters as union politics, emotional attitude, sheer ignorance or poor calculation, which are pertinent, are not decisive—one would expect settlement where

---

[30] George W. Taylor, "Is Compulsory Arbitration Inevitable?" *Proceedings of the First Annual Meeting, Industrial Relations Research Association*, 1948, p. 64.

for both parties the cost of agreement equals, or is only slightly greater than, the cost of disagreement.[31]

Effect of Tax Support Benefits

In such a situation, it is reasonable to assume that welfare or unemployment payments to strikers could alter the calculation to both parties, but in opposite directions. For the union and its members, the prospective costs of disagreement would be lowered. Losses to the individual members would be notably lessened by their access to tax supported benefits. There would also be less pressure on unions to pay strike benefits, or to increase such benefits. If the strike lasted over a long period, employee morale would probably be bolstered by welfare payments and back to work movements not considered worthwhile. Instead of recriminations for a long strike, the union leadership would be likely to reap praise for the tax supported benefits. On the other hand, the employer would surely note that while he was losing sales, his employees were obtaining compensation in lieu of wages and therefore were under less pressure than would otherwise be the case during a strike.

It would seem, therefore, that the cost of disagreement for the union could be less, and for the company more, if public funds are utilized to pay strike benefits to workers. Three possible results are likely: (1) settlement would be reached at a higher figure, closer to the union demands; (2) a strike would occur and last longer, and be settled closer to the union demands; or (3) a strike would occur and end fairly promptly because the employer would see that strikers were not being severely hurt economically and could continue to hold out, there-

---

[31] Dr. Allan M. Cartter's work, *Theory of Wages and Employment* (Homewood, Ill.: Richard D. Irwin, 1959), has been helpful here. He defines each party's bargaining attitude as follows:

$$\text{X's bargaining attitude} = \frac{\text{cost of disagreeing with Y}}{\text{cost of agreeing on Y's terms}}$$

When one's bargaining attitude is equal to unity it is just as costly to disagree as to agree on the other's terms, and we can anticipate that when either party finds itself in this position the bargaining may be completed on the other bargainer's offered terms. (Page 117.)

In fact, because strike length is indeterminate, experienced negotiators will come to an agreement even when the cost of agreement somewhat exceeds the cost of disagreement. The former is relatively known; the latter, relatively unknown.

fore, the employer would be willing to settle closer to the union demands. In all three cases, whether or not a strike occurred, the settlement would be higher because of the tax supported benefits available to strikers.

In actuality, many factors other than pure economic calculations determine the levels of settlements or whether negotiations result in settlements or strikes. The presence or absence of tax supported strike benefits may not necessarily be decisive. It does seem perfectly logical, however, that the potential of such benefits must be a factor in the bargaining and calculations which precede the decision by both parties whether to settle and on what terms.

Impact on Strikes

If it seems logical to assume that the existence of tax supported benefits for strikers can tip the bargaining scales in favor of strikers, it appears utterly realistic to understand that they contribute substantially to the resolve of strikers to remain out once they have left their jobs, and to hold out for their demands instead of compromising the issues in the hope of achieving early settlement. In this, the timing of the receipt by strikers of tax supported benefits is very important.

Assume, for example, that a strike occurs in a major plant. Immediately, those strikers in the poorest financial condition would be eligible for food stamps, and as time goes on and striker resources decline, others would become eligible. Moreover, anyone in dire economic straights could apply for, and obtain, general or emergency assistance to care for his problems. Thus the resolve to remain on strike would be strengthened, and the propensity to pressure union officials to negotiate a compromise settlement would be lessened.

After thirty days, one would expect declining striker resolve to hold out and increased pressure for a settlement. At this time, however, when strikers' wives might be grumbling and upset about loss of income, the strikers in most of the more heavily industrialized states become eligible for benefits provided by AFDC. These involve, in addition to welfare payments, such extra benefits as free medical assistance. It is quite likely that many of the strikers who qualify for these welfare benefits will find their overall economic situation only slightly worsened because of the strike. Under such circumstances, one could expect little pressure from the strikers to force a compromise settlement.

If the strike occurred in New York or Rhode Island, the strikers' resolve would likely become even stronger at the seventh and eighth week when they become eligible for unemployment compensation. Many would be able to receive these benefits and still be eligible for food stamps. One would expect strikers under these circumstances to have little incentive to compromise, but rather to resolve most strongly to hold out for their demands.

WHERE THE STRIKE DOES NOT
PERFORM ITS FUNCTION

From our short theoretical analysis, it would appear that tax supported benefits to strikers can prevent the strike from performing its function of being, in Dr. Taylor's words, "the motive power which induces a modification of extreme positions and then a meeting of minds." What happens to the collective bargaining system when this occurs? Such situations have not been analyzed in terms of tax supported benefits to strikers, but we can theorize by analogy to other situations. For example, Dr. Taylor has described what occurs when third party determination or intervention is substituted for the collective bargaining system:

> When the rights to strike and to lockout are withdrawn, as during a war or under compulsory arbitration, a most important inducement to agree is removed. The penalties for failing to agree—stoppage of production and employment—are waived. Even more devastating consequences result. Each party is reluctant to make any "concessions" around the bargaining table. That might "prejudice" its case before whatever Board is set up to deal with labor disputes. In addition, the number of issues is kept large and formidable. Demands that customarily "wash out" in negotiations are carefully preserved for submission to the Board. Why not? There is everything to gain and nothing to lose by trying to get one's unusual demands approved without cost.[32]

There are other situations when the strike does not serve its purpose. This can occur if a strike exerts greater pressure upon the public or the government than it does on the parties. "The

---

[32] Taylor, *op. cit.*, pp. 64-65. See also Northrup, *op. cit.*, p. 183.

parties can hold out longer than the public or the government. In consequence, a strike which creates a public emergency exerts primary pressure upon the government to intervene and also to specify the terms upon which production is to be resumed." [33] Such situations, which have been well described in the literature, have resulted in a great variety of strike control legislation and legislative proposals. [34]

Still other situations exist where, although the strike cannot entirely serve its function, the parties are operating within their traditional boundaries and have adjusted to each other's tactics. For example, during a strike, a company is free to ship from inventory stockpiled before the strike began. Thus under certain business conditions, it might have little incentive to settle until the inventory was largely disposed of. The ability to stockpile, however, is circumscribed by warehousing costs, and ability to sell from stockpiles can be impeded by union picketing and boycotts. On the other side, unions may reduce the "pain" of a strike to the workers by paying strike benefits and this may reduce the propensity to reexamine bargaining demands and seek compromise settlement. Strike benefits are limited in amount, however, and can easily be dried up during a protracted dispute. Some companies have countered by purchasing strike insurance of their own.

Although these and similar company and union activities during strikes do weaken the effectiveness of the strike mechanism, the extent depends on the direct economic power of the parties involved. It is only when one of the parties can extend leverage beyond its own economic power that the results of collective negotiations become imbalanced.

TAX SUPPORT OF STRIKERS AS A NEW COLLECTIVE BARGAINING DIMENSION

We may look at tax support of strikers as a new dimension which has the theoretical potential of undermining the role of the strike by providing one party to a dispute economic leverage far beyond its own economic power. The amounts of funds and the duration of payments could even be so great as to raise

---

[33] Taylor, *op. cit.*, p. 65.

[34] See, e.g., Northrup, *op. cit.*, pp. 184-187. Such legislation has been much more successful in disrupting collective bargaining than in curbing strikes.

the fundamental question of whether the strike can continue to serve a useful role in the future. Essentially, our theoretical analysis indicates that the payment of government benefits to strikers may be expected to reduce materially the cost of disagreement which a strike imposes on union members and to increase those costs to employers.

Part Two of this book will demonstrate what does happen in strikes when government benefits to strikers are a significant factor. If our theoretical analysis of the probable consequences are correct, we would expect higher and more inflationary settlements, and either longer and more costly strikes, or if employers become convinced of the futility of resistance, higher settlements without such strikes. If by insulating unions and union members against the costs of strikes the strike can no longer serve the function of being the catalyst for agreement, there would seem to be no incentive to tolerate strikes, nor to retain the collective bargaining system.

PART TWO

The Empirical Evidence

How Tax Supported Welfare Payments to Strikers
Developed and Expanded and Case Studies of
Such Payments to Strikers

From Occasional Use to Commonplace Occurrence: The New Deal to The 1969 General Electric Strike

Between the early New Deal days of the 1930's and the General Electric strike of 1969, a number of forces have worked to make the payment of welfare to strikers a commonplace occurrence. Foremost among these have been: (1) the attitudes and precedents established during the 1930's; (2) the careful planning and program development by organized labor to achieve public financial support for strikers; (3) the reorganization of welfare in 1961 which made families with unemployed fathers eligible for Aid to Families with Dependent Children funds; (4) the revolution in thinking, greatly enhanced by the Johnson Administration's "war on poverty," toward making welfare a "right," and (5) the Food Stamp program established in the 1960's. How these forces combined to create the present situation is described in this chapter.

THE FORMATIVE POLICY YEARS, 1933-1940

The New Deal of Franklin D. Roosevelt ushered in a whole new era of labor relations. Legislation, commencing with the National Industrial Recovery Act of 1933 and culminating in the National Labor Relations (Wagner) Act of 1935, protected workers from management discrimination because of union activity and required companies to bargain with unions chosen by employees. Concurrently, government further aided union growth and power by granting strikers the right to receive public assistance.[35] Although the Taft-Hartley Act of 1947, and

---

[35] There is at least one pre-New Deal instance where public relief was paid to strikers. Strikers in Illinois received public benefits as early as 1904. *City of Spring Valley* v. *County Bureau*, 115 Ill. App. 545 (Ct. App. 1904), cited in Robert W. Clark III, "Welfare for Strikers: *ITT* v. *Minter*," *University of Chicago Law Review* (Fall 1971, forthcoming), p. 79, n.2.

later the Landrum-Griffin Act of 1959, attempted to balance union rights and duties, there was no legislative impairment of the right of strikers to sustain their absence from work with tax supported welfare payments.

The Federal Emergency Relief Administration

In July 1933, soon after the Roosevelt Administration began, the federal government adopted its first position regarding relief to strikers. Harry Hopkins, the administrator of the Federal Emergency Relief Act, in response to a request for direction from the executive director of the Pennsylvania State Emergency Board, made the following statement concerning a strike in Montgomery County, Pennsylvania:

> The Federal Emergency Relief Administration is concerned with administering relief to the needy unemployed and their families. Each case applying for relief to the local emergency relief agencies should be treated on its merits as a relief case wholly apart from any controversy in which the wage earner may be involved.
> The FERA will not attempt to judge the merits of labor disputes. State and Federal agencies, as well as courts, exist which are qualified to act as arbiters and adjusters in such disputes.
> Unless it be determined by the Department of Labor that the basis for the strike is unreasonable and unjustified, the FERA authorizes local relief agencies to furnish relief to the families of striking wage earners after careful investigation has shown that their resources are not sufficient to meet emergency needs.[36]

In October 1933 and in September 1934, this policy was reaffirmed in Washington [37] and, under the short-lived federal emergency relief program, some state and local emergency relief boards adhered to it. Thus it was found that in the fall of 1933, the California State Relief Administration provided supplies to strikers against cotton growers after the strikers were evicted from their employers' properties. This was "perhaps the first time in American history that strikers were fed at public expense, the cause of bitter criticism." [38]

---

[36] Josephine Chaplin Brown, *Public Relief 1929-1939* (New York: Henry Holt and Company, 1940), p. 270.

[37] U.S. Works Progress Administration, *Chronology of the Federal Emergency Relief Administration* (Washington: Government Printing Office, 1937), pp. 22 and 25.

[38] Irving Bernstein, *The Turbulent Years: A History of the American Worker, 1933-1941* (Boston: Houghton Mifflin, Sentry Edition, 1971), p. 158. Bernstein was apparently unfamiliar with the *Spring Valley* case cited above.

Hopkins claimed that his policy contributed to law and order, and had little effect upon the incidence or duration of strikes, and that it cost almost nothing while being overwhelmingly approved in most communities.[39] That these points were then, as now, at least debatable is shown by the uproar that arose when on August 27, 1934, newspapers across the United States announced that the federal government would give relief to strikers in the United Textile Workers strike set for September 1934.[40] This public pronouncement evoked critical responses from around the nation. A Georgia attorney representing textile interests wrote the President that "The strike would have never been called . . . without the . . . financial support from the Federal Government." The Illinois Manufacturers Association told Hopkins that his policy imposed "an undue and indefensible burden upon . . . taxpayers."[41] The Alabama Relief Administration ordered payments to strikers stopped,[42] a move which apparently contributed to the defeat of the union.

The position taken by Hopkins and the New Deal Administration toward welfare payments to strikers was consistent with their belief that sound public policy required governmental assistance to unions if collective bargaining and equality of union power with that of management were to be achieved. Just as the Wagner Act sought to encourage collective bargaining by enhancing union power, so welfare payments to strikers sought to sustain unions when they required assistance. Of course, long after the justification for such overt assistance to union power has expired, the policy of payment of welfare benefits to strikers has endured:

> This policy, which made so clear a distinction between the issues of relief and labor, was adhered to throughout the entire emergency program by the Federal Relief Administration. In many localities, from time to time, there were departures from the general principle and in some cases local officials, yielding to pressures from labor or from industry, gave or refused relief to strikers on some basis

---

[39] *Ibid.*, p. 307.

[40] *Ibid.*

[41] *Ibid.*, pp. 307-308.

[42] *Ibid.*, p. 312. Dr. Bernstein, completely accepting the Hopkins view, terms the dispute over welfare aid to the 1934 textile strikers as an "absurd amplification of a circumstance with little inherent significance." (Page 307.) Yet his own analysis demonstrates that then (as now) both unions and companies believed that such welfare payments play a significant role.

other than need. On the whole, however, the Federal policy was
followed in local practice and did much to clarify thinking in regard
to the relation between the administration of relief and labor disputes. It also had a strong influence on the position of the officials
in the later permanent state and local public welfare agencies when
it became necessary for them to deal with similar situations.[43]

The Social Security Act

In August 1935, Congress enacted the Social Security Act
which remains today the basis for our old age, unemployment
insurance, and public welfare system. The Federal Emergency
Relief Administration was terminated, and a Social Security
Board created. No provision was made for or against payment
of unemployment compensation or welfare to strikers. The
legislative history gives no indication that the issue was discussed. Consequently, the matter was left up to the states
which administer both the unemployment compensation and welfare provisions of the Act.

As was pointed out in Chapter I, two states and the railroad
system pay unemployment compensation to strikers and others
provide such payments if the stoppage is deemed a lockout, or
if direct involvement, narrowly construed, is not found. Although administrative regulations affect the issue of compensation for strikers, the basic guidelines have been established by
state legislatures pursuant to the 1935 federal Act and subsequent amendments. Insofar as welfare is concerned, the rules
are largely administrative, and date back to the 1930's. At
that time, welfare officials were not only guided by the precedents established by Harry Hopkins and the Federal Emergency
Relief Administration, but were themselves sympathetic to unions and their aims. In the absence of congressional direction
to the contrary, welfare aid to strikers was not only assured
in most states, but on some occasions, even promised before
hand. Thus on July 5, 1936, Thomas Kennedy, who then was
both Secretary-Treasurer of the United Mine Workers of America and Lieutenant Governor of Pennsylvania, told a meeting
of the Steel Workers Organizing Committee in Homestead,
Pennsylvania, that the strikers could count on public relief if
SWOC called a strike.[44] By 1940, the precedents were thus
clearly established.

---

[43] Brown, *op. cit.*, p. 270.

[44] Bernstein, *op. cit.*, p. 434.

ORGANIZED LABOR'S COMMUNITY SERVICES PROGRAM

During World War II and the postwar period another series of events took place which assist in explaining the development of the public support of strikers. In contrast to the thirties, where government action was largely responsible for strikers receiving welfare, during the forties organized labor assumed the initiative. Since then, unions have become an active participant in our nation's welfare system.

Organized labor established a working relationship with the National War Fund and American Red Cross in 1942. Through the CIO War Relief Committee and the AFL Labor League for Human Rights, the American labor movement sponsored war relief type projects in coordination with labor organizations in 15 foreign countries.[45] Because of this experience, organized labor moved directly from war relief work to community services activities following the war. Leo Perlis, who was in charge of the CIO war relief project, has headed this effort ever since, first for the CIO, and then after the merger for the AFL-CIO.

Organized labor began the development of its Community Services Program in 1945. The course of action, as during the war, was to establish a working relationship with public and private relief organizations. The goals of the program were primarily to prepare for the strikes that were expected to follow the end of the war, and to create a labor program which could always be ready to provide aid to needy union members.

In the fall of 1946, the CIO officially founded the Community Services program. The CIO Executive Board approved an annual budget of $13,500 and appointed Leo Perlis as the program director.[46] Figure 3 summarizes the purpose of the CIO program, which has been carried over to the merged federation.

In a Labor News Conference on August 10, 1971, Mr. Perlis presented some examples of the labor movement's early efforts to utilize an organized approach to obtaining aid for strikers. Answering a question as to how long strikers have been receiving public assistance, Mr. Perlis said, "Well, in a more or

---

[45] Based upon an interview with Leo Perlis, Director, AFL-CIO Department of Community Services, July 15, 1971, and an article he was preparing for *The Shipbuilder* (forthcoming).

[46] *Ibid.*

less organized and disciplined fashion, since 1945. This approach was developed by the labor movement in the fall of
1945, in the case of the General Motor strike. The following
year it was applied in the case of the United Steelworkers
strike in basic steel . . . also, in 1948, in the case of the Electrical Workers in the GE plant in Erie, Pennsylvania. From
that point on, [it has been used] in hundreds of thousands of
cases right across the country . . . ." [47]

It is interesting to note that it was primarily within the
CIO that the community services effort was enthusiastically accepted and promoted. It was the CIO that first officially adopted
the Community Services program, and it was CIO affiliated
unions which Leo Perlis described as being the first to approach
the use of public aid during a strike in an organized manner.
(See Figure 3.) Even today, former CIO unions are stronger
supporters of the community services effort. Their efforts and
success as participants in the country's welfare system have
been clearly revealed during the authors' study of the welfare
and strikers issues.

Operational Impact

The story of welfare and strikers reached its denouement in
the late 1960's but only after a sequence of important developments in the welfare and labor movements. Although the foundation for strikers to receive public aid had been constructed
during the first two decades in the life of our national welfare
system, the superstructure was not laid into place until the
fifties and sixties. Thus Mr. Perlis points out:

> At the founding convention of the AFL-CIO in December 1955,
> which witnessed the merger of the American Federation of Labor
> and Congress of Industrial Organizations, the delegates unani-
> mously adopted a resolution which dedicated the AFL-CIO "to the
> proposition that what is good for the community is good for labor."
> . . . The resolution declared that the objectives of the AFL-CIO
> "in the area of community organization for health, welfare and
> recreation" include a) assisting "union members, their families
> and other citizens in time of need," and b) cooperating "with

---

[47] *Labor News Conference*, Mutual Broadcasting System, Series 11, Tuesday,
August 10, 1971.

FIGURE 3. *Community Services Committee*
CIO Policy

Purpose of the Community Services Program

CIO union members face serious personal problems during strikes, lockouts, shutdowns, unemployment and general industrial instability. Your local union will want to use every method available to help meet those problems.

Public and private community organizations are set up to aid the citizens of your community in meeting just such situations as those faced by your membership. BUT THEY OFTEN ARE NOT UTILIZED BECAUSE UNION MEMBERS DO NOT KNOW THEY ARE THERE.

The CIO Community Services Program is designed to tell you how you can bring the services of these agencies to your members, when their need for them is made greater by industrial unrest.

It is not meant to suggest that the services of these agencies will replace all or many of the services provided by your union through its own resources. It does suggest that the services of the agencies can supplement and increase the aid given by the union.

It suggests that by bringing community services to your members you can help them over the period when wages are not coming in.

CIO Policy

The policy of the National CIO Community Services Committee is that these community services, administered by public and private agencies, should be available on the basis of need alone. REGARDLESS OF THE CAUSE OF THAT NEED and regardless of RACE, COLOR OR CREED.

This is also the publicly stated policy of most public and private welfare agencies. But there are instances when agencies do not follow that policy.

In dealing with community services agencies, CIO representatives should insist that the publicly stated policy is firmly established and followed. Upon the basis of that policy, the public and private agencies are obligated to aid CIO members in need, just as they must aid any other citizen in need, REGARDLESS OF THE CAUSE.

Source: California CIO Industrial Union Council, Community Services Committee, *Hand Book for Union Counsellors*, (mimeo, ca. 1950), pp. 1-2.

other agencies in dealing with and in solving social and health problems." [48]

In 1956 the AFL-CIO Department of Community Services began the development of its nationwide program. One of its first objectives was to establish a network of full-time AFL-CIO Community Services representatives throughout the country. The representatives were to be selected from and chosen by the labor movement. Their duties were to "work with the labor movement and local community agencies, . . . develop programs, . . . train volunteers, . . . [and] raise funds for local services." [49]

> In cooperation with United Community Funds and Councils of America (now the United Way of America) the AFL-CIO negotiated, through local central labor bodies, with local community chests and united funds the appointment of such full-time AFL-CIO Community Services representatives. Today there are 180 in 144 communities. . . . A number of international unions, state central labor bodies and some local unions also have full-time AFL-CIO-CSA staff. [50]

Essentially, there are two organizational structures within the AFL-CIO Community Services program: the Community Services Committees of local labor bodies and local unions, and union members who serve as full-time personnel on private welfare agencies. Through these structures, unions have become active participants in community welfare organizations and, accordingly, have become knowledgeable of the services and policies of these agencies. As a result, the availability of public funds as strike benefits has become an integral part of organized labor's strike planning. Figure 4 uses materials from the United Steelworkers to illustrate this point.

---

[48] Perlis, *Shipbuilder, loc. cit.* It should be pointed out that it is not the authors' intent to discredit or to diminish the many fine accomplishments of the labor movement's community services, community action, and welfare programs. It is fully recognized that union involvement in community affairs and welfare programs extends far beyond union recognition that participation will probably be rewarded during a strike. Only one objective exists in the discussion of labor's community services activities: to disclose that a program which was established to meet "the day-to-day personal and family needs of union members" is also designed to bring the services of public as well as private agencies to union members during strikes.

[49] *Ibid.*

[50] *Ibid.*

FIGURE 4. *Strike Assistance and the*
Community Services Committee
United Steelworkers of America

First Step

ORGANIZING FOR STRIKE ASSISTANCE

A good strike assistance program, like any insurance policy, anticipates and prepares for the future. The Union will strive to gain its demands through peaceful negotiations, but if a strike is necessary, the Union is prepared.

The objective of such a program is to meet the health and welfare needs of striking members and their families. The local union with a day-to-day community services program helps its members use social service facilities in resolving family and personal problems. A strike assistance program is nothing more than the broadening of the local union's ongoing community services program, if one exists.

A local union Community Services Committee (CSC) can save considerable time in the event of a strike:

First, the local union CSC is informed on the community's social services. Committee members are acquainted with state welfare laws and local welfare provisions. They will know the local relief director and his staff.

Second, the Committee will have trained union counsellors who can be used as strike counsellors and to staff the strike assistance headquarters.

· · ·

If the Community Services Committee assumes responsibility for the strike assistance program, the CSC officers will, of course, continue to function in that capacity.

· · ·

Summary of the First Step

There can be no effective strike assistance program without a responsible and active committee.

A strike assistance program can best be handled by the local union's Community Services Committee.

Source: United Steelworkers of America, *Beyond the Picket Line: How to Organize a Strike Assistance Program,* Pamphlet No. PR-304 (n.d.), pp. 3-4.

The Community Services program also operates as an effective lobbying and pressure mechanism for the labor movement. Because of the program's elaborate organizational structure and diversified activities, labor has access to a variety of interest groups which can bring pressure to bear on local, state, and national officials and politicians. Full utilization of the community services organization is made when unions are attempting to influence decisions regarding public aid programs that can provide funds to strikers.

The 1959-60 Steel Strike

The first great strike that enabled the AFL-CIO Department of Community Services and its programs to establish their worth to organized labor was the 1959-60 steel strike. This dispute lasted 116 days and involved approximately 500,000 union members. According to I. W. Abel, then Secretary-Treasurer of the United Steelworkers (now President), outside sources of aid "made the strike endurable . . . [and] provided the major part of strike relief."[51]

Public assistance payments, unemployment insurance, aid from united funds and community chests, and union strike benefits all helped to support the striking Steelworkers. It was reported that public assistance amounted to more than $22.7 million, aid from voluntary agencies provided $118,712, and direct payments from state and county agencies were in excess of $12 million. Approximately 35,000 New York Steelworkers received $9 million in unemployment insurance. "Mr. Abel reported that 105,114 families of strikers got 7,133,210 pounds of surplus food valued at 1.4 million dollars."[52]

> Officials of the Pennsylvania public welfare department told *U.S. News and World Report* that striking Steelworkers in that State had collected about 18 million dollars in public assistance during the 116-day walkout. At the peak period, 16,489 families of steel strikers were on the relief rolls, with aid going to a total of 69,186 persons. Average payment to a family during the strike was about $30 per month.[53]

---

[51] Quoted in *U.S. News and World Report*, October 3, 1960, p. 101. See also Neil W. Chamberlain and James W. Kuhn, *Collective Bargaining* (New York: McGraw-Hill, 1965), p. 174, which credited federal, state, and local benefits to strikers of at least $22,750,000 in this strike.

[52] *U.S. News and World Report*, October 3, 1960, pp. 101-103.

[53] *Ibid.*, p. 102.

The array of assistance provided by public agencies "exceeded by far the amount that the union poured into the districts and the locals. Had the union not secured assistance for its members from these agencies, the union's treasury would have been much more severely depleted." The Steelworkers' Union, which did not pay strike benefits as a matter of right, but rather on a basis of need, spent approximately $20 million in strike aid. Mr. Abel believed that government assistance was in excess of $45 million.[54]

Public funds were available in many strike locations and the Steelworkers' Union utilized its Community Services Committee to secure relief for its members. In his report before the Union's convention, Mr. Abel noted that by maintaining a year-around relationship with welfare officials, the Steelworkers could insure that public aid is provided to their members during strikes. He suggested that union officials become involved in greater political activity relating to private and public welfare agencies. He recommended also that pressure be exerted on welfare agencies which rebel at the thought of providing public funds to strikers.[55]

Thus during the 1959-1960 steel strike, public funds exceeded in tactical importance the aid which unions could provide striking members from their own resources. Union officials were beginning to understand clearly that their participation in community services activities paid off during strikes, as they were well aware of the importance of public aid and community srevices as an effective strike assistance program.

AFDC-U, FOOD STAMPS, AND THE NEW ATTITUDE TOWARD WELFARE

An array of reform programs and policies which significantly expanded the scope of public aid and modified public attitudes toward welfare and the receipt of welfare payments emerged during the 1960's. As a result of some of these programs, special advantages were provided to organized labor. The programs and policies instituted to enlarge the scope of the public relief system increased the number of programs available to striking

---

[54] *Ibid.*, pp. 101-102.

[55] *Ibid.*

workers. In addition, the changes provided for greater financial benefits while on strike.

Surplus Food Commodities

Two welfare reform programs adopted during the Kennedy
Administration proved to be valuable sources of strike relief.
One was the program which improved the distribution of surplus food commodities and led eventually to the introduction of
the Food Stamp program. The other, and much more important, was the modification of the AFDC program.

AFDC-U

The Kennedy Administration secured a federal program to aid
financially those states willing to extend the coverage of the
AFDC program to families with an ablebodied, but unemployed,
father.[56] This may well have been the most significant federal
government contribution to organized labor's strike assistance
program since Harry Hopkins' 1933 FERA policy regarding
strikers. Although there was no immediate rush by the states
to adopt the AFDC-U program, 22 states currently do so,[57] and
only one of these denies benefits to persons because of their
involvement in a labor dispute.[58] In addition, a number of
states which do permit strikers to participate in the AFDC
program, but do not offer the AFDC-U option, have instituted
their own form of aid to families with an unemployed father.

The War on Poverty Impact

The welfare reform developments of the war on poverty period were without a doubt especially beneficial to the labor
movement's strike capability. President Johnson's 1965 Anti-

------

[56] Section 607, Subchapter IV, Title 42, Social Security Act.

[57] The details of this program are found in Appendix A.

[58] One state denies AFDC-U benefits to those whose need is as a result of
their involvement in a strike, two states deny benefits to strikers unless the
dispute is because of an employer lockout and two states will not grant benefits to strikers if the walkout is considered "illegal." *Francis* v. *Davidson*,
Civil No. 71-853-K, U.S. District Court, District of Maryland, January 28,
1972, p. 22. This recent litigation may require all states which have AFDC-U
to pay welfare to strikers unless Congress intervenes. See Chapter VIII.

poverty Program promoted efforts to expand the welfare system and to provide the general public with an adequate knowledge of aid available through public relief. In addition, there was a government commitment to eliminate the stigma associated with going on welfare. Eligibility procedures and requirements were adjusted to reduce or eliminate embarrassments, complications, or unpleasantness for clients. Although perhaps salutary and something even administratively more efficient, the easing of eligibility procedures and requirements had the side effect of encouraging a number of persons who would otherwise not do so to participate in the welfare system. Thus this federal effort to overcome poverty in the United States, in addition to opening the way to organized labor and providing cash assistance, food, medical, and housing programs to aid strikers at the taxpayer's expense, also eliminated the roadblocks of personal inhibition to accepting it.

One of the most significant accomplishments of the Antipoverty Program was this alteration of the public's attitude toward receiving welfare relief. The status of public assistance was elevated and those individuals in need of financial or other forms of aid were invited to join the relief rolls. They became "clients," not handout recipients. A number of changes were made in existing welfare programs, and new relief programs were introduced in an effort to support existing cash aid programs. Accordingly, the federal government's commitment to wage a war on poverty brought the issues of need and welfare into public focus. The nation became knowledgeable of the different benefits available through the multiplicity of welfare programs. Moreover, organized labor became aware of the magnitude of aid encompassed within a comprehensive public relief system which was sympathetic to strikers.

Food Stamps

One of the "relief-in-kind" programs adopted during the "war on poverty" period was food stamps. Since 1964 this Department of Agriculture program has aided the needy by providing stamps which could be exchanged for food at community grocery stores. Food stamps were made available to low income households as well as to full-time clients of public assistance programs. Although the original legislation was silent as to the eligibility of strikers, Congress on at least three occasions has

since declined to make strikers ineligible,[59] and they now are
specifically included.

It did not take organized labor long to discover that food
stamps were available to strikers and offered almost immediate
financial relief. Because the Food Stamp program was generally
introduced on a county by county basis, many strikers were
not exposed to this new form of government aid until their
counties adopted them in the late sixties. The program is not
a part of the welfare structure under the Department of Health,
Education and Welfare. From the very start it was not promoted as a welfare program, but was introduced as part of
the government's effort to distribute surplus food and to encourage domestic consumption of farm products. Welfare officials have not earmarked food stamps as a welfare program and
food stamps have not carried with them the same "stigma"
that has been attached to public assistance programs. The effect
during strikes has been to eliminate much of the strikers' earlier hesitation to apply for public aid. Now food stamps are an
accepted form of strike benefits. Moreover, stamps are distributed by welfare offices, bring workers into these offices, and
often serve to introduce them to other welfare programs as
well as to reduce the stigma attached to receiving government
aid.

The New Attitude Toward Welfare

Along with the "war on poverty," the internal and external
political, social, and economic development of the last half of
the sixties appear to have encouraged increased use of welfare
aid by striking workers. Certainly this combination of changes
occurring within and outside of our nation apparently influenced
individual attitudes toward accepting welfare relief. In speaking to one of the authors, Leo Perlis stated that for many
years union leaders had almost to twist arms to get workers to

---

[59] Since 1968 there have been at least three unsuccessful attempts to amend
the Food Stamp Act by adding a provision prohibiting strikers from participating under the Food Stamp Program. In 1968 Congressman Teague (R-
California) offered a motion. It was defeated by a vote of 158 to 187.
(*Congressional Record-House*, September 25, 1968, pp. H9080-H9088.) Congressman Abbit (D-Virginia) offered a similar motion in December 1970.
It was defeated by a vote of 172 to 183. On June 23, 1971, an amendment
which would have made strikers ineligible for food stamps, offered by Congressman Michel (R-Illinois), was defeated by a vote of 172 to 225 (*Congressional Record-House*, June 23, 1971, pp. H5805-H5810).

apply for public assistance, but that in recent years the attitude has changed and now it is much easier to promote public aid.[60]

The attitude change on the part of union members toward accepting public relief has been aided significantly by organized labor, welfare rights organizations, and public welfare agencies. The labor movement has lobbied long and hard, at all levels of government, to encourage liberalizing eligibility requirements for strikers. In addition, union community services groups have promoted legislation and administrative changes which would make more public funds available to their members. Welfare rights organizations and union groups have continually emphasized that welfare was a matter of right, based on need regardless of cause. Social workers have insured that striking workers are completely aware of all public funds available to them. During the processing for food stamps, for example, strikers are often counseled as to the other aid existing under the welfare system. Union community services committees join with welfare agencies to distribute information on all public aid programs that strikers may be qualified to receive. The rank and file are also given classes by community services personnel or welfare officials as to eligibility requirements for public aid programs.

One aspect of the new attitude toward welfare was the growth of an organization established to represent the interests of welfare recipients—the National Welfare Rights Organization. With local branches in most industrial centers and at state capitals, the NWRO has been able to mobilize welfare mothers for marches, lobbying, and confrontations. This appears to have helped to achieve administration more sympathetic to welfare recipients, political support for higher benefits, and a greater knowledge among potential recipients of available benefits. NWRO has regularly supported welfare payments to strikers as a means of furthering its aim of universal welfare payments "as a right." To this end, locals of NWRO have appeared on union picket lines, lobbied in defense of welfare payments to strikers, urged strikers to apply for welfare, and served as a liaison between strikers and local welfare department administrators.

Figure 5 shows how each of these above mentioned factors affected the welfare costs and rolls during the 1960's. Although

---

[60] Interview, July 15, 1971.

FIGURE 5. *Welfare Costs and Rolls*
1955-1970

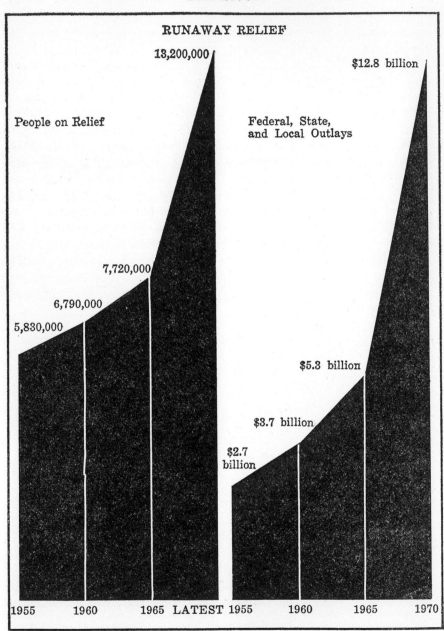

RUNAWAY RELIEF

13,200,000

$12.8 billion

People on Relief

Federal, State,
and Local Outlays

7,720,000

6,790,000

5,830,000

$5.3 billion

$3.7 billion

$2.7
billion

1955   1960   1965 LATEST 1955   1960   1965   1970

Reprinted from *U.S. News & World Report*, February 8, 1971, p. 31. Copyright
© 1971, U.S. News & World Report, Inc.

this was at a time our nation was experiencing its greatest and most prolonged prosperity, relief rolls and costs soared to unprecedented heights.

THE NONFERROUS METALS AND THE GENERAL ELECTRIC STRIKES

The effect of the welfare reform period on strikes began to coalesce in the last half of the 1960's. At least two major strikes which occurred during that period showed the influence of welfare and how the use of an expanding number of different public assistance programs spread rapidly. The 1967-1968 nonferrous metals or "copper" strike and the 1969-1970 General Electric strike brought the impact of strikers obtaining welfare into public focus and laid it on the doorsteps of taxpayers and many government officials. As these strikes progressed into their second, third, and fourth months, relief costs soared.

The 1967-68 Copper Strike

About 37,000 workers in five western states were idled for 316 days in the nonferrous metals (copper) strike of 1967. The primary issue of the strike was the structure of the collective bargaining unit, as the unions attempted, without success, to force the companies to bargain on an industry-wide coalition basis. Twenty-five unions were involved, with the United Steelworkers of America by far the most important, along with the four major copper mining companies (American Smelting and Refining, Anaconda, Kennecott, and Phelps Dodge). The work stoppage affected ninety percent of all our country's copper mining, as well as the mining and refinery of zinc, lead and other metals. Work finally resumed when a three-tier, three-year settlement was reached upon the recommendation of an extra-legal panel appointed by the Secretaries of Labor and Commerce following President Johnson's intervention outside the framework of the Taft-Hartley Act.[61]

---

[61] For an account of this strike and the issues involved, see William N. Chernish, *Coalition Bargaining*, Industrial Research Unit Study No. 45 (Philadelphia: University of Pennsylvania Press, 1969), Chapter IX. The union demand which precipitated the strike was later found to be an unfair labor practice. See *United Steelworkers of America (Kennecott Copper Corp.)* NLRB Case No. 27-CB-453 (April 8, 1969); *Phelps-Dodge Corporation,* 184 NLRB 106 (1970).

Understandably, the copper industry shutdown had a severe economic impact on all parties involved. Strikers expected to get along on union benefits ranging from $10 to $30 per week, part-time or full-time jobs that could be found, and personal savings. As anticipated by the unions, many stores, banks, and landlords deferred collections during the strike. And, strikers in some of the states found assistance was available from public funds.

As the strike continued and personal savings disappeared, more and more strikers turned to public welfare to reduce the economic pressures. Strikers discovered that food stamps or surplus food were available in most states, and public assistance was apparently obtainable in all of the states affected by the strike except Arizona. Complete reports on the amount of public aid are not available but fragmentary data indicate that it was substantial. Thus, five months after the strike commenced, *U.S. News & World Report* reported that in Butte, Montana, "Welfare payments totaling $50,065 went to 594 families in August, $64,520 to 649 families in September, and $62,287 to 629 families in October." [62]

The 316-day strike nearly exhausted Utah's welfare reserves. Utah's Department of Health and Welfare reported in June 1968 that 584 strikers and their families had received financial assistance sometime during the long dispute. The Welfare Department said that the cost of this assistance totaled $411,725, of which federal funds contributed sixty percent and state funds forty percent. In addition, 85 strikers received food commodities only.[63] Figure 6 shows how the number of strikers on welfare progressed during the copper strike. Utah's Welfare Department said that approximately 11 percent of the state's total strike force applied for assistance.[64]

Undoubtedly, the capacity of the nonferrous metal union coalition to sustain their long strike was materially enhanced by the availability of tax supported strike benefits made available in substantial amounts. Yet the use of such benefits, as great as it was, became dwarfed by the massive injection of welfare for General Electric strikers in 1969-1970.

---

[62] *U.S. News & World Report*, December 11, 1967, p. 96.

[63] Utah State Department of Health and Welfare, Research and Statistics Division, *Re Stat Report*, June 5, 1968.

[64] *Ibid.*

FIGURE 6. *Copper Strike*
Number of Strikers on Welfare
Utah, October 1967-April 1968

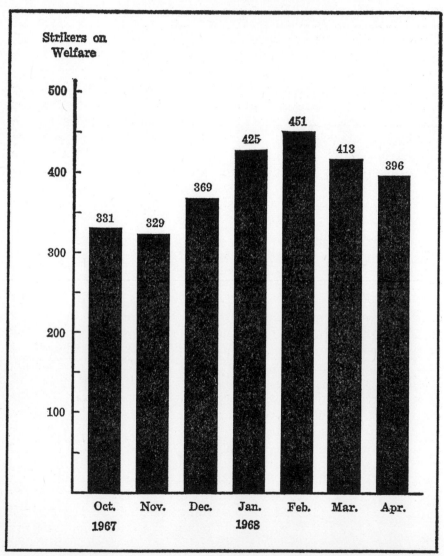

Source: Utah State Department of Health and Welfare, Research and Statistics Division.

Note: The copper strike began on July 15, 1967 and lasted until April 1, 1968.

The 1969-70 General Electric Strike

On October 26, 1969, approximately 164,000 workers walked off their jobs at the General Electric Company and stayed off for 122 days. Ten unions were involved in this economic dispute which affected plants in over thirty states. The General Electric strike was to represent the most massive and skillful campaign waged up to that time by organized labor in order to obtain public benefits for strikers. According to Leo Perlis, the labor movement mobilized "unprecedented support" for strikers from welfare and public agencies in 33 states.[65] Less than two months after the strike had begun Perlis said in a newspaper interview that strikers were reciving as much or more from public welfare and similar sources as they were from union strike benefits.[66] Our research more than sustains Perlis' claim. Actually, public support of strikers amounted to substantially more than was paid in union strike benefits. Indeed, almost every conceivable form of public aid was utilized by the General Electric strikers: food stamps, surplus food, public assistance, unemployment compensation, veterans' benefits, and even social security benefits were reported to have been used. Although state welfare programs and laws vary throughout the United States, generally strikers everywhere received some form of support from public service agencies. According to Mr. Perlis, strikers encountered difficulties in only a few places. Food stamps and surplus commodities were denied at first to strikers in Tyler, Texas; Louisville, Kentucky; Jackson, Mississippi; and Hickory, North Carolina; but these problems were cleared away either through federal court order or "the good efforts of the Department of Agriculture." [67]

Government officials at local, state, and federal levels were quite helpful to strikers. They stepped in to insure that strikers were "properly aided" in accordance with welfare rules and policies. The *Boston Globe* reported in December 1969 that welfare officials in Massachusetts were abiding by an HEW ruling of 1968 that held that families of strikers are entitled to AFDC.[68] When New York County Welfare commissioners

---

[65] Quoted in *The Christian Science Monitor*, December 13, 1969, p. 6.

[66] *Berkshire Eagle* (Pittsfield, Massachusetts), December 17, 1969.

[67] Quoted in *The Christian Science Monitor*, December 22, 1969.

[68] *Boston Globe*, December 6, 1969.

questioned the payment of public benefits to strikers they were informed that "any welfare department which denies otherwise eligible strikers assistance will jeopardize reimbursements for the total program." [69] Social services grants to strikers were made in New York under a 1946 state law.[70] An officer of General Electric said that the company "had much the same experience in all thirty-three states in which [they] operate" when they questioned such practices.[71]

Almost two months in advance of the General Electric strike, union leaders had begun meeting with public and private welfare agencies to discuss "the problems strikers might run into during a predictably long strike, and how they might be helped." [72] Union officials and community services representatives who had a working relationship with public service agencies experienced little difficulty in integrating public programs and resources into their strike assistance effort. Other unions formed committees to coordinate strike assistance and public welfare programs. A Massachusetts strike leader stated: "We didn't twist arms or suggest that our favors in the past ought to be returned. We didn't have to. We only pointed out that strikers should be considered for help on the same basis as others in need of temporary help." [73] The AFL-CIO labor representative to the Philadelphia United Fund Torch Drive said that General Electric strikers in his area received significant aid and good cooperation from Pennsylvania welfare agencies. He explained that he acted as the liaison between public and private service agencies and the union's strike assistance or community services committee.[74]

Speaking before a luncheon sponsored by the AFL-CIO Maritime Trades Department in December 1969, Leo Perlis said that in the General Electric strike then in progress community benefits averaged $50 per striker per week, bringing the weekly

---

[69] *Syracuse Post Standard*, October 29, 1969.

[70] *Schenectady Gazette*, November 13, 1969.

[71] Letter to Elliot L. Richardson, Secretary of Health, Education and Welfare, from Virgil B. Day, Vice President, General Electric Company, dated August 20, 1970.

[72] *The Christian Science Monitor*, December 13, 1969, p. 6 .

[73] Quoted in *ibid*.

[74] Interview, Philadelphia, June 8, 1971.

outlays by the voluntary and public agencies well above the $5 million mark.[75] What this consisted of can be understood by examining events which occurred in Massachusetts and New York, where about 33 percent of the General Electric strikers were found.

Massachusetts

Joseph W. Chamberlain, Director of the Massachusetts Department of Public Welfare, reported to the Associated Press in February 1970 that his state had paid out $2,307,823 in benefits to the 5,070 General Electric workers who were on strike.[76] About one GE worker in four participated in these payments.

At the time of the General Electric strike, Massachusetts had not yet adopted the food stamp program, but benefits were available under the Surplus Commodities Program. They could receive 150 pounds of food per month for a family of four. It was estimated that in Pittsfield, 400-500 strikers were receiving surplus foods in January 1970, and strikers' children were receiving free school lunches under the federal free lunch program. In Lynn, site of another large General Electric facility, an estimated 24 tons of surplus food per week were being distributed to General Electric strikers as of January 1970.[77]

Massachusetts, at that time, provided welfare aid of $240 per month for a family of four.[78] Strike benefits, however, were deducted. The *Boston Globe* reported on December 6, 1969, about six weeks after the strike commenced, that "More than $1 million in welfare benefits has been paid to at least 3,000 striking General Electric workers in Massachusetts. . . ."[79] As mentioned above, by the end of the strike the amount of aid to strikers had more than doubled. Thus during the first week of December, the Massachusetts Welfare Department reported that one or more electrical workers in thirty or thirty-six communities in eastern Massachusetts were aided and that the suburban Boston total was 2,038. The *Globe* reported that at

---

[75] *Seafarers Log*, January 1970.

[76] *North Adams Transcript* (Massachusetts), February 4, 1970.

[77] These data are found in an unpublished study in the authors' possession.

[78] *Berkshire Eagle*, December 17, 1969.

[79] *Boston Globe*, December 6, 1969.

several of the plants, members of the National Welfare Rights Organization and the Massachusetts Wage Supplement Organization informed picketers of the public relief available to them.[80]

On January 11, 1970, the *Lynn Sunday Post* disclosed that "$1 million in public assistance payments have been made to 2,648 striking General Electric workers in seven North Shore communities since the start of the walkout . . . ." In Lynn, where the case load included 2,087 strikers, $813,000 had been distributed. In addition, 90 cases received war veterans assistance amounting to between $12,000 and $13,000.[81]

In contrast to New York, Massachusetts does not provide unemployment compensation to strikers. The program is being mentioned at this time because a lobbying effort has been underway for a number of years in Massachusetts to pass legislation entitling strikers to unemployment benefits. The "strikers' Benefit Bill" was defeated in 1970 by a one vote margin. A novel reason put forward by state welfare officials was that strikers should receive unemployment compensation, as a replacement for welfare, because the General Electric strike had depleted the state's welfare resources.

New York

The Empire State's experience with subsidizing strikers was quite similar to other states during the early part of the General Electric strike. County welfare officials were informed by the state welfare office that eligible strikers must be permitted to receive public assistance and surplus food. Consequently, soon after the strike started, welfare offices began receiving applications for aid. In less than two weeks, strikers had applied for assistance at the social services department of Warren, Washington, and Saratoga counties. By November 13, 1969, the Schenectady County Welfare Office had approximately 300 applications for public relief from strikers.[82] As of December 5, 1969, Onondaga County (Syracuse) had paid $78,951 to 431 strikers' families.[83] This cost included flat grant payments and

---

80 *Ibid.*

81 *Lynn Sunday Post (Massachusetts),* January 11, 1970.

82 *Schenectady Gazette,* November 13, 1969.

83 *Syracuse Herald-Journal,* December 8, 1969.

rental payments. The commissioner of the Schenectady County Department of Social Services reported that by December 23, 1969, his office had paid strikers $78,805 in public benefits. This represented 218 AFDC cases for November and 339 AFDC cases at the close of the third week of December.[84]

After December 23, 1969, the remaining 43 days of the General Electric strike took on a different complexion in New York, for on that date about 26,000 New York GE strikers became eligible for unemployment compensation. New York and Rhode Island are the two states which provide unemployment compensation to strikers.

Strikers in New York had to wait until the second day after the seventh week of the strike to file. Once benefits began, General Electric strikers could receive up to $65 per week in unemployment compensation, to supplement their $12 per week in union strike benefits.[85] In other words, the striker's monthly income could average about $333.00. The state director of unemployment security estimated that 21,500 strikers were drawing $1.2 million a week in unemployment benefits.

The impact of unemployment compensation on General Electric strikers was evidenced by an incident that occurred in early February 1970. The *Syracuse Post-Standard* reported that leaders of a Cleveland, Ohio, union local group told their members that the rejection of a recommended national settlement by the Syracuse and Schenectady IUE locals was because New York strikers were receiving unemployment benefits. In a call for a vote on the contract, one of the local union officials supporting acceptance of the contract was said to have shouted "To Hell with Schenectady." [86]

As mentioned previously, General Electric's experience with welfare assistance and public aid to strikers was quite similar in most states. Only Texas, Virginia, and Wisconsin showed any disposition to bar strikers from collecting state welfare benefits. California, Connecticut, Georgia, Illinois, Indiana, Ohio, Pennsylvania, and Vermont were reported to have been providing various forms of public aid to General Electric strikers. Because public resources were provided to strikers in different

---

[84] *Schenectady Gazette*, December 23, 1969.

[85] *Syracuse Herald-Journal*, December 11, 1969. Maximum benefits have since been raised to $75 per week.

[86] *Syracuse Post-Standard*, February 5, 1970.

forms and quantities in many communities in these states, an exact dollar figure for the amount of public funds distributed during the strike is not available. Nevertheless, taking into consideration Leo Perlis' estimate of public aid support and the unemployment compensation provided strikers in New York, one could conservatively estimate that about $25 million in public aid was divided among the General Electric strikers.

THE IMPACT OF THE GENERAL ELECTRIC STRIKE

The fact that many states were subsidizing strikers and this government policy was costing the public many millions of dollars is only a part of the General Electric story. The other part, and that which was responsible for stimulating concern and interest in the welfare for strikers situation, can best be explained by an individual involved in public aid to General Electric strikers. Thomas Spirito, a Massachusetts County Welfare Director, declared during the strike, "I've seen nothing like this in the 16 years I've been here." [87] Many other people as well had never witnessed such a massive organized approach to collecting public benefits which were apparently designed for individuals and families who did not have the ability or opportunity to support themselves. Here were organized groups of ablebodied men and women at welfare offices applying for and taking public funds. These men and women had jobs but they were not working at those jobs because they had decided to strike for higher wages and greater benefits. They were effectively utilizing not only organized labor's tools and powers to insure that they were economically protected as they exercised their right to strike but also those of the welfare system. For several months communities watched thousands of General Electric strikers sustain a labor dispute that had incorporated public aid into the labor movement's General Electric strike assistance fund or war chest.

Until the General Electric strike, few public officials, businessmen, or taxpayers had experienced the impact of a modern day strike assistance program on public welfare: a striker-welfare program which can drain public resources, affect public services, and influence the length and cost of a strike. Although strikers had received public help from tax dollars for many years, the

---

[87] *Boston Globe*, December 6, 1969.

earlier incidents did not involve much public relief, many strikers, or such an elaborate and organized union campaign to provide strikers with public aid programs. This explains, at least in part, why until recently there apparently was little interest in, opposition to, or concern over public policies which permitted strikers to obtain welfare.

The experiences of the General Electric and nonferrous metals strikes confirmed that organized labor had discovered the welfare system and compelled a recognition that most future strike assistance for union members is likely to come not from unions, but from public sources. Leo Perlis informed one of the authors that large national and international unions must depend on public funds in order to utilize the strike as a tool of collective bargaining. He said that the cost of engaging in a nationwide strike is too high to permit large unions to support members through their own funds. He affirmed that public aid is a much more important source of strike support than is the union strike fund.[88] The case studies which follow support this contention.

---

[88] Interview with Mr. Leo Perlis, July 15, 1971.

CHAPTER IV

Westinghouse Strike, Lester, Pennsylvania August 28, 1970 to January 25, 1971

August 28, 1970 marked the beginning of a 160-day strike at Westinghouse Electric Corporation's Steam Division by 5,132 members of the United Electrical, Radio and Machine Workers of America, Local 107 (UE). This strike exemplifies a union's capability to sustain a prolonged strike without paying any strike benefits. Although when the strike was called Local 107 did not possess a well-organized strike assistance program, given the proper direction, it developed the machinery and proficiency necessary to make public assistance a valuable strike fund. To the public, this assistance meant a cost of at least $2.5 million.

Westinghouse's Lester Plant has been located in Delaware County, Pennsylvania (a few miles south of Philadelphia) for 53 years. Consisting of 3 manufacturing divisions (large turbine; small gas and steam turbine; and heat transfer and auxiliary product manufacturing) and one nonmanufacturing division (power generator service division), it is the largest employer in the Delaware County area. Prior to the strike, the plant's industrial relations office claimed that Westinghouse had one of the highest average wages and one of the lowest turnover rates in the area.[89]

THE STRIKE

On February 23, 1970, Westinghouse reached agreements on national contracts with three unions including the UE. Under the UE national agreement, however, locals are free to negotiate for local settlements and to bargain for wages suitable to their

---

[89] Interview, management representative, Westinghouse Electric Corporation, Lester, Pennsylvania, April 16, 1971.

areas. If no agreement is reached, locals under this arrangement are free to strike. When bargaining began at the Lester
plant, on March 1, 1970, Local 107 demanded such items as
upward changes in pay levels, adjustments of job descriptions,
and an increase in hourly wages. Westinghouse would not accept these demands and on August 28, 1970, UE Local 107
struck. (All other local settlements within the Westinghouse
Electric Corporation were completed without a strike.)[90]

As the strike began, 5,500 hourly workers walked off their
jobs. (Although only 5,132 were members of UE Local 107,
all hourly employees are part of the bargaining unit.) In addition, 2,200 salaried employees left their jobs. According to a
plant management representative, "When the strike began our
salaried employees' association pledged to honor the UE picket
line. They did so for three weeks and one day. At that time,
Local 107 released them from their pledge and all 2,200 salaried
employees returned to work. It was necessary, however, to fur-
lough 800 due to a lack of work."[91]

Arranging for Welfare

From the start of the Westinghouse strike, members of Local
107 knew that no financial assistance would be afforded them
by their union since the UE constitution prohibits the payment
of strike benefits. According to a Local 107 officer, the only
aid the union was able to provide during the 160-day strike
was a load of coal for the truly destitute and a free meal at
the union hall for members on picket duty.[92]

"At the time the strike was called," a union official said, "we
did not know if we would be eligible for welfare benefits." He
added that during the strike, a committee was formed to determine what benefits strikers were entitled to under public assistance.[93]

---

[90] For an analysis of the methods of bargaining and settlement in the
electrical products industry, see Herbert R. Northrup, *Boulwarism* (Ann
Arbor: University of Michigan, Bureau of Industrial Relations, 1964); and
William N. Chernish, *Coalition Bargaining*, Industrial Research Unit Study
No. 45 (Philadelphia: University of Pennsylvania Press, 1969), Chapter VI.

[91] Interview, Lester, Pennsylvania, April 16, 1971.

[92] Interview, union official, Local 107, United Electrical, Radio and Machine
Workers of America, Essington, Pennsylvania, April 27, 1971.

[93] Interview, April 27, 1971.

The Delaware County Board of Assistance had not been contacted prior to the strike either to ascertain the legal right of striking workers to receive welfare assistance or to determine what public aid programs might be available to strikers. The memorandum set forth in Figure 7 makes it clear that strikers were eligible to receive welfare aid. When the strike began, Local 107 lacked both the information and organization necessary for strikers to make full and immediate use of public aid. Other factors, however, such as increasing public awareness of welfare programs, recognition that during recent strikes welfare aid was paid to strikers, and the decreasing stigma attached to accepting welfare (especially in the form of food stamps) resulted in a large number of striking UE members converging on the Delaware County welfare offices in Chester, Pennsylvania, to apply for food stamps and other relief. According to a newspaper report:

> The Department of Public Assistance in Chester was forced to close its offices at 1 p.m. Friday because of overflow crowds of strikers from the Westinghouse Corp.'s Lester plant applying for emergency funds and food stamps.
> On Thursday, when the processing of the strikers' applications began, 83 were processed before the end of the day. As the processing began on Friday morning, 64 were put through at 12th and Crosby Sts. and 79 at 5th and Penn Sts.
> At 12th and Crosby Sts. nine intake workers were receiving applications, instead of the normal five persons, plus a supervisor. At 5th and Penn Sts., five persons plus a supervisor were processing applications.[94]

This was corroborated by an official of the county welfare department:

> The crowds by the end of the first week of the strike were impossible to handle. Our office was not equipped to process so many extra applications. Even before the Westinghouse strike, application duties were heavy due to strikes at General Electric and in construction, general economic conditions in the area, and a hiring freeze in the Department of Public Welfare ordered by Governor Raymond Shafer last April. Therefore, during the heaviest influx of strikers, the office had to stop taking applications at about 10 a.m. each day and tell remaining applicants to return the next day. On Friday, August 4, 1970, approximately two-thirds of all applications for the money payment division were Westinghouse strikers.[95]

---

[94] *Philadelphia Inquirer*, September 15, 1970.

[95] Interview, Chester, Pennsylvania, April 21, 1971.

FIGURE 7.   *Welfare for Strikers*
Delaware County Board of Assistance Memorandum
May 6, 1970

SUBJECT: STRIKERS

A Memorandum from Mrs. Irene F. Pernsley, Region I Director, to CBA Executive Directors dated April 23, 1970, points up the following policy about providing benefits to strikers.

The purpose of this memorandum is to clarify the Department's position with regard to assistance for strikers.

1. There is no change in the Department's long-standing policy that a strike-bound job is not available employment and therefore does not affect eligibility.

2. A person who voluntarily leaves his job on what is known as a "wildcat strike" is not eligible for assistance because he has available employment.

3. When an employer curtails operations or shuts down completely for any reason, including a "wildcat strike," the jobs are no longer available and these people are eligible for assistance if all other conditions are met.

It is appreciated that in some labor disputes, there may be difficulty ascertaining the facts so as to apply the above principles. In case of doubt follow the usual rule that to be eligible for assistance an employable person must seek, accept and retain employment. A person who voluntarily refuses suitable employment is not eligible for assistance.

. . . .

Source: Delaware County Board of Assistance, Chester, Pennsylvania.

Union Strike Assistance Committee

Charged with the responsibility of organizing the strikers' efforts to obtain public aid, Local 107's newly formed strike assistance committee began constructing the required machinery. Although the UE is not affiliated with the AFL-CIO, the committee sought assistance from the federation's Community Services representative who had assisted numerous other Delaware County unions in developing strike assistance committees. This man was familiar with the requirements of strikers and knew what public agencies would be available to provide assistance. He provided the strike assistance committee with instructions on what to do and valuable information on whom to contact.

The strike assistance committee then met with representatives of area welfare agencies to learn about welfare aid available, application procedures and requirements, and methods of coordinating union and welfare department efforts. Utilizing the information and guidance provided, Local 107's strike assistance committee embarked on the development of a program, the purpose of which was to systematize the employment of public dollars as strike benefits.

The third week of the strike reflected the significant progress which the Delaware County Welfare Board and Local 107 strike assistance committee had made toward achieving their similar goals. Functioning as an effective arm of the Department of Public Welfare, the strike assistance committee was insuring that eligible Local 107 strikers were being processed for welfare benefits. Expanding its capabilities to handle applications and to provide public aid, the welfare office was meeting the demands of its clients. The two organizations were coordinated as to procedures and objectives.

The strike assistance committee distributed written information to strikers on available public aid. It provided counseling services to assist strikers in determining the extent of their eligibility for welfare benefits and established a telephone message service in order to provide Local 107 members with up-to-date information and instructions. In addition, the committee and Local 107 strikers assisted the welfare office in applying group instruction, application, and certification methods. The union hall was utilized to process welfare applications.

According to the executive director of the county welfare office:

The Delaware County Welfare Office adjusted to the crisis. Seven to ten workers were provided each day from other agencies within the department to assist the five workers taking applications. The Department of Welfare also approved the employment of ten additional clerks, despite the "hiring freeze" being experienced by public agencies within Pennsylvania. They remained on the payroll for an average of four and one-half months. In addition, five retired clerical supervisors were asked to return to work, and stayed on the job for about six months. Also, a special overtime pay package was approved by the Commonwealth of Pennsylvania in order that the staff could work an extra two hours each day.[96]

When the welfare office needed an additional facility in which to handle the swollen stream of applicants, Local 107 suggested using the Union Hall to handle strikers. By closing the welfare office to applications about 10:00 a.m. each day, the office was able to perform additional screening in an attempt to discover those cases in desperate need. The county accepted other union assistance and suggestions, such as initiating a procedure to recertify food stamps through the mail.

According to a Delaware County Board of Assistance official, "Most of the strikers who requested assistance applied for food stamps, while only a few sought cash grants."[97] It was believed that this was attributable to several reasons. First, people were most familiar with the aid provided through this program; second, the strike had not been in effect long enough for a large number of strikers to be in need of cash assistance; third, it is easier to qualify for food stamps; and fourth, there appears to be less of a stigma attached to accepting food stamps than there is to receiving other forms of public aid. As the strike continued, however, more and more strikers sought and obtained cash, as well as food stamp benefits.

EFFECTS AND IMPLICATIONS

Results of this welfare distribution were viewed differently depending on the viewpoint of the respondent. This can be illustrated by reproducing selections from interviews held with a Local 107 official, a representative of the Lester plant management, and an official of the Delaware County Board of Assistance in April and June, 1971.

---

[96] Interview, Executive Director, Delaware County Board of Assistance, Chester, Pennsylvania, June 4, 1971.

[97] Interview, June 4, 1971.

Union Viewpoint

Interviewer:	Could the union have withstood the economic pressures of the strike without the assistance of welfare funds?
Union Official:	Welfare assistance was the only assistance our strikers had. I like to think we could have stayed out for the twenty-two weeks without welfare, but it would have been rough.
Interviewer:	Do you think providing welfare to strikers makes strikes longer?
Union Official:	No, but coupled with a good cause they certainly augment our position.
Interviewer:	What influence, in your opinion, does furnishing welfare aid to strikers have on collective bargaining?
Union Official:	There is little effect. They merely act to counterbalance management's past advantages.
Interviewer:	Are union members more likely to vote for a strike recognizing that welfare programs will provide financial assistance?
Union Official:	No. The issue is of primary importance. I do not think we would call for a strike if we did not feel it was our only means to reach an agreement.
Interviewer:	Considering your experience with welfare aid during a strike, do you think there will be increased reliance on welfare programs as a strike subsidy?
Union Official:	This was the first time our members received welfare benefits while on strike. Our experience with them has been very favorable. Yes, I think our membership now relies on welfare. After all, for twenty-two weeks these programs put food in their mouths and roofs over their heads.

Interviewer: What is the union's reaction to efforts to make strikers ineligible for welfare?

Union Official: We are not happy with this. We feel we are entitled to these benefits since our tax dollars support these programs.

Management Viewpoint

Interviewer: Should strikers be eligible for welfare benefits?

Management Official: No, they should not. When you consider the fact that strikes are voluntarily self-imposed to begin with and that work is available, it does not follow that strikers should receive outside assistance when engaged in an economic struggle within the guidelines of our system of collective bargaining.

Interviewer: What effect does welfare payments to strikers have on collective bargaining?

Management Official: Welfare payments have a negative effect on collective bargaining. Collective bargaining, as we know it in the private enterprise system, is essentially two parties bargaining freely for their respective interests without unfair advantage to either side, and with a minimum of government influence. If we assume that economic benefits to "people in need" are in the national interest and that strikers should be compensated, then we must assume also that the above definition of collective bargaining is no longer applicable.

Interviewer: Does public aid to strikers lengthen or encourage strikes?

Management Official: Welfare benefits to strikers lengthen strikes, and also have a tendency to spread strikes. We are convinced that the welfare benefits received by our employees during the recent strike played a major role in reducing the economic pressures to settle. Further, our salaried employees, who were not on strike, supported the UE strike for the first three weeks and participated in the Food Stamp program during that period of time.

Interviewer: Do you believe, then, that welfare aid to strikers reduces the strikers' willingness to settle?

Management Official: Welfare benefits definitely reduce the economic pressures to settle. In looking back at our recent strike, the union negotiating committee commented on a number of occasions during the negotiations that the food stamp and welfare assistance benefits received by their members greatly reduced the economic pressures to settle.

Interviewer: Earlier, you mentioned that collective bargaining depends on a minimum of outside influence. Is the payment of welfare benefits to strikers a form of government intervention in labor-management negotiations?

Management Official: Yes, because it helps create an unbalanced condition between the parties involved in collective bargaining with respect to the union's demands and their attitude during the negotiations.

Interviewer: Did public subsidies to strikers affect the bargaining environment?

Management Official: These subsidies increased labor-management conflict by enabling labor to put up greater resistance. In our case, it not only gave the union greater confidence, it also strengthened their attitude in respect to the size of their demands. Talk was common in union circles throughout the strike that because of the welfare assistance to strikers the negotiating committee should hold out longer for a better settlement.

Interviewer: Do welfare benefits to strikers make settlements more expensive?

Management Official: In local management's opinion, they do make
settlements more expensive. The local union
operates with the concept that the longer a
strike lasts, the more money the company
must put in the "pot" in order to reach a
settlement. Further, welfare benefits are
supported in part by corporate taxes.

Welfare Agency Viewpoint

Interviewer: What were the immediate effects on your
department when the strike began?

Welfare Official: The strike inconvenienced the entire welfare
department. The non-striker recipient was
also inconvenienced in that by 10:00 a.m. in
the early days of the strike our office could
accept no more food stamp applications.

Interviewer: Could you please explain some of the problems you encountered?

Welfare Official: We were not equipped to handle the number
of applications which we were receiving.
Neither our staff nor our facility is sufficient to process so many people.

We had to borrow from the staff of other
agencies, which affected their operations.
These people were not familiar with our procedures and had to be trained. There was a
job freeze in effect and it was some time before we were able to hire additional clerks.
Once our request for additional employees
was approved, we hired ten temporary clerks
and five retired clerical supervisors. An overtime pay package was also requested and
aproved by the Department of Public Welfare in Harrisburg. I also found it necessary to pull some of my staff off the permanent eligibility cases. These people could
not keep up with the new regulations and
an audit recently taken disclosed that there
were a number of errors in our permanent
cases.

We were in the process of developing a new social services program. The strike imposed a serious threat of disrupting it. However, I refused to remove the staff assigned to it and fortunately I did not have to.

The strike was a strain on our facility. On September 9, 1970, we set up a temporary office at a different location to handle food stamp applications and distribution. At the union's suggestion we also utilized the union hall.

Interviewer:

You mentioned previously that your staff became frustrated with the situation. Would you please expound on their reaction to the situation?

Welfare Official:

Our staff had mixed feelings on the situation. They did not like to neglect the old age or disabled cases; this is one reason why it was so important that we acquire additional help. The attitude of many strikers was demanding and arrogant. Many strikers were defensive. There was also an obvious appearance of well-being on the part of strikers in comparison to our typical applicants. Accordingly, our staff almost walked out when they began receiving complaints from non-striker recipients that strikers were receiving more than they were. In some cases it was true.

Interviewer:

What are your feelings on allowing strikers to receive welfare?

Welfare Official:

The union should be primarily responsible for providing strike benefits. Then, if great need arises, under present rules we must provide aid. I was skeptical about the real needs of many of the strikers.

Our ability to handle and take applications varied day to day. Therefore, I was afraid the strikers were affecting the people who were really desperate. Some people were inconvenienced but, hopefully, not harmed.

Interviewer: In order to handle the heavy administrative
                        load during the strike was it necessary to
                        loosen certification requirements or utilize
                        new procedures?

Welfare Official: No, the standards were not loosened. How-
                        ever, we did adopt a few new procedures.
                        We held group instruction and application
                        sessions for strikers. Also, at the union's
                        suggestion and at the approval of our re-
                        gional office, we instituted a program of re-
                        certifying food stamp recipients through the
                        mail.

Interviewer: How many strikers received welfare assist-
                        ance from your office?

Welfare Official: Exact numbers are not available, but we es-
                        timate that between 2,000 and 2,500 strikers
                        were certified for the Food Stamp program.

Interviewer: Can you estimate the cost of providing wel-
                        fare aid to the Lester plant strikers?

Welfare Official: Most strikers who applied for aid applied
                        for the Food Stamp program. Therefore, the
                        United States Department of Agriculture
                        bore most of the financial burden. An esti-
                        mate of the cost to this program can be de-
                        rived by using a family of four as the typi-
                        cal welfare payment.

                        Some strikers found it necessary to utilize
                        the services of state funded programs. Most
                        avoided it, however, for they felt the strike
                        would end soon and their creditors were al-
                        lowing a grace period. I would not be able
                        to estimate the amount of aid provided un-
                        der these programs.

                        The general assistance program, which is
                        entirely state funded, was the program which
                        qualified strikers seeking cash grants were
                        originally placed on. However, we made a
                        significant effort to transfer people from
                        general assistance to the other public as-
                        sistance programs, such as AFDC and Aid
                        to the Disabled, since the general assistance

program is the only public assistance program not federally supported.

Emergency assistance grants were provided for those strikers in immediate need of cash aid. Unlike the other programs, emergency assistance is operated under budget restrictions. This emergency fund of $150,000 was exceeded during the strike and we were forced to request additional funds from the bureau in Harrisburg. About $45,-000 was borrowed.

The Commonwealth of Pennsylvania also encountered an extra administrative expense because of the strike. This was due to the hiring of additional personnel as well as the requirement for overtime pay. I am not certain what the additional administrative costs were to the department. An estimate could be made by determining the amount of wages paid to the additional help that was hired. You could also add the cost of the two hours of overtime that was worked each day by each employee in this office.[98]

Interviewer: What influence has the strike had on future plans for your department?

Welfare Official: We recognize that there should be some type of system developed to handle such situations. There should be a method of quickly acquiring temporary help. There is a need for better coordination between the state, regional, and local offices, and with the union. We ran out of forms during the strike. There should be a way to prevent such an occurrence. However, the state does not have a plan to handle such an emergency situation.

The only plan we can make is in regard to our budget requests. The possibility of another strike occurring in our area has been considered in our budget request.

[98] These costs are calculated in Table 6.

Interviewer: Are there any additional comments that you
                                wish to make regarding the payment of wel-
                                fare to strikers?

Welfare Official: Many of the strikers are now aware of the
                                income supplementation programs and medi-
                                cal assistance coverage available through the
                                welfare department. We found at the end
                                of the strike that we could not close all the
                                Westinghouse cases since some Lester plant
                                employees were notified that they were still
                                eligible for aid and they chose to continue
                                receiving benefits. There may still be West-
                                inghouse employees on one of the public as-
                                sistance programs.

WESTINGHOUSE STRIKERS ON WELFARE— NUMBERS AND COSTS

The Department of Public Welfare, Commonwealth of Pennsylvania, does not require its county welfare offices to record,
on a continuous basis, the number of strikers on welfare or to
distinguish striker from nonstriker welfare participants. This
can probably be attributed to the fact that department officials
claim that "an insignificant proportion of strikers actually apply
for and receive assistance grants. Denial of assistance would
have little effect on the settlement of the strike. . . ." [99]
Accordingly, a request for data as to the number of Lester
plant strikers participating in Delaware County's welfare programs yielded only estimates which had been made during the
strike by officials of the County Board of Assistance. Rather
than relying exclusively on these estimates, official monthly statistical reports were procured from the Commonwealth of Pennsylvania Department of Public Welfare and from the United
States Department of Agriculture. Utilizing these reports, as well
as data on unemployment and labor-management disputes, empirical analysis produced a very accurate measurement and description of the number of Lester strikers receiving food stamps,
general assistance, and AFDC. This analysis also provided an
estimate of the expenditures made to strikers under these pro-

---

[99] Memorandum from Department of Public Welfare to Delaware County
Board of Assistance, April 12, 1971.

grams. Contrary to the views held by Pennsylvania Public Welfare officials, there were a significant number of strikers participating in welfare programs and the cost to the public was far from insignificant, amounting to more than $2.5 million.

Of the 5,500 Lester plant strikers, approximately 40 percent, or 2,200, reside in Delaware County and the rest live in one of four other counties in the Delaware Valley area. Nearly 90 percent are residents of the Commonwealth of Pennsylvania.[100] Therefore, most of the strikers had access to the same welfare programs. Although welfare programs in Pennsylvania are administered by county boards of assistance, certification requirements, rules, and procedures are essentially uniform.

Delaware County was selected for statistical analysis because of the high concentration of strikers in this county, and because Delaware County had available considerable welfare data and information and could show the impact of the Westinghouse strike on the County Welfare Office. Based on information gathered in other case studies in the Philadelphia labor market area, the authors feel that the conclusions drawn from a study of Delaware County can be applied to the other Pennsylvania counties in which Lester plant strikers reside.

Food Stamp Program

Table 2 shows the total number of persons participating in Delaware County's food stamp program during the period April 1970 through April 1971. These figures are presented in a graph in Figure 8. Non-public assistance persons, as distinguished from public assistance persons, are those individuals not receiving financial aid under public assistance programs.

Food stamp participation began climbing after the Westinghouse walkout began and did not start to decline until the month following the Westinghouse-UE settlement. By January 1971, over 18,000 persons were receiving food stamps in Delaware County, representing a 164 percent increase over the number of participants in August 1970. Initially most of the Lester Plant strikers sought public relief only from the food stamps. This accounts for the incredible 375.2 percent change in non-public assistance participation from August to September, as compared to a 7.5 percent increase for public assistance persons, as shown in Table 2. Generally, the ratio of non-public to public assistance

---

[100] Interview, Lester, Pennsylvania, April 16, 1971.

TABLE 2. *Westinghouse Strike*
Food Stamp Participation
Delaware County, Pennsylvania
April 1970-April 1971

		Persons Participating			Percent Difference from First Month of Strike [a]		
Year	Month	Public Assistance	Non-Public Assistance	Total	Public Assistance	Non-Public Assistance	Total
1970							
	April	4,533	569	5,102	—18.8	—54.0	—25.2
	May	4,939	613	5,552	—11.6	—50.4	—18.6
	June	5,154	769	5,923	— 7.7	—37.8	—13.2
	July	5,474	999	6,473	— 2.0	—19.2	— 5.1
	August	5,585	1,237	6,822	—	—	—
	September	6,003	5,878	11,881	7.5	375.2	74.2
	October	7,525	7,607	15,132	34.7	515.0	121.8
	November	7,295	8,015	15,310	30.6	547.9	124.4
	December	8,818	8,543	17,361	57.9	590.6	154.5
1971							
	January	9,640	8,384	18,024	72.6	577.8	164.2
	February	9,645	7,658	17,303	72.7	519.1	153.6
	March	9,793	4,804	14,597	75.3	288.4	114.0
	April	9,825	4,848	14,673	75.9	291.9	115.1

Source: U.S. Department of Agriculture, Food and Nutrition Service.

[a] August 1970 was the first month of the strike and January 1971 was the last.

food stamp participants is quite low in Delaware County. As an example, the mean ratio was approximately 14.6 percent for the four months preceding the Westinghouse strike. In September 1970, however, this ratio climbed to 98 percent and then to a high of 110 percent in November 1970. As is apparent from Figure 8, in October the number of non-public assistance persons participating in the Food Stamp program exceeded public assistance participants and it was December before the non-public assistance line moved back to a position below the public assistance line.

FIGURE 8. *Westinghouse Strike*
Food Stamp Participation
Delaware County, Pennsylvania
April 1970-April 1971

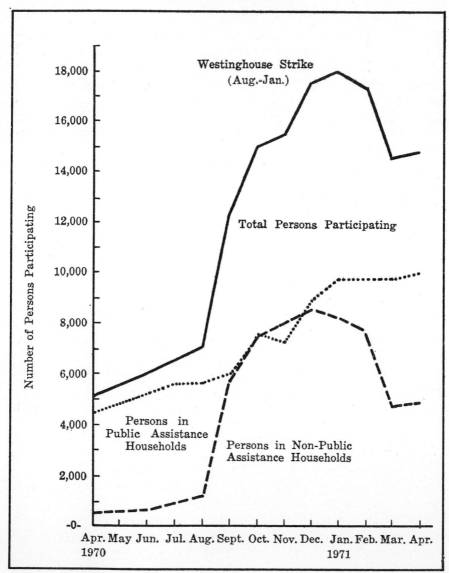

Source: Table 2.

Note: Dates express monthly averages.

Figure 8 also discloses that the number of food stamp recipients in the public assistance category did not increase sharply until October 1970, about one month following the acute rise in non-public assistance participants. The October public assistance participation was up more than 25 percent, over September, compared to monthly increases from 2 to 9 percent for the preceding five months. This change in the food stamp recipient ratio between those on public assistance and those not is the result, not of strikers ceasing to obtain food stamps, but of strikers who already were receiving food stamps obtaining welfare payments as well. Since regulations generally require a thirty-day wait to obtain welfare (AFDC), the changing character of food stamp recipients and welfare set forth in Table 2 and Figure 8 follow expected developments.

The November data would seem inconsistent with this explanation since they show a 3 percent drop in public assistance participants receiving food stamps. One would expect more Westinghouse strikers, not less, to be receiving public assistance. Actually, we believe this occurred. The data, however, reflect the end of concurrent strikes in a large nearby General Electric facility and in Philadelphia-area construction. Removal of persons associated with these strikes is believed to explain the temporary data aberration in November. In December, and thereafter, the number of persons on public assistance receiving food stamps continued sharply upward.

To present a more vivid illustration of the impact of the Westinghouse strike on the Food Stamp program, Delaware County food stamp participation for the period April 1970 through March 1971 was compared to that of Lancaster County, Pennsylvania (Table 3). According to work stoppage data from Pennsylvania's Bureau of Employment Security, Lancaster County did not experience any major strikes during the period under consideration. Therefore, it accommodates a comparison to identify the impact of a strike on food stamp participation.

First, a ratio between food stamp participation in Delaware County and Lancaster County was calculated; second, these ratios were used to establish an average ratio or benchmark from the figures derived for non-strike months; and third, the percent difference between the benchmark and the ratios calculated for each month was computed. This was done, as shown in Table 3, for each food stamp participation category: public assistance, non-public assistance, and total.

TABLE 3. *Westinghouse Strike*
Food Stamp Program Comparative Analysis
Delaware and Lancaster Counties, Pennsylvania
April 1970-March 1971

		Percent Difference from Comparative Mean Ratio [a]		
Year	Month	Public Assistance Participants	Non-Public Assistance Participants	Total Participants
1970				
	April	—2.8	—16.4	—4.4
	May	—3.7	—22.5	—5.7
	June	—3.2	4.2	—2.2
	July	—5.5	28.3	—1.8
	August	—6.5	59.2	0.4
	September	—5.1	586.1	65.4
	October	12.0	718.9	97.8
	November	6.9	683.9	95.6
	December	19.4	639.2	103.9
1971				
	January	24.0	686.7	103.5
	February	15.7	566.9	82.0
	March	0.9	203.3	30.3

Source: U.S. Department of Agriculture, Food and Nutrition Service.

[a] The comparative mean ratio is the mean of the proportion of food stamp participants in Delaware County to those in Lancaster County for the five months preceding the start of the Westinghouse strike. The comparative mean ratios, or benchmarks, are 2.17, 3.60, and 2.28 for PA, Non-PA, and Total food stamp participants respectively. August 1970 was the first month of the strike and January 1971 was the last.

The number of strikers applying for food stamps one month after the walkout began is again clearly shown by the 586 percent difference shown for non-public assistance participation from the benchmark ratio in September 1970. Table 3 also shows the approximate one-month lag in the effect of the Westinghouse strike on public assistance participation. There was a 12 percent positive difference in October 1970 as compared to negative differences during the five preceding months. The impact of the strike on public assistance food stamp participation during the months following October reveals the certification of strikers and their families for public assistance benefits.

Table 3 shows that non-public assistance participation reached a peak in October 1970. The upward movement in food stamp participation by public assistance households, however, did not peak until January 1971.[101] The speed at which non-public assistance participation reached its apex during the strike can be partially explained by the fact that within two months after a work stoppage occurs one can expect to find a majority of the strikers using the food stamps. As the strike enters its second, third, and fourth months, a number of strikers became eligible for AFDC or General Assistance. Therefore, as strikers become clients of public assistance they are transferred from the non-public assistance food stamp participation category to public assistance participation. This administrative process accounts for part of the decline in the non-public assistance rolls.[102]

Looking at the data in Tables 2 and 3 for the months of February, March, and April 1971, we find another interesting and costly aspect of providing food stamps for strikers. One would expect that when the strike ended there would be a decline in the food stamp rolls comparable to the increase noted when the strike commenced. Yet that did not happen for three reasons. First, there is commonly a lag of about thirty days before food stamp and other welfare cases can be administratively closed following the end of a strike.[103] This administrative delay in removing strikers from the welfare rolls is a mechanical difficulty encountered by most welfare offices. A second reason for the delay is that Pennsylvania's Department of Public Welfare has made it a policy to provide at least one additional welfare payment to strikers after they have returned to work and have received a paycheck from their employer.[104] Obviously, this adds to the cost of paying welfare benefits to strikers. A third reason is that a number of Westinghouse employees remained on welfare after the strike, because they discovered they had been entitled to income supplements even before they went on strike

---

[101] The fall from October to November 1970 in PA participation, as explained previously, was primarily attributed to the removal from food stamp rolls of individuals who had been engaged in other strikes throughout the Delaware Valley.

[102] Interview, Chester, Pennsylvania, June 4, 1971.

[103] Interview, June 4, 1971.

[104] Telephone conversation, Director, Public Relations, Department of Public Welfare, Commonwealth of Pennsylvania, October 20, 1971.

or they became eligible because of the strike.[105] Hence, the decline in welfare participation by employees involved in a labor dispute after a strike will often neither be rapid nor complete.

Table 4 shows Delaware County's food stamp sales and costs during the period of the Westinghouse strike. In terms of public cost the impact of providing strikers with food stamps is best indicated by the change in the bonus value of coupon sales after August 1970. Bonus value represents the difference between the amount a participant must pay for food stamps and their actual dollar value. For example, one month after the work stoppage began, a striker with a family of four and certified for food stamps could have received $106 in stamps for a cost of about $33.68. As illustrated in Table 4, the bonus value of his purchase (the public's cost) would have been $72.32.

A brief additional comment regarding bonus stamps may be of value at this point. The sizeable increase in the average bonus per person evident in September 1970 reflects the United States Department of Agriculture's "Special Introductory Offer Program" instituted in 1967. This program offers a 50 percent discount off the required food stamp purchase price for an individual's first month of participation,[106] which permitted strikers to receive additional aid during their first month on food stamps.

Number and Costs of Strikers Aided by Food Stamps

The determination of the number of Westinghouse strikers aided by food stamps and the dollar amount of that aid required statistical estimation techniques. The basic reason for the need of a statistical inference procedure is that the Pennsylvania county welfare offices involved in the strike did not maintain a record of the number of Lester Plant strikers who obtained food stamps. From the information and data provided by the Delaware County Board of Assistance and the U.S. Department of Agriculture it was possible to obtain the desired estimates.

It is estimated that between 1,000 and 2,000 Westinghouse strikers residing in Delaware County, from 50 to 98 per cent of all strikers resident there, received food stamps during and immediately following the walkout. February, the month subse-

---

[105] Interview, Executive Director, Delaware County Board of Assistance, Chester, Pennsylvania, June 4, 1971.

[106] Control Systems Research, Inc., *The Food Stamp Program and How It Works*, Vol. 1, No. 2 (February 1971), p. 41.

TABLE 4. *Westinghouse Strike*
Food Stamp Sales and Expenditures
Delaware County, Pennsylvania
April 1970–April 1971

Year	Month	Total Value	Bonus Value	Average Bonus	Average Bonus per Family [a]	Percent Difference from First Month of Strike in Bonus Value [b]
1970	April	$119,415	$ 43,272	$ 8.48	$33.92	—37.4
	May	130,576	48,315	8.70	34.80	—30.1
	June	142,137	55,364	9.35	37.40	—19.9
	July	157,872	64,763	10.01	40.04	— 6.3
	August	166,588	69,139	10.13	40.52	—
	September	336,566	214,783	18.08	72.32	210.7
	October	379,643	234,652	15.51	62.04	239.4
	November	408,461	248,279	16.22	64.88	259.1
	December	439,570	261,658	15.07	60.28	278.5
1971	January	439,106	250,967	13.92	55.68	263.0
	February	441,200	244,649	14.14	56.56	253.9
	March	351,570	163,413	11.19	44.76	136.4
	April	352,845	162,889	11.10	44.40	135.6

Source: U.S. Department of Agriculture, Food and Nutrition Service.

[a] Derived by multiplying the average bonus per person times four (the estimated average size of a family participating in the Food Stamp program).

[b] August 1970 was the first month of the strike and January 1971 was the last.

TABLE 5. *Westinghouse Strike*
Number of Strikers Receiving Food Stamps
and Financial Aid Provided—Estimated
Delaware County, Pennsylvania
September 1970-February 1971

Year	Month	Estimated Number of Striker Participants	Percent of Delaware County Strikers	Average Bonus Value per Striker	Total Estimated Aid
1970					
	September	1,115	50.7	$72.32	$ 80,637
	October	1,700	77.3	62.04	105,468
	November	1,750	79.5	64.88	113,540
	December	2,100	95.5	60.28	126,588
1971					
	January	2,150	97.7	55.68	119,712
	February	2,000	90.9	56.56	113,120
	Total aid				$659,065

Source: Tables 2 and 4.

quent to the contract settlement, was included because of the large number of strikers who remained on the Food Stamp program for about thirty days after the end of the work stoppage.

The estimates presented in Table 5 were derived by analyzing the characteristics of the Delaware County food stamp data for a 28-month period. To test our estimating technique, a comparative analysis was made of the impact of the 1969-1970 General Electric strike on Delaware County, Pennsylvania, and that of the 1970-1971 Westinghouse strike as shown in Figure 9. This comparative inquiry substantiated the reasonability of our estimations. Although there were not as many striking General Electric employees living in Delaware County as there were Westinghouse strikers, both strikes had a similar impact on county welfare rolls. An analysis of the monthly increases in Delaware County relief rolls, in light of area unemployment problems before, during and after these two lengthy work stoppages, revealed that all but a small percent of the added welfare clients during the General Electric and Westinghouse strikes

were striking workers. Figure 9 cannot disclose the full impact
of these two strikes on public aid programs, but it does illustrate
the common characteristics associated with long strikes.

Table 5 also shows that by January 1971 nearly all the Westinghouse strikers residing in Delaware County were food stamp
participants. This seems quite probable in light of the fact that
the strikers' union was not providing any benefits and by January Westinghouse employees had been off their jobs for five
months. Even if some strikers were able to find part-time or
full-time jobs and although some strikers may have had working
wives, it is reasonable to suspect that between 95 and 100 percent of the strike force was qualified for food stamp aid.

The estimated cost of aiding strikers through the food stamp
program, also shown in Table 5, was more than $650,000. This
represents the bonus value of the coupons distributed—the actual
value of the stamps to the striker recipient and the cost of this
aid to the public. It should be noted, however, that this is only
the cost for strikers living in Delaware County, which means
that it is approximately 40 percent of the total food stamp cost.
We estimate the bonus value of the aid furnished all Westinghouse strikers through the food stamp program at approximately
$1.6 million. These cost figures do not include the thousands of
dollars expended by county welfare offices as a result of the
increased administrative and logistical demands made by the
strike. The unanticipated personnel costs incurred by the Delaware County Board of Assistance alone, presented in Table 6,
totaled $31,170, and do not include overtime pay.

Public Relief Programs

Once the UE-Westinghouse dispute had continued beyond
thirty days, a number of strikers became clients of public assistance programs, as well as the food stamp program. Although
not as many strikers were able, or willing, to qualify for public
assistance as for food stamps, the cash grants and other benefits provided through such programs as General Assistance or
AFDC-U shielded a significant proportion of the strikers from
severe economic hardship. Figure 10 delineates the impact of
the Westinghouse strike on both the General Assistance and
AFDC-U programs.

The Delaware County Welfare Office apparently utilized General Assistance as a sort of catch-all and emergency aid program
during the Westinghouse strike. When strikers began to request

FIGURE 9. *Westinghouse and General Electric Strikes*
Food Stamp Participation
May 1969-April 1971

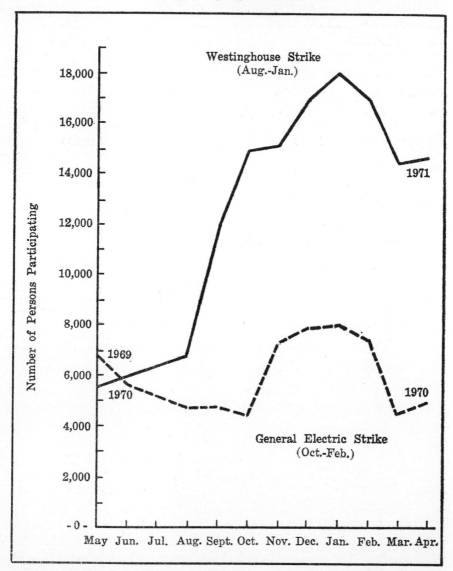

Source: Department of Public Welfare, Commonwealth of Pennsylvania.

Note: Dates express monthly averages.

TABLE 6. *Westinghouse Strike*
Added Personnel Cost
Delaware County Board of Assistance
August 1970-January 1971

Cost Item	Expenditure
Hiring of 10 Temporary Clerks	
Length of service: 3-6 months	
Pay: approximately $340 per month	
Approximate total cost	$15,300
Temporary Reemployment of 5 Newly Retired Personnel	
Length of service: 6 months	
Position: clerical supervisors	
Pay: approximately $529 per month	
Approximate total cost	15,870
Total Cost[a]	$31,170

Source: Delaware County Board of Assistance, Pennsylvania.

[a] In addition to the personnel costs presented herein, a special overtime pay package was required for the Delaware County Board of Assistance. Data as to the dollar amount of overtime pay package were not available.

cash aid from the welfare office, they were processed initially through the General Assistance program. If the striker, having qualified for cash benefits, intended to remain on public assistance, an attempt was made to transfer him from General Assistance because this is a state funded program while such programs as AFDC and Aid to the Disabled are supported by federally matched funds. Unfortunately, for purposes of analysis, the transferring of strikers made it extremely difficult to determine the effect of the strike on public assistance. As with the food stamps, the County Welfare Department made no attempt to distinguish striker from non-striker clients. Because of program eligibility requirements, however, it can be assumed that most strikers on welfare were enrolled in either General Assistance or AFDC-U.

FIGURE 10. *Westinghouse Strike*
AFDC-U and General Assistance Participation: A Comparison
Delaware County, Pennsylvania
April 1970-April 1971

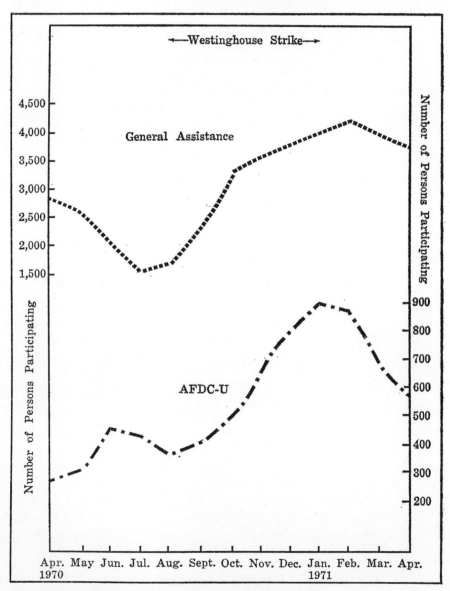

Source: Department of Public Welfare, Commonwealth of Pennsylvania.

Note: Dates express monthly averages.

TABLE 7. *Westinghouse Strike*
General Assistance Participation
Delaware County, Pennsylvania
April 1970-April 1971

Year	Month	Persons Participating	Percent Change from Previous Month	Percent Difference from First Month of Strike [a]
1970				
	April	2,780	— 5.4	68.3
	May	2,545	— 8.5	54.1
	June	2,078	—18.3	25.8
	July	1,524	—26.7	—7.7
	August	1,652	8.4	—
	September	2,245	35.9	35.9
	October	3,237	44.2	95.9
	November	3,628	12.1	119.6
	December	3,883	7.0	135.0
1971				
	January	4,013	3.3	142.9
	February	4,213	5.0	155.0
	March	4,038	— 4.2	144.4
	April	3,909	— 3.2	136.6

Source: Department of Public Welfare, Commonwealth of Pennsylvania.

[a] August 1970 was the first month of the strike and January 1971 was the last.

Table 7 shows the number of persons participating in Delaware County's General Assistance program before, during and after the Westinghouse strike. The impact of the strike on this program is clearly indicated by the 35.9 percent increase in the number of persons receiving General Assistance one month after the walkout took place. There was an even more alarming rise between September and October, 44.2 percent, representing a 95.9 percent increase over August. As illustrated in Figure 11, after October the General Assistance caseload continued to move upward, but at a decreasing rate. Hence, the greatest shock of the strike was felt by the General Assistance program during the first two months of the UE-Westinghouse dispute. Figure 11 shows the similarity between the effect of the General Electric

FIGURE 11. *Westinghouse and General Eléctric Strikes*
General Assistance Participation
Delaware County, Pennsylvania
May 1969-April 1971

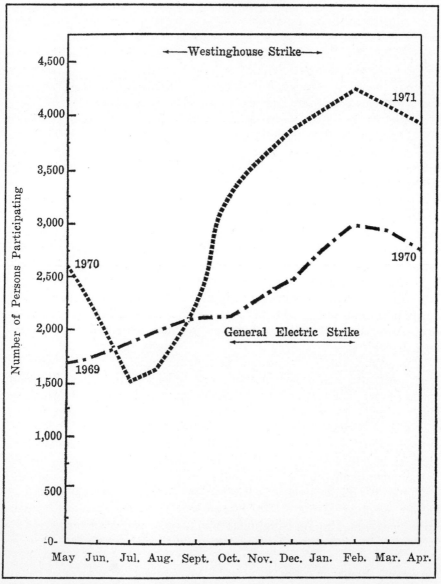

Source: Department of Public Welfare, Commonwealth of Pennsylvania.

Note: Dates express monthly averages.

strike on General Assistance participation and that of the West-inghouse strike. This same parallelism was characteristic of the effect of both strikes on the food stamp program (Figure 9).

Figure 12 provides another illustration of the dramatic rise in Delaware County's General Assistance rolls during the West-inghouse strike. It is often difficult to realize and assess the relative significance of monthly welfare increases during a period when relief costs and caseloads are soaring. Figure 12 allows a comparison of Delaware County's skyrocketing rolls with those of Pennsylvania as a whole. When compared to a somewhat normal trend in General Assistance participation, the severe impact of the Westinghouse strike is clearly evident.

Table 8 shows the expenditures made to General Assistance participants for the period April 1970 through April 1971. The amount of General Assistance aid distributed during October and succeeding months of the Westinghouse strike was significantly higher than any preceding month.

Table 9 gives the estimated number of Lester Plant strikers residing in Delaware County who are believed to have received cash grants from General Assistance. The same statistical estimation techniques that were used for food stamp striker recipients were utilized here. The total cost figure presented in Table 9 is the estimate for Delaware County only, where about 40 percent of the Westinghouse striking employees were living. It is estimated that up to 16.8 percent of these strikers received General Assistance benefits, aid which totaled $190,006 over a six-month period.

The other public assistance program which provided strikers with cash aid and other benefits was AFDC-U. Although a few strikers are believed to have entered the regular AFDC program, the majority of Westinghouse workers who qualified for AFDC aid did so because of the unemployed father option. It is assumed, therefore, that the greatest increase in AFDC participation because of the strike will be observed in the unemployed father segment.

Table 10 displays the participation data for the unemployed father segment of the AFDC program. As in the General Assistance program, the Westinghouse strike was reflected by startling increases in the number of persons enrolled in AFDC-U during the last four months of 1970 and January 1971. The AFDC-U program, however, did not feel the impact of the strike as quickly as did General Assistance, as indicated in the graphs in

FIGURE 12. *Westinghouse Strike*
Percent Difference from First Month of Strike
in General Assistance Participation
Delaware County and the Commonwealth of Pennsylvania
April 1970-April 1971

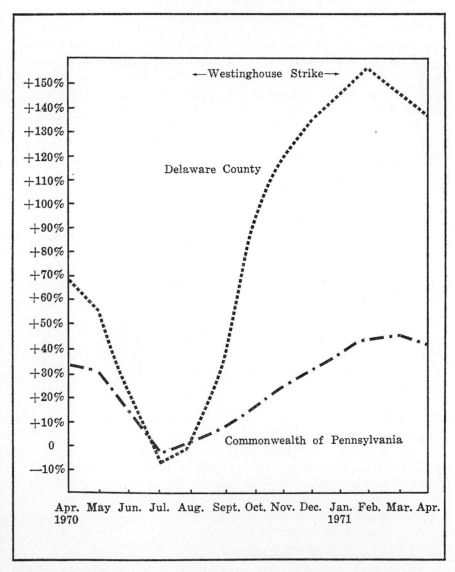

Source: Department of Public Welfare, Commonwealth of Pennsylvania.
Note: Dates express monthly averages.

TABLE 8. *Westinghouse Strike*
General Assistance Expenditures
Delaware County, Pennsylvania
April 1970-April 1971

Year	Month	Total Expenditures	Percent Change from Previous Month	Percent Difference from First Month of Strike [a]	Average Payment per Case
1970					
	April	$289,539	—3.2	35.5	$104.15
	May	255,625	—11.7	19.6	100.44
	June	252,295	—1.3	18.0	121.41
	July	155,191	—38.5	—27.4	101.83
	August	213,752	37.7	—	129.39
	September	243,316	13.8	13.8	108.38
	October	346,067	42.2	61.9	106.91
	November	347,365	0.4	62.5	95.75
	December	412,223	18.7	92.9	106.16
1971					
	January	430,500	4.4	101.4	107.28
	February	442,235	2.7	106.9	104.97
	March	409,644	—7.4	91.6	101.45
	April	387,273	—5.5	81.2	99.07

Source: Department of Public Welfare, Commonwealth of Pennsylvania.

[a] August 1970 was the first month of the Westinghouse strike and January 1971 was the last.

Figure 10. The large AFDC-U increases occurred from October 1970 through January 1971. The variations between the effect of the strike on AFDC-U and General Assistance corroborate what has already been stated about the certification procedure followed by the Delaware County Welfare Office. The General Assistance program was used as the striker's first source of cash aid. Then, if the striker recipient remained on public assistance, an effort was made to transfer him to a program which received financial support from the federal government.

In any event, AFDC-U rolls increased rapidly from the beginning of the Westinghouse strike until its end, as illustrated in

TABLE 9. *Westinghouse Strike*
Number of Strikers
Receiving General Assistance and Financial Aid Provided—
Estimated
Delaware County, Pennsylvania
September 1970-February 1971

Year	Month	Estimated Number of Striker Participants	Percent of Delaware County Strikers	Average Payment per Striker	Total Estimated Aid
1970					
	September	113	5.1	$108.38	$ 12,247
	October	328	14.9	106.91	35,066
	November	364	16.5	95.75	34,853
	December	370	16.8	106.16	39,279
1971					
	January	370	16.8	107.28	39,694
	February	275	12.5	104.97	28,867
				Total cost	$190,006

Source: Tables 7 and 8.

Figure 13. Even in February 1971, the month following the contract settlement, there were still 142.4 percent more persons on AFDC-U than in August 1970. This extraordinary level for AFDC-U rolls is clearly evident in the graphical illustrations presented in Figures 13 and 14. Figure 13 depicts how the effects of the General Electric strike on AFDC-U parallel those of the Westinghouse strike. Figure 14 indicates the consequence of permitting strikers to obtain financial help through public assistance by plotting AFDC-U participation in Delaware County against that of Pennsylvania as a whole.

Expenditures made by Delaware County to those enrolled in the AFDC-U program during the period April 1970 through April 1971 are shown in Table 11 along with the average payment made to each recipient during these months. The average payment per case ranged from a low of $263.25 in the month before the strike to a high of $308.10 during August, the first month of the strike. The total monthly expenditures on AFDC-U

TABLE 10. *Westinghouse Strike*
AFDC-U Participation
Delaware County, Pennsylvania
April 1970-April 1971

Year	Month	Persons Participating	Percent Change from Previous Month	Percent Difference from First Month of Strike a
1970				
	April	284	—11.5	—21.8
	May	303	6.7	—16.5
	June b	460	51.8	26.7
	July	446	—3.0	22.9
	August	363	—18.6	—
	September	404	11.3	11.3
	October	492	21.8	35.5
	November	681	38.4	87.6
	December	807	18.5	122.3
1971				
	January	893	10.7	146.0
	February	880	—1.5	142.4
	March	659	—25.1	81.5
	April	587	—10.9	61.7

Source: Department of Public Welfare, Commonwealth of Pennsylvania.

a August 1970 was the first month of the strike and January 1971 was the last.

b The increase in AFDC-U rolls in June 1970 reflects the impact of the Philadelphia Construction Industry strike which began on May 1, 1970 and lasted forty-two days. Source: U.S. Department of Labor, Bureau of Labor Statistics and Delaware County Board of Assistance.

FIGURE 13. *Westinghouse and General Electric Strikes*
AFDC-U Participation
Delaware County, Pennsylvania
May 1969-April 1971

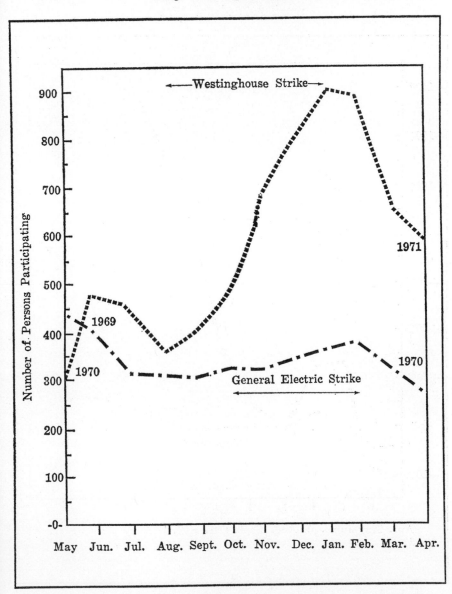

Source: Department of Public Welfare, Commonwealth of Pennsylvania.

Note: Dates express monthly averages.

FIGURE 14. *Westinghouse Strike*
Percent Difference from First Month of Strike
in AFDC-U Participation
Delaware County and the Commonwealth of Pennsylvania
April 1970-April 1971

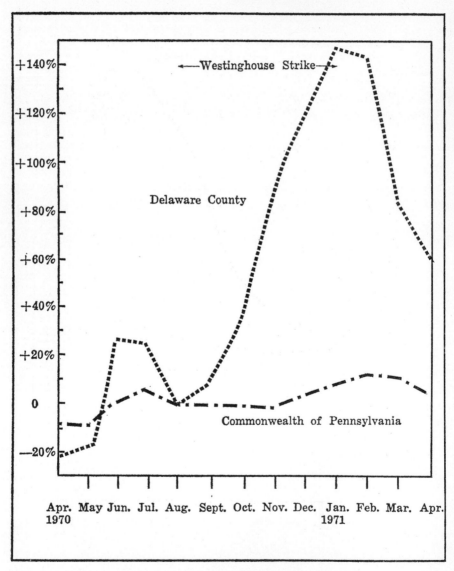

Source: Department of Public Welfare, Commonwealth of Pennsylvania.

Note: Dates express monthly averages.

climbed to more than $260,000, a 132.5 percent rise over August 1970. This peak was reached in February 1971, after which the effects of the strike on welfare rolls began to subside considerably.

TABLE 11. *Westinghouse Strike*
Expenditures for AFDC-U Program
Delaware County, Pennsylvania
April 1970-April 1971

Year	Month	Total Expenditures[a]	Percent Change from Previous Month	Percent Difference from First Month of Strike[b]	Average Payment per Case
1970					
	April	$ 78,341	—18.7	—30.0	$275.85
	May	86,491	10.4	—22.7	285.45
	June	128,938	49.1	15.3	280.30
	July	117,410	—8.9	5.0	263.25
	August	111,840	—4.7	—	308.10
	September	109,464	—2.1	—2.1	270.95
	October	134,587	23.0	20.3	273.55
	November	192,451	43.0	72.1	282.60
	December	229,349	19.2	105.1	284.20
1971					
	January	249,281	8.7	122.9	279.15
	February	260,040	4.3	132.5	295.50
	March	194,504	—25.2	73.9	295.15
	April	158,960	—18.3	42.1	270.80

Source: Computed from Table 10 and U.S. Department of Health, Education and Welfare, Social and Rehabilitation Service, *Public Assistance Statistics* (monthly), Table 8.

[a] Total expenditures for the AFDC-U Program were derived by multiplying the average payment per person times the number of persons receiving AFDC-U aid in Delaware County, Pennsylvania (see Table 10).

[b] August 1970 was the first month of the strike and January 1971 was the last.

Table 12 presents the estimated number of Lester Plant strikers living in Delaware County who participated in the AFDC-U program. The statistical methods used to approximate the number of Westinghouse strikers obtaining aid from the General Assistance and Food Stamp programs were again utilized. In January 1971 an estimated 119 strikers (representing 5.4 percent of strikers living in Delaware County) received an average payment of $279.15, total aid of $33,219. Total AFDC-U assistance to these strikers over the six-month period is estimated at $126,783. Since this only represents what happened in one county where about 40 percent of the total number of strikers resided, the total for all strikers could be more than double this amount.

The relatively small proportion of striking Delaware County residents who were on AFDC-U rolls is unusual when compared to the other long strikes which have been studied. A strike of the duration experienced at Lester would generally have resulted in between 15 and 20 percent of the strike force entering AFDC-

TABLE 12. *Westinghouse Strike*
Number of Strikers
Receiving AFDC-U and Financial Aid Provided—Estimated
Delaware County, Pennsylvania
September 1970-February 1971

Year	Month	Estimated Number of Striker Participants	Percent Delaware County Strikers/ Residents	Average Payment per Striker	Total Estimated Aid
1970					
	September	8	0.4	$270.95	$ 2,168
	October	31	1.4	273.55	8,480
	November	75	3.4	182.60	21,195
	December	108	4.9	284.20	30,694
1971					
	January	119	5.4	279.15	33,219
	February	105	4.8	295.50	31,027
				Total	$126,783

Source: Tables 10 and 11.

U. However, something else was different about the Delaware County situation. An unusually high percentage of the Westinghouse strikers received aid from General Assistance. This program has usually been found to be of less use to strikers than either food stamps or AFDC-U. Yet, in Delaware County it appears to have been second only to food stamps. This situation reflects the processing procedure utilized by the Delaware County welfare office during the strike. In addition, although 50 percent of the cash aid provided through the AFDC-U program is paid for by the federal government, it was still less expensive for Pennsylvania to aid an individual through the General Assistance program because AFDC-U participants received monthly payments over twice as large as those received by General Assistance participants. (Compare Tables 8 and 11.)

Total Estimated Costs

Table 13 gives the total estimated public cost of supporting strikers living in Delaware County through the Food Stamp, General Assistance, and AFDC-U programs. Considering the almost one million dollar cost figure presented pertains only to 40 percent of the Westinghouse strikers, the total cost of subsidizing the strikers through these programs probably amounted to nearly

TABLE 13. *Westinghouse Strike*
Total Estimated Cost of Providing Public Aid
to Strikers
Delaware County, Pennsylvania
September 1970-February 1971

Program	Expenditure	Percent of Total
Food stamps	$659,065	67.5
General assistance	190,006	19.5
AFDC-U	126,783	13.0
Total a	$975,854	100.0

Source: Tables 5, 9, and 12.

a Does not include the added administrative and logistical costs caused by the strike, or the cost of aiding strikers through other public aid programs. For example, aid from the regular AFDC program and medical benefits.

$2.5 million, not including the added administrative or logistical costs of handling these cases. In addition, it does not account for the cost of the special benefits afforded welfare recipients, such as medical assistance.

The Food Stamp program was responsible for 67.5 percent of the total cost of aiding Westinghouse strikers, General Assistance for 19.5 percent, and AFDC-U for 13 percent. Although the two public assistance programs together accounted for only about 33 percent of the total cost, they aided only 5 to 17 percent of the total strike force. Food Stamps, however, were aiding more than 50 percent of the Westinghouse strikers just one month after the walkout started, and nearly all of them by the fifth month. Thus, although welfare offices may not have had to process or service as many public assistance striker clients as Food Stamp striker participants, the cost of the aid per striker was significantly higher. If in future strikes of the length and magnitude of the Westinghouse-UE dispute, strikers are more willing and prepared to obtain financial aid from public assistance than they were during the work stoppage at Lester, one can expect the public's cost of supporting strikers to be much higher than $2.5 million.

SUMMARY AND CONCLUSION

It is evident from a review of the Lester Plant strike that public subsidies played a key role in the union's strike assistance program. As a consequence, the union now plans to rely on public financial support during a strike. From once having used public dollars in an organized manner, Local 107 now recognizes both the value of welfare aid and the necessity for a well-developed, continuously functioning welfare committee. Both union officials and members indicated that it would be difficult, if not impossible, to sustain a prolonged strike without welfare benefits.

The availability of public resources for strikers during the Westinghouse strike provided support both to the local and international union. Welfare benefits reduced the strikers' economic pain, providing union officials and the union bargaining committee with greater flexibility in contract negotiations. In addition, public dollars to strikers relieved the local and international union of the financial pressure connected with giving aid to needy strikers. Although there were some strikers who expressed dissatisfaction with the UE for not providing a strike benefits program, welfare eliminated much of the demand for union financial help.[107] The union could rely on the welfare department to care for strikers who experienced economic hardships. The union and the striker, therefore, were relieved of much of their financial responsibility in preparing for and supporting the strike. The public assumed this responsibility.

Impact on Striker Resolve

Although difficult to prove qualitatively, it can be easily perceived that welfare benefits had an effect on the strikers' resolve. The Lester Plant strike began in August, yet lasted through Christmas and well into the middle of a cold winter. Despite the fact that no union strike benefits were provided, strikers were able to remain off their jobs for 160 days. Public aid supported their cause by protecting them from severe economic hardship. The striker recognized that, no matter how long the strike lasted, his family would be provided food, shelter, clothing, medical aid, and basic necessities. There is little doubt that such economic protection had an effect on the striker's decision either to hold out in support of his bargaining committee or to return to work.

It is the "average" to "low" wage earner who is afforded the greatest assistance by welfare during a strike. Unlike many union strike benefit programs (where financial aid is distributed evenly to all members based only on whether single, married, or married with a family), public aid is directed to that striker who is first financially hurt by a strike. Thus, as a strike progresses, an increasing number of strikers become clients of the welfare department. The family man with a large number of debts, little savings, and a low income prior to the strike may be certified for public support shortly after a walkout occurs, while the older worker who may have few debts, owns his own home, and has accumulated sizeable liquid savings may not become eligible for public aid during a long strike. Accordingly, in a strike situation, the individual who has prepared for the strike by saving and by being thrifty will be discriminated against by the welfare department.

---

[107] Interview with members of Local 107, April 27, 1971.

Impact on a Typical Striker

Prior to the strike the average wage of an hourly employee at Westinghouse's Steam Division was $4.12 per hour. The average work week was 37.5 hours. Therefore, an average employee received a weekly gross pay of $154.50. His net weekly wage would be about $131.50 (net wage was computed assuming that the wage earner was married and claiming five[108] deductions: Federal Tax—$13.50, Social Security—$8.00, and union dues—$1.50).

The records of the U.S. Department of Health, Education and Welfare reveal that in November 1970 an average Pennsylvania AFDC-U case received approximately $282 in cash assistance. There is no reason to believe that a striker meeting the necessary requirement for certification to the AFDC-U program and having a family of four did not receive an equal amount of cash benefits. In addition, an AFDC-U recipient could have received $106.00 in food stamps for about $41.00.[109] Therefore, the total amount of welfare aid provided would be $347.00 per month or about $85.00 per week.[110]

When compared to the weekly net wage of the striker described in step one above, $85.00 in public assistance represents about 65 percent of the striker's working wage. The availability of such a sizeable amount of financial aid while on strike cannot but reduce the economic hardship experienced by a striker. Although it can be legitimately argued that not all strikers who received welfare assistance were provided as much financial help as indicated above, it can also be justifiably inferred that there were strikers who may have received more than 65 percent of their weekly net salary. The case presented is based on an average hourly worker. Those strikers on welfare who made less than the average hourly wage employee at Westinghouse would have received even greater assistance from welfare benefits.

A number of Steam Division strikers made some surprising discoveries when they became clients of the welfare department. After a short glimpse of what aid was available through welfare, many found double benefits. First, they were eligible either for

---

[108] A family size of five was selected for this example for it was the average size of a family participating in the AFDC-U program in November 1970. Source: Department of Public Welfare, Commonwealth of Pennsylvania.

[109] See Table 4 for average bonus values.

[110] This aid is tax free.

food stamps or for some other form of income supplement before they went on strike. Second, they could receive almost as much weekly income while on strike as when working. For example, a striker working for a standard hourly wage of $3.12 per hour, with a family of five members and meeting all requirements for the AFDC-U program discovered he could receive assistance amounting to 90 percent or more of his working income. According to an official of the Delaware County Welfare Department, this situation prompted some Westinghouse workers to remain on welfare rolls even after the strike had ended.

There are a number of factors which can affect the length of a strike. Hence, it cannot be said that welfare payments to strikers were the exclusive cause of the long strike at Westinghouse's Steam Division. The financial assistance provided Westinghouse strikers by welfare seems obviously, however, to have affected their determination and strength of mind during the dispute and that the latter had an effect on the length of the strike and on its cost.

CHAPTER V

General Motors Strike
September 14—November 12, 1970

On September 14, 1970, labor contracts with the big three auto makers expired. One hundred thirty-seven General Motors plants in the United States became the target of a United Auto Workers nationwide strike. Leonard Woodcock, head of the UAW, led 329,000 GM employees on a 71-day walkout which was termed the biggest and costliest strike suffered by our nation in over a decade.[111] Observers believed that financial pressures on strikers, the UAW, General Motors, and the nation would force an early settlement. Yet, no urgency seemed to exist within the UAW to settle. When the strike began, General Motors demanded that local contracts at 54 key plants be completed before a national settlement could be reached. UAW officials agreed. It was nearly the end of October, however, before the national leaders of the UAW attempted to speed up sluggish local negotiations.[112] Until that time there was little evidence of pressure to settle on local or national union negotiators; only 26 of 54 key plants had new contracts seven weeks after the strike began.[113]

Pressure for a settlement finally came from national UAW officers. They pressed to secure local contracts at key GM plants to permit a national settlement by the middle of November. The November date was apparently an attempt to avert a complete drain of the UAW's $121 million "war chest" and the payment of another $26 million in life and medical insurance premiums on striking members.[114] Both the union and company appeared

---

[111] *Time*, November 23, 1970, p. 94; and U.S. Bureau of Labor Statistics, *Work Stoppages in 1970*, January 11, 1971.

[112] *Wall Street Journal*, November 9, 1970, p. 4.

[113] *Wall Street Journal*, November 2, 1970, p. 28.

[114] General Motors agreed to continue paying life and medical insurance premiums for strikers during the strike, but only on condition that the UAW was obligated to reimburse GM with interest.

concerned that if the strike went past mid-November, it might get out of control and continue well into 1971.

The number of local contracts secured by early November satisfied General Motors' management. A national settlement was reached on November 12, 1970, but even then thirty nonkey plants still did not have contracts, and the union had spent over $156 million from its strike fund and other sources.[115] The national contract was ratified on November 23, 1970.[116]

A number of factors may be said to be responsible for the length of the 1970 UAW-GM strike. It is unlikely that any one factor can be isolated and identified as the single determinant of the strike's duration. Yet in the 1970 General Motors strike, there appeared to be an abnormal lack of pressure on union bargaining committees; reports from the press and personal interviews with union officials and management representatives involved in the strike all noted this phenomenon. It was repeatedly suggested that the low level of pressure was caused by the absence of an expressed urgency or eagerness to settle on the part of strikers and striker families. Said a union official in Flint, Michigan, "It is unusual to get so little pressure during a long strike like this." [117]

THE MICHIGAN STORY

Of the thirty states with General Motors plants and parts depots, Michigan has the greatest concentration of General Motors facilities and employees. The 1970 strike directly idled nearly 170,000 Michigan workers, representing more than 18 percent of the state's manufacturing work force.[118] Striking employees of General Motors plants located in three Michigan counties (Genesee, Okland, and Wayne) accounted for nearly 70 percent of the Michigan UAW strike force and over a third of the nation's UAW strike force.

Obviously, the 71-day strike had severe economic effects on the state of Michigan and especially on those Michigan counties with a high concentration of General Motors plants. In addition, a significant share of the cost of the strike had to be paid by

---

[115] *Philadelphia Bulletin*, February 12, 1971.

[116] *U.S. News and World Report*, December 7, 1970, p. 72.

[117] Interview, Flint, Michigan, March 16, 1971.

[118] *U.S. News and World Report*, November 23, 1970, p. 17.

Michigan and United States' taxpayers. The UAW walkout had a twofold, negative impact on federal, state, and local finances. First, as anticipated, there was a costly decline in sales and income tax revenues. For Michigan these losses were estimated to have amounted to about $5 million per week.[119] Second, Michigan experienced a startling increase in welfare expenditures, an added public expense estimated to be almost $15.7 million.[120] Some repercussions of these combined revenue losses were described by *U.S. News and World Report* in November 1970:

> Michigan's Governor, William Milliken, recommended cuts of 50 to 60 millions in State spending. Pontiac, home of four GM plants, laid off 200 city employees. Saginaw put some departments on a 32-hour week. Officials in Flint were considering a 1.8 million dollar cut in their budget.[121]

The sharp decline in tax revenue during a prolonged strike is not a new experience for Michigan. The state has frequently paid that price for the presence of the unionized auto industry which employs approximately 10 percent of its total labor force.[122] In addition, the 1970 GM strike introduced Michigan taxpayers to the cost of providing welfare aid to striking workers.

Actually, Michigan has been distributing public funds to strikers for many years. Opinions in 1946 and 1948 by the Michigan attorneys general of those periods held that strikers were eligible to receive welfare assistance.[123] Information from the Michigan Department of Social Services verifies the fact that Michigan strikers had been receiving various forms of public aid long before the 1970 General Motors strike. Nevertheless, it was during the 1970 dispute, when striker participation in welfare programs far exceeded welfare officials' expectations, that it became quite apparent that strikers were more than willing to take advantage of state and federal policies which permitted them to receive welfare. This was Michigan's first real encounter with the problem of public support of strikers.

---

[119] *Business Week*, November 7, 1970, p. 19.

[120] See Table 21.

[121] *U.S. News and World Report*, November 23, 1970, p. 17.

[122] State of Michigan Employment Security Commission reports.

[123] *Flint Journal*, October 11, 1970. We previously noted a statement by Leo Perlis that the 1945 General Motors strike was one of the earliest organized efforts by labor to utilize welfare funds during a strike.

Strikers on Welfare in Michigan: Numbers and Costs

At least 54 of Michigan's 83 counties provided some form of public aid to General Motors strikers.[124] County welfare offices were contacted prior to the strike by a union official or a representative of the local union's community services, strike assistance, or welfare committee. Meetings were then arranged between representatives of the welfare office and the local union at which welfare representatives enumerated both the welfare programs available to strikers and the requirements for eligibility. In turn, the union advised the welfare office as to the expected number of striker applicants and additionally offered the services of union personnel and property to facilitate the processing of striker applications.

Accordingly, as the strike began, most strikers were well aware that food stamps would be available to them right away. It was no surprise when welfare offices were immediately swamped with food stamp applications. What was startling, however, was how vastly the number of applications exceeded prestrike estimates. For example, an official of the Genesee County Welfare Office said that his agency had anticipated 10-12,000 applicants but had received instead approximately 30,000.[125] 000.[125]

Some strikers were astonished to discover that they had been eligible for public relief benefits before the strike began. A few were informed by social workers that they were entitled to income supplements under certain provisions of the AFDC program even though they were employed in full-time jobs. Others were counseled on the various income adjustments which would have made it possible for them to receive food stamps while working steadily. Consequently, a number of strikers remained on various public aid programs after the General Motors strike was settled.[126]

In addition to the Food Stamps program, thousands of General Motors employees within three months were also receiving benefits under the AFDC and General Assistance programs. Combined with weekly union strike benefits ($30 if single, $35 if married with no children, and $40 if married with children),

---

[124] Michigan Department of Social Services.

[125] Interview, Flint, Michigan, March 19, 1971.

[126] Interview, March 19, 1971.

public funds assisted up to 50 percent of the Michigan General Motors strikers in sustaining a 71-day labor dispute with minimum economic hardship.[127]

Food Stamp Program

As in the case of Westinghouse, the impact of the strikers' use of food stamps is shown by the great increase in the number of non-public assistance (Non-PA) household participants immediately after the strike began and an increase of public assistance (PA) participants later as strikers became eligible for public assistance. Figure 15 and Table 14 show that non-PA participation increased more than 208 percent from September to October 1970, just one month following the commencement of the strike.

The participation data presented in Table 14 and illustrated in Figure 15 represent the average number of persons receiving food stamps each month, as reported by the U.S. Department of Agriculture. In order to exhibit only the normal monthly changes in food stamps participation and the effect of the General Motors strike, food stamp participation data presented has been adjusted so as to exclude Michigan counties which introduced the program after April 1970.[128]

Figure 15 shows that approximately thirty days after the sharp climb in Non-PA rolls there occured an acute upward movement in PA participation (see also Table 14). We have already noted that this is the time period necessary for a sizeable proportion of a strike force to become eligible for cash relief and begin receiving aid.

As was the case in the Westinghouse strike, strikers were slower to leave programs than to join them. Indeed, some stayed on for a considerable time after the strike was over. An official of Michigan's Department of Social Services explained the situation following the General Motors strike:

> Many . . . striker cases were not closed effectively until the second half of December 1970 [the strike officially ended November 20, 1970] i.e., families received a check for one-half of the month

---

[127] Data from Michigan Department of Social Services.

[128] Not all Michigan counties administer the Food Stamp program. In May 1970 57 Michigan counties had the program as compared to 63 at the end of 1970. Most counties not providing food stamps aided strikers by supplying surplus commodities.

TABLE 14. General Motors Strike
Food Stamp Participation (Adjusted)
State of Michigan
May 1970-April 1971

Year	Month	Total Participating Counties [a]	Persons Participating			Percent Difference from First Month of Strike [b]		
			Public Assistance	Non-Public Assistance	Total	Public Assistance	Non-Public Assistance	Total
1970	May	57	195,001	64,322	259,323	—21.1	—50.8	—31.4
	June	57	206,515	82,455	288,970	—16.4	—37.0	—23.6
	July	57	207,566	107,209	314,775	—16.0	—18.1	—16.7
	August	57	231,861	108,774	340,635	—6.2	—16.9	—9.9
	September	57	247,163	130,825	377,988	—	—	—
	October	57	269,560	403,404	672,964	9.1	208.4	78.0
	November	57	309,470	431,122	740,592	25.2	229.5	95.9
	December	57	335,619	252,578	588,197	35.8	93.1	55.6
1971	January	57	307,031	163,657	470,688	24.2	25.1	24.5
	February	57	321,260	177,213	498,473	30.0	35.5	31.9
	March	57	333,167	170,908	504,075	34.8	30.6	33.4
	April	57	346,145	168,836	514,981	40.0	29.1	36.2

Source: Department of Agriculture, Food and Nutrition Service.

[a] Michigan counties admitted to the Food Stamp Program after May 1970 are eliminated from the participation data presented.

[b] September 1970 was the first month of the strike and November 1970 was the last.

FIGURE 15. *General Motors Strike*
Food Stamp Participation
State of Michigan
May 1970-April 1971

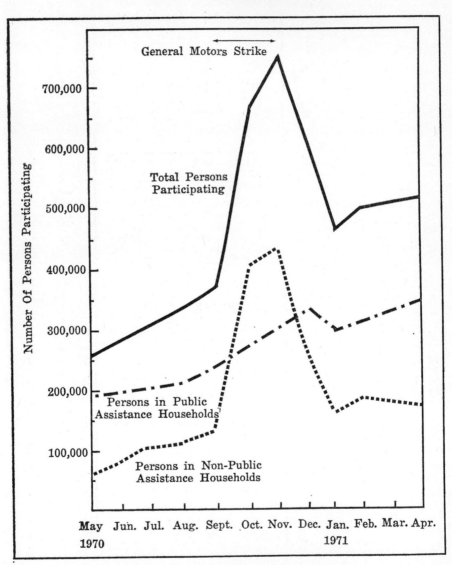

Source: U.S. Department of Agriculture, Food and Nutrition Service.

Note: Dates represent monthly average.
           Michigan counties admitted to the Food Stamp Program after May
           1970 are eliminated from the participation data presented.

of December prior to case closing. This overlay was caused by the tremendous amount of paperwork involved in respect to closure of these cases.[129]

Figure 15 shows that the decline in food stamp participation following the strike is not as sharp as the increase in participation at the strike's beginning. Also, food stamp rolls in the PA category do not fall until some time after the strike is over. Although there was some unemployment in Michigan caused by the strike, food stamp rolls in December 1970 and January 1971 were still unusually high. This means that in accordance with the eligibility requirements and income adjustment procedures of the food stamp program, some General Motors workers had been entitled to food stamp aid before the strike began and/or the economic impact of the lengthy labor dispute on some strikers' asset position was severe enough to qualify them for food stamps for some time following their return to work.

Table 15 shows the food stamp sales and expenditures for Michigan during the General Motors strike. The dramatic increase of 115.3 percent from September to October in the bonus value of coupon sales discloses clearly the impact of the strike on food stamp costs. As already noted, it is the bonus value of food stamps which indicates the cost of the coupon to the government and the value of the coupon to the welfare recipient. In addition, Table 15 shows the average bonus paid per family, which discloses the approximate average monthly dollar worth of food stamps to a striker. Many strikers, however, received a greater bonus contribution than the average because of the special food stamp regulation which at that time provided a 50 percent discount off the purchase price for the individual's first month of participation.[130]

The Michigan Department of Social Services was not able to provide a precise monthly count of the number of General Motors strikers who participated in the Food Stamp program. The estimates presented in Table 16 were calculated using the data and information provided by the Michigan Department of Social Services, the U.S. Department of Agriculture, UAW local

---

[129] Letter from Supervisor, Statistical Reports Section, Michigan Department of Social Services, July 12, 1971.

[130] This was offered by the Department of Agriculture until January 1, 1971. Almost all strikers qualified for this special benefit. See Control Systems Research, Inc., *The Food Stamp Program and How It Works*, Vol. 1, No. 2 (February 1971), p. 41.

TABLE 15.   *General Motors Strike*
Food Stamp Sales and Expenditures (Adjusted)
State of Michigan
May 1970-April 1971

Year	Month[a]	Total Value	Bonus Value	Average Bonus	Average Bonus per Family[b]	Percent Difference from First Month of Strike in Bonus Value[c]
1970						
	May	$ 5,971,938	$ 3,020,738	$11.65	$46.60	—30.6
	June	6,790,311	3,479,668	12.04	48.16	—20.1
	July	7,487,642	3,973,638	12.62	50.48	—8.8
	August	7,670,843	3,970,598	11.66	46.64	—8.8
	September	8,447,829	4,355,240	11.52	46.08	—
	October	15,204,303	9,375,584	13.93	55.72	115.3
	November	16,881,847	10,125,375	13.67	54.68	132.5
	December	12,656,961	6,709,406	11.41	45.64	54.1
1971						
	January	10,598,948	5,253,974	11.16	44.64	20.6
	February	11,334,546	5,597,896	11.23	44.92	28.5
	March	11,991,038	5,840,689	11.59	46.36	34.1
	April	12,090,618	5,873,907	11.41	45.64	34.9

Source: U.S. Department of Agriculture, Food and Nutrition Service.

[a] The sales and expenditures data for Michigan counties admitted to the Food Stamp program after May 1970 were eliminated.

[b] Derived by multiplying the average bonus per person, as reported by the U.S. Department of Agriculture, times four (the average size of a family participating in the Food Stamp program).

[c] September 1970 was the first month of the strike and November 1970 was the last.

TABLE 16. *General Motors Strike*
Number of Strikers Receiving Food Stamps and Financial Aid
Provided—Estimated
State of Michigan
September-December 1970

Month	Estimated Number of Striker Participants	Average Bonus Value per Striker	Total Estimated Aid
September	15,000	$46.08	$ 691,200
October	70,000	55.72	3,900,400
November	82,000	54.68	4,483,760
December	35,000	45.64	1,597,400
		Total	$10,672,760

Source: Estimated from Tables 14 and 15.

officials, and company management representatives. They are very conservative and undoubtedly lower than the actual number of strikers who obtained food stamps.[131]

A brief comparison of Tables 15 and 16 demonstrates the significance of a federal commitment to provide food stamps to striking workers. For example, the bonus value of the food stamps distributed in November 1970 to about 50 percent of the total number of strikers in Michigan—$4,483,760—was higher than the total cost of Michigan's Food Stamp program during any one month from May to October 1970. Also, the nearly $11 million in food stamps provided Michigan General Motors strikers could have financed Michigan's program for the months May, June, and July 1970.

---

[131] The estimates presented in Table 17 are considered conservative for at least two reasons. First, the monthly food stamp statistics used to calculate these estimates are average monthly figures and not absolute figures. Thus, the impact of a strike on food stamp rolls is submerged because monthly participation figures are determined by dividing the number of persons obtaining food stamps at the two allotment periods during a single month by two. The effect of a large number of strikers receiving only one food stamp payment during a month, therefore, will be partially concealed.

Second, the data used to compute these estimates were adjusted so as to exclude certain Michigan counties (see Table 15). According to the Michigan Department of Social Services at least three of these excluded counties provided public aid to General Motors strikers.

Public Assistance Program

General Motors strikers were slower to accept public assistance than food stamps, as were their Westinghouse counterparts. Accordingly, even after the required waiting period, it was late October and early November before such programs began to bear a significant share of the cost of supporting GM strikers. They soon, however, took on a sizeable share. Thanks to the exceptionally good records of the Michigan Department of Social Services, the overall impact of the strike is clearly distinguishable.

Taking first the AFDC program, Table 17 shows the number of striker families who were participants as reported by the Michigan Department of Social Services. Since Michigan also extends aid to families with dependent children under the unemployed father option, most of the strikers were enrolled in the AFDC-U segment of the program. The participation data in Table 17 includes AFDC-U recipients. Table 18 and Figure 16 show the great increase in AFDC-U rolls during the time of the strike. The most severe shock was felt in November, but General Motors employees who were still on AFDC-U in December continued to hold rolls high a month after the strike was settled. In other words, the Michigan Department of Social Services was unable to remove many of these strikers before they had received a public assistance payment for December.

The total of the AFDC cash payments to General Motors striker families in Michigan was more than $4 million. Table 19 shows that the approximate monthly value of these payments to a participating striker ran from $93.82 to $102.73. These AFDC recipients were also eligible for food stamps, medical benefits, and other forms of welfare assistance. Thus, as an example, with union strike benefits it was possible for approximately 13 percent of the General Motors strikers to have received about $325 in nontaxable financial aid in November 1970.

Approximately 2,800 strikers received cash payments from the General Assistance program in November 1970.[132] It is difficult to determine the precise number of strikers participating in this program in October and December, but it is estimated that, like AFDC, the combined number of striker cases for October and December 1970 about equalled the number of GM employees

---

[132] Letter from the Michigan Department of Social Services to James R. Konneker, December 28, 1970.

TABLE 17. *General Motors Strike*
Number of Striker Families Receiving AFDC by County
State of Michigan
October, November, and December 1970

County	Number of Families		
	October	November	December
Entire state	2,851	22,797	18,817
Alcona	1	4	2
Alger	12	36	39
Allegan	1	11	21
Alpena	2	2	3
Antrim	1	3	4
Arenac	—	14	10
Barry	1	28	27
Bay	148	767	605
Berrien	3	9	7
Branch	1	1	—
Calhoun	1	31	46
Charlevoix	—	1	—
Clinton	1	46	62
Eaton	33	222	142
Emmet	—	2	4
Genesee	1,445	8,829	6,879
Gladwin	—	1	2
Grand Traverse	—	—	2
Gratiot	6	139	111
Houghton	—	2	2
Huron	—	9	11
Ingham	118	660	687
Ionia	—	87	60
Iosco	—	1	1
Isabella	2	16	18

TABLE 17—*continued*

| County | Number of Families | | |
	October	November	December
Jackson	—	2	2
Kalamazoo	—	3	5
Kent	14	127	159
Lapeer	35	299	327
Lenawee	1	5	11
Livingston	—	12	20
Macomb	9	107	119
Manistee	—	—	2
Mecosta	—	2	3
Midland	8	120	150
Monroe	5	90	67
Montcalm	—	5	3
Montmorency	1	2	1
Muskegon	—	3	4
Newaygo	—	8	9
Oakland	165	3,261	2,599
Ogemaw	—	6	7
Oscoda	—	1	1
Ottawa	—	9	14
Roscommon	—	4	3
Saginaw	385	3,016	2,399
St. Clair	9	23	27
St. Joseph	—	4	3
Shiawassee	78	501	487
Tuscola	2	184	169
Van Buren	—	9	15
Washtenaw	2	194	170
Wayne	361	3,877	3,294
Wexford	—	2	2

Source: Department of Social Services, State of Michigan.

TABLE 18. *General Motors Strike*
AFDC-U Participation
State of Michigan
May 1970-March 1971

Year	Month	Number of Families	Total Payments	Average Payment per Family
1970				
	May	3,147	$ 857,941	$272.62
	June	3,357	920,454	274.19
	July	3,591	965,506	268.87
	August	3,902	1,073,822	275.20
	September	4,188	1,255,412	299.76
	October	7,056	1,698,400	240.70
	November	19,138	3,807,759	198.96
	December	22,107	3,526,186	159.51
1971				
	January	7,601	2,202,588	289.78
	February	8,019	2,395,747	298.76
	March	9,045	2,732,150	302.06

Source: Department of Social Services, State of Michigan.

Note: September 1970 was the first month of the strike and November 1970 was the last.

TABLE 19. *General Motors Strike*
AFDC Cash Assistance to Striker Families
State of Michigan
October, November, and December 1970

Month	Number of Striker Families	Average Payment per Family	Total Payments
October	2,851	$102.73	$ 292,871
November	22,797	98.36	2,242,231
December	18,817	93.82	1,765,467
		Total	$4,300,569

Source: Department of Social Services, State of Michigan.

FIGURE 16. *General Motors Strike*
Percent Change in AFDC-U Participation
Over the Same Month of the Previous Year
State of Michigan
August 1970-January 1971

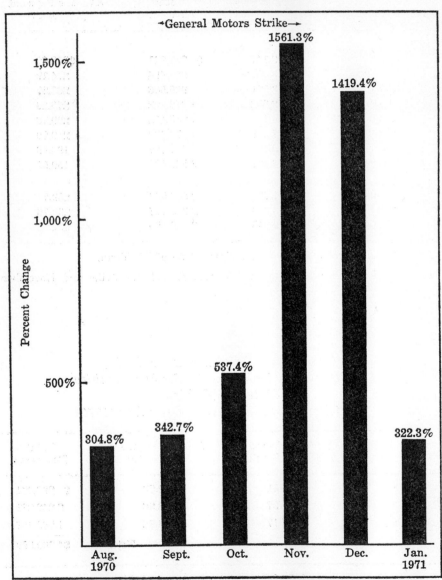

Source: Department of Social Services, State of Michigan.

enrolled in the General Assistance program in November. Therefore, utilizing the cash payment data presented in Table 20, it is estimated that the support of GM strikers through the General Assisance program amounted to about $700,000. Unlike the financing of the AFDC program, which is federally subsidized, Michigan and its counties had to pay for the entire cost of this General Assistance aid.

As strikers were certified for either the General Assistance or AFDC programs they automatically became eligible for Medicaid benefits. When authorized, a medical assistance card was issued to the striker's household. Information as to the number of strikers who received medical assistance and the cost of such aid is too sketchy to permit an estimate of the costs involved; but we know that at least some strikers on public assistance did avail themselves of medical assistance benefits, including hospital care, clinical prescription drugs, physicians, dental care, and other forms of medical aid.

Table 21 presents a summary indicating that $15.7 million in public funds were provided Michigan General Motors strikers through the various welfare programs. This does not take into consideration the thousands of public dollars that were expended for the administrative costs of distributing public relief to strikers, or the medical benefits used. Therefore, not only is the total cost of $15.7 million a conservative figure because of the methods used to compute it, but it also does not encompass the entire cost of subsidizing Michigan General Motors strikers.

TABLE 20. *General Motors Strike*
Number of Strikers Receiving General Assistance and Financial Aid Provided—Estimated
State of Michigan
October, November, and December 1970

Month	Estimated Number of Striker Participants	Average Payment per Striker		Total Estimated Aid
October	1,860	$128.93		$239,810
November	2,800	124.09		347,452
December	940	111.90		105,186
			Total	$692,448

Source: Estimates computed from data provided by the Michigan Department of Social Services.

TABLE 21. *General Motors Strike*
Total Estimated Public Funds Distributed to Strikers
State of Michigan
September-December 1970

Program	Expenditure	Percent of Total
Food stamps	$10,672,760	68.1
General assistance	692,448	4.4
AFDC	4,300,569	27.5
Total	$15,665,777	100.0

Source: Tables 16, 19, and 20.

The cost summary shown in Table 21 provides a comparison of the financial contributions made by each program to General Motors strikers. The AFDC program, which is supported partially from federal funds, and the Food Stamp program, which is supported entirely from federal funds, provided strikers with the greatest money assistance, 95.6 percent of the total. Only General Assistance costs were met solely by the taxpayers of Michigan. Taxpayers throughout the country thus picked up most of the tab of aiding Michigan General Motors strikers. The situation was generally the same for other states experiencing the GM-UAW dispute.

THE LOCAL IMPACT IN MICHIGAN

The effects of General Motors employees' receiving millions of dollars in public relief funds were felt throughout the state of Michigan. However, the greatest impact of this long strike fell on only a few counties and communities.

Flint, Michigan

At the time of the strike, General Motors employed approximately 55,000 employees in eight facilities in Flint, Michigan. The UAW did not call out its members at the AC Spark Plug Division there, however, on the stated grounds that it was producing parts for other companies which could be shut down if such parts became unavailable. Since, however, over 50 percent of the production of this plant was for General Motors facilities that were struck, General Motors was forced to lay off or put on short time many of the Spark Plug plant's employees. Obviously, the selective strike tactics of the UAW relieved the union and many strikers (a number of other plants were similarly treated) of sizable financial pressures by keeping them at work during part of the strike.

General Motors strikers in Flint also made extensive use of public aid programs during the 71-day strike. One month after the work stoppage began, 1,480 strikers (representing 2.7 percent of the total number of General Motors strikers in the Flint SMSA, which includes Genesee and Lapeer counties) were enrolled in the AFDC program [133] and about 10,000 strikers, more than 18 percent of the area's strike force,[134] were receiving food stamps. In November the average number of General Motors employees on strike in Flint (Genesee County) declined to 48,670,[135] as plants began to return to work. Although the number of individuals on strike had dropped, the AFDC rolls for General Motors striker families climbed to 9,128 or 18.8 percent of the strike force (Table 17). The average AFDC payment in November amounted to $207.22 for Genesee County, but most of the strikers participating in the AFDC program were covered under the unemployed parent segment. The average AFDC-U payment for November 1971 in Genesee County was $171.76.[136]

The first line of aid for strikers came from the Food Stamp and General Assistance programs. The number of individuals receiving food stamps but living in non-public assistance households expanded by 7,875.0 percent from September to October, as indicated by the graph in Figure 17. Then, from October to November an additional 10,990 persons were admitted as food stamp participants. This represented an increase of 82,184 people or 9,091.0 percent over September. Public assistance household participation climbed from 22,858 persons in November to 50,509 persons in December. Food stamp rolls did not decline until January 1971, although the strike ended in November 1970.[137]

---

[133] Table 17 and Michigan Department of Social Services.

[134] *Pontiac Press*, October 14, 1970.

[135] Letter from Director of Personnel Relations, General Motors Corporation, May 13, 1971.

[136] Michigan Department of Social Services.

[137] U.S. Department of Agriculture, Food and Nutrition Service.

FIGURE 17.   *General Motors Strike*
Food Stamp Participation
Genesee County, Michigan
July 1970-February 1971

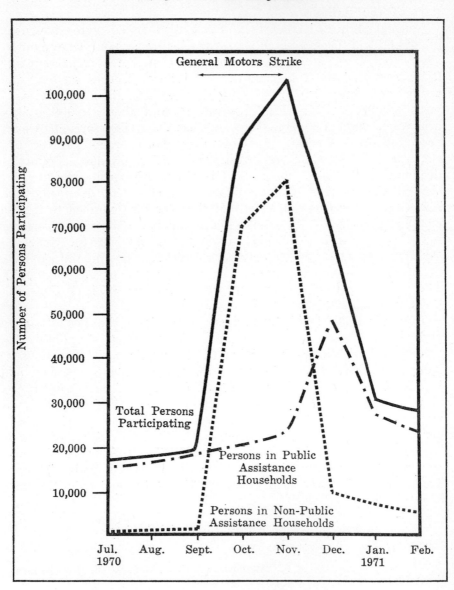

From September to October 1970 the number of General Assistance cases in Genesee County increased by over 74 percent. The average October payment to a General Assistance client was $71.53. Only a small proportion of the strike force, in comparison to the AFDC and Food Stamp programs, maintained an active participation in general assistance as the county made every effort to get eligible strikers enrolled in public assistance programs which receive federal government aid.[138]

The impact of the strike on AFDC-U rolls in Genesee County is shown in Figure 18. By the end of October AFDC-U enrollment had increased more than 423.0 percent over August 1970. In November the AFDC-U case load went up an additional 231.0 percent (representing 5,319 families), a 1,633.0 percent gain over August. The number of families on AFDC-U in Genesee County reached a peak of 6,520 in December, falling to 857 families in January 1971, as shown in Figure 19. Since there were 6,879 General Motors striker families receiving benefits from the AFDC program in Genesee County in December 1970 (Table 17), 400 to 500 striker families must have been enrolled under special provisions of the regular AFDC program. Many of these families probably discovered that they qualified for income supplements whether the head of household was on strike or not, and therefore, many could have remained on AFDC after the strike was settled.

The increase in the number of families receiving AFDC-U in Genesee County in November 1970 over October 1970 represented an increase of $672,041 in the cost of operating the program; $900,000 was distributed to AFDC-U clients in November, a climb of 804 percent in cash relief since August. Participation and payments can be compared for December and January between the strike period and a year previously from the data in Figure 19. In 1970, payments to families totaled $764,909 ($117.32 per family) in December and dropped to $234,646 in January. A year earlier the trend and the cost were quite different. In December 1969, there were only 231 Genesee County families on AFDC-U, receiving $43,442. In January 1970, AFDC-U rolls climbed to 383 families, who received $72,003 in public relief.

---

[138] Michigan Department of Social Services.

FIGURE 18. *General Motors Strike*
AFDC-U Participation
Genesee County, Michigan
July 1969-February 1970 and July 1970-February 1971

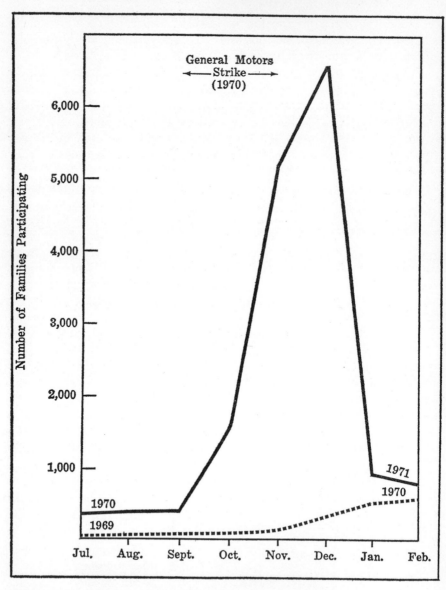

Source: Department of Social Services, State of Michigan.

Note: Dates express monthly averages.

FIGURE 19. *General Motors Strike*
AFDC-U Participation and Expenditures
Genesee County, Michigan
December-January

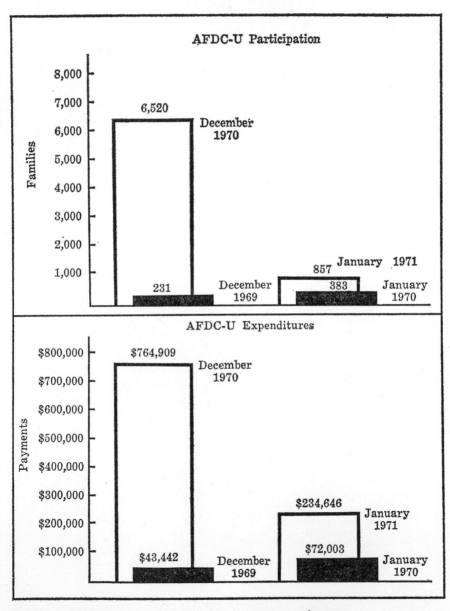

Source: Department of Social Services, State of Michigan.

Community Impact

A lengthy strike involving a community's primary employer is certain to produce a number of serious problems for local businesses and government agencies. Considering General Motors strikers represented nearly 30 percent of the total non-farm employment for the Flint metropolitan area, the 71-day UAW-GM dispute was no exception.[139] *Business Week* reported in November 1970 that Flint's merchant business was off 25 to 30 percent. Flint's City Manager, Tom Kay, said that during the strike the city was losing $110,000 a week in withholding taxes alone.[140] Public revenue losses associated with the strike, in the form of lost income taxes and welfare payments to strikers, had an adverse effect on both city and county government operations.

An official of the Genesee County Department of Social Services stated that the strike had several immediate and long-range effects on his agency. One of the immediate impacts of the strike was felt by individuals who were regular participants of the county's welfare program; the Welfare Department found that it could not properly service nonstrikers. A welfare official explained, "The lines each morning during the strike were set up on a number basis. The union members were best organized and thus, were first in line. The telephone company recorded nearly 24,000 busy signals each day. There were many complaints from welfare clients who could not be assisted."[141] The Welfare Department disclosed that before the strike each caseworker was handling about 100 cases, but during the strike each caseworker had to process at least 400 cases. Applications for assistance were taken at the Welfare Department's main office, at a temporary welfare office established in an old hospital building, at union halls, and at temporary processing facilities in trailers located on General Motors plant grounds. In order to service the thousands of applicants, the Genesee County Welfare Office added thirty people to its staff and worked about one-third of its work force overtime. Accordingly, in addition to the hundreds of thousands of dollars distributed to strikers

---

[139] Michigan Employment Security Commission.

[140] *Business Week*, November 7, 1970, p. 19.

[141] Information on the impact on the Genesee welfare system is from an interview, the assistant director, Genesee County Department of Social Services, Flint, Michigan, March 19, 1971.

in the Flint area in the form of public assistance, and the estimated $2 million in food stamps issued there to strikers every two weeks, each of the administrative and logistical actions required to support the Welfare Department's striker assistance program added to the public's cost of subsidizing these strikers.

Genesee County welfare offices also loosened certification procedures and adopted some new methods of handling cases:

> It was impossible, because of the large number of people applying, for us to do an adequate investigative job. . . . During the strike we could not accommodate our normal cases. Case workers could not keep up to date with changes in programs. In addition, it was not possible to keep up with reports that were due. Hopefully through our audits we can determine and recover any overpayments.

The assistant director of Genesee County's Department of Social Services believed that the distribution of welfare aid to General Motors strikers set a precedent. He found that the attitude toward receiving welfare changed and that the Food Stamp program now draws a lot of interest. Now that union officials recognize the extent to which the welfare system can be of help during a strike, there will be increased use of public aid programs to support future strikes. The welfare official provided the following example: "There was a hospital strike called during the General Motors strike and the striking hospital workers wanted the same service provided them as was provided the UAW. Therefore, it was necessary to dispatch a case worker to their union hall to accompish certification requirements."

UAW Programs in Action

The UAW unions were significantly helpful in getting their members certified for assistance during the General Motors strike.[142] An officer of UAW Buick Local 599 in Flint reported, "Our Community Services Committee assisted the Welfare Department in channeling qualified workers. It assisted in the screening process and in certification procedures." Another Buick local officer said that counseling was a key in obtaining welfare services for strikers. He maintained that if the applicant was

---

[142] Information on union efforts in obtaining welfare assistance is from interviews with officers of UAW Buick Local 599, Flint, Michigan, March 16 and 17, 1971.

not acquainted with the various programs offered through the
Department of Social Services, a striker would generally not
obtain the full benefits to which he or she was entitled. Accordingly, the union enlarged its education program and through
its Community Services Committee developed a counseling service for striking members. Union counselors provided members
with information and direction on both private and public relief
services available. In addition, the Department of Social Services sent counselors to the local union hall to aid in the union's
informational and screening program.

The Community Services Committee of the local union played
a vital role in getting union members to utilize public agencies
as part of the strike assistance program. As a Buick local officer disclosed, strikers have more faith in seeking and getting
help from their union than from a welfare agency. Strikers
will usually turn first to their union for help. In addition, for
many workers, a stigma is still attached to "being on welfare."
As one union official said, "Many union members did not feel
right by having to request welfare assistance. They were
raised in families where welfare was looked at as something
to be used only in dire need." But these attitudes are changing.
By applying for help through the union along with other strikers, seeking aid becomes a part of the union strike assistance
program. Public funds become a union "war chest" and as one
union official described the situation, "Now, many are stating
that they want their share, for it is owed them."

Buick Local 599's program to incorporate public relief funds
into their strike assistance effort was certainly successful. Although union officials could not estimate how many of their approximately 16,500 striking members received welfare aid, they
did say that food stamps and public assistance were a significant help to many strikers. One union officer said that there
were fewer complaints expressed by union members about being
on strike than he had encountered in previous strikes. He maintained that he had gotten more pressure from members during
strikes lasting two weeks than he received during the 71-day
General Motors strike. A Buick local officer was asked if welfare payments to Buick strikers reduced the economic pressures
of the strike and, therefore, affected the speed of the settlement. The union official responded, "There is a lot of desire to
get back to work. However, when workers are receiving welfare assistance there is not as much economic hardship on mem-

bers. Therefore, there is not as much pressure on our bargaining unit to settle."

Need, regardless of cause, was the common justification of Buick union leaders for a public policy which permits strikers to receive welfare. "When I am in need, regardless of how I become in need, I should be able to receive assistance," said one union official. A strike is viewed as a critical economic period for workers, no different from any other economic crisis. Accordingly, since a strike is a time of need, welfare payments should be made available to help ease that need. An officer of Buick Local 599 said that regulations regarding strikers receiving public aid should be liberalized and men on strike should be able to receive unemployment compensation. Their theory is that when the striker is under less economic hardship, greater pressure will come to bear on management and, therefore, the strike will be shorter.

Notwithstanding the claim by union officials that public relief should be provided strikers on a basis of need only, Buick Local 599 did not distribute union strike benefits to its members on a basis of their need. The full UAW strike assistance program, promulgated in December 1969, explained that strike assistance from the UAW's "war chest," to which union members had contributed, was "based on right in accordance with the rules and regulations approved by the [UAW] International Executive Board." [143] Only if the striker were recognized as a member in good standing and met certain qualifications would he or she receive the following benefits: a single person, $6.00 per day; a couple, $7.00 per day; and a family, $8.00 per day. In addition, these benefits were provided the striker "for each day he is on strike, beginning with the eighth day of the strike, Monday through Friday."

The UAW Strike Assistance Program made it clear that aid to union strikers is not provided on the basis of need alone or regardless of the cause of that need. If one does not or has not lived up to the various requirements of the union, strike benefits are withheld as a form of punishment. Even the UAW's Emergency Fund is not founded on meeting the needs of members in extreme financial difficulty. The amount available is trivial; funds are provided in accordance with a prespecified rate and not on a basis of the individual's need; and union

---

[143] See Appendix B for the entire strike assistance document, describing rules and regulations, penalties, and other aspects of the program.

emergency funds are only obtainable after the striker has exhausted all public relief possibilities. Thus, although leaders of the UAW and its locals assert that public relief should be provided striking workers solely on a basis of need, they have established a strike assistance program which has a foundation of rules, regulations, restrictions, rates, and various qualifications.

Detroit and Pontiac

Nearly 40 percent of the Detroit metropolitan motor vehicle and equipment industry labor force was idled by the 1970 strike. The Detroit SMSA consists of the counties of Wayne, Oakland, and Macomb, and includes the cities of Pontiac and Detroit. Over 67,000 men and women, representing more than 13 percent of the area's total manufacturing labor force, work at General Motors plants.[144]

As was the situation in Flint, retailers in Pontiac and Detroit found their pre-holiday business falling short of expectations. Many merchants were forced to lay off employees. Tax losses in Wayne, Oakland, and Macomb Counties had a severe impact on public agencies. *Business Week* reported in November 1970 that Detroit was losing $500,000 a week and Pontiac $50,000 a week in income taxes alone. The loss in tax revenues and the large expenditures for welfare aid to strikers forced the municipal government of Pontiac to lay off 173 city workers, and firemen and policemen.[145] According to the *Wall Street Journal*, Pontiac was finally forced to borrow $2.4 million in order to maintain its services to the public, even though it had made substantial budget cuts during the strike.[146]

Soon after the UAW walkout, hundreds of General Motors strikers began to apply for food stamps and other forms of public aid at county welfare offices throughout the Detroit metropolitan area. The director of the Oakland County Department of Social Services said that from September 21 through November 25, 1970, her office certified 10,198 striker families for food stamps. The Oakland County Welfare Office services the Pontiac area, where between 23,000 and 26,000 General Motors

---

[144] Michigan Employment Security Commission.

[145] *Business Week,* November 7, 1970, p. 19.

[146] *Wall Street Journal,* November 12, 1970, p. 2.

employees were on strike.[147]   Therefore, at least 39 percent of all General Motors strikers in Oakland County were using food stamps during the strike. In September 1970, Wayne County (Detroit) approved 3,619 General Motors strikers for food stamps. Then in October, 13,162 striker families were approved from 13,909 applications. As shown in Figure 20, by the end of the strike the cumulative total of striker participants reached 18,102, after 1,321 strikers were admitted to the Food Stamp program in November. The average size of the General Motors strike force in Wayne County was 31,500.[148] Although all of these workers may not have resided in Wayne County, one can conservatively estimate that more than 55 percent of the Wayne County General Motors strikers were getting food stamps.

In November 1970, there were still more than 56,000 General Motors employees on strike in the Detroit area. In the same month nearly 13 percent (7,245) of these strikers were enrolled in the AFDC program. (See data for Macomb, Oakland, and Wayne Counties in Table 17.) Pontiac had also approved 123 strikers for General Assistance.[149] It is estimated that in November more than 28,000 General Motors strikers were clients of the Michigan Department of Social Services. The impact on the County's Welfare Office was substantial, as described by the director of the Oakland County Welfare Department:

> All I can say is it has been a *long* 47 days; however, I have only praise for the employees of this agency who worked long hours and hard hours. Many days we opened our emergency strike office at 7:00 a.m. and closed at 11:00 p.m. . . . During the period from September 21, 1970 through November 25, 1970, this agency utilized 4,258 hours of overtime. . . . Unless you were in the crisis the problems that arise are hard to visualize. For example, the security needed, the officers to handle traffic and the extra space needed to open the emergency office, in order that work could go on as usual at the regular office.[150]

There were other effects. Although policemen had to be laid off because of budget cuts brought on by the strike, the police

---

[147] Letters from Director, Department of Social Services, Oakland County, Michigan, to J. R. Konneker, December 1, 1970, and from Director of Personnel Relations, General Motors Corporation, May 13, 1971.

[148] General Motors letter, May 13, 1971.

[149] Oakland County, Michigan, Department of Social Services, letter December 1, 1970.

[150] *Ibid.*

FIGURE 20.   *General Motors Strike*
New Applicants Approved for Food Stamps
Wayne County, Michigan
August-December 1970

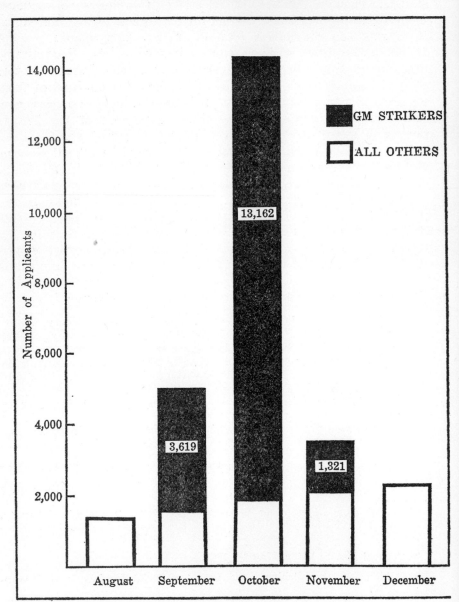

Source: Department of Social Services, Wayne County, Michigan.

department was called upon to provide security and traffic control for crowded welfare offices. While other city agencies were forced to send employees home, welfare departments had to hire additional personnel in order to cope with the amazing number of strikers applying for relief. The Detroit Food Stamp Office had to employ an extra 100 workers and create two special offices so that it could distribute food stamps to strikers.[151]

UAW locals in the Detroit area were well prepared for the 1970 General Motors strike. Their Community Services or Welfare Committees quickly and skillfully became an integral part of the strike assistance effort. The year-round participation of union members in public and private relief agencies, boards, and programs had helped to develop an atmosphere favorable to the UAW's cause. The conferences, institutes, and training classes on welfare programs and issues, conducted under the UAW's Community Service Program, provided many locals with the information and skills so vital to the operation of a strike assistance program which effectively incorporates public relief. Having witnessed other unions throughout the country taking advantage of state and federal welfare programs, the UAW was ready and willing to get its share in order to support the strike against General Motors.

UAW Cadillac Local 22 (Detroit) is one example of the many unions that provided members, through the union's Community Service Committee, with the information and assistance necessary for many of them to qualify and obtain public funds. Figures 21 and 22 are examples of a few of the tools UAW Local 22 used to encourage and aid members to obtain welfare during the General Motors strike.

THE IMPACT IN OTHER STATES AND AREAS

The General Motors strike put major burdens on other areas besides Michigan. Experiences with public welfare payments to strikers in some of those states and areas are discussed in the balance of this chapter.

California

A significant number of the nearly 12,000 UAW members who struck General Motors plants in the Oakland and Los

---

[151] *Yakima Washington Republic*, October 9, 1970.

FIGURE 21.   *General Motors Strike*
Form Used by Cadillac Local 22, UAW,
to Aid Its Members in Obtaining Public Relief

Cadillac Local 22, UAW

TO WHOM IT MAY CONCERN:

This is to certify that ....

of ....
                              Address   City

a member of Cadillac Local 22, UAW, and an employee of Cadillac Motor
Car Division.

☐ is not eligible for strike assistance for the duration of the current
  G. M. strike.

☐ will not become eligible for strike assistance until ....
  and will receive the first check on ....

He (she) is the head of a household, and claims .... dependents
other than himself (herself), and to our knowledge has no other source of
income than employment at Cadillac, and last worked on ....

Any consideration extended in this emergency will be greatly appreciated.

                                                    Respectfully yours,

                                    _____
                                    Title of Union Representative Certi-
                                    fying above ....

opeiu42/v

Source: Copy of original in authors' possession.

FIGURE 22.   *General Motors Strike*
Flyer Distributed by Cadillac Local 22, UAW,
to Its Members During the General Motors Strike

ATTENTION

LOCAL 22 MEMBERS

Recently a UAW spokesman pointed out that many UAW members are missing out on benefits that they are entitled to under State and Federal laws. The UAW spokesman pointed out, for instance, that many GM strikers are not aware of the ADCU program—Aid to Dependent Children of the Unemployed. This program triggers in after the 4th week that a member has been on strike.

Upon being asked how the locals could inform the members who were qualified for the ADCU Benefits, the UAW spokesman pointed out that the best criteria to use is that almost everyone who qualifies for food stamps also qualifies for ADCU.

TO APPLY FOR ADCU YOU MUST GO TO THE SAME PLACE WHERE YOU SIGNED UP FOR FOOD STAMPS. STATE FAIR GROUNDS OR WAYNE COUNTY GENERAL

For further information inquire inside the food stamp trailer in the Local Union parking lot.

LOCAL 22, UAW

opeiu42/plk

Source: Copy of original in authors' possession.

Angeles areas received public relief during the lengthy 1970 auto dispute. With the financial contributions of the AFDC program alone, at least $475,848 was obtained from public funds to subsidize the UAW's strike effort in three Colifornia counties alone.[152]

San Francisco-Oakland Bay Area

Some 4,200 members of UAW Local 1364 walked off their jobs at the General Motors Assembly Plant in Fremont on September 14, 1970. Another 350 Autoworkers struck the General Motors Parts Division Center in Oakland. Mr. William Rainey, assistant director of the Alameda County Welfare Department (servicing both the Fremont and Oakland areas) reported, "We're in a heck of a mess with this sudden caseload. . . . The number of new cases from the strikers is consuming manhours equivalent to 16 welfare workers." [153] Although over three-fourths of the General Motors workers lived outside of Fremont, by October 2,400 Autoworkers had applied for aid at Alameda County's Fremont Welfare Office.[154] Approximately 1,160 General Motors strikers were enrolled in the AFDC-U. The cost of AFDC-U aid to these strikers in October and November 1970 respectively was $35,000 and $46,000.[155] In Santa Clara County (south of Fremont), 542 General Motors strikers were admitted to the welfare rolls at a cost of $172,000.[156] Since strikers can qaulify for food stamps without being certified for public assistance and those who are on public relief are eligible for food stamps, even greater numbers of General Motors strikers were undoubtedly receiving aid from the Food Stamp program. For example, Alameda County witnessed an addition of 4,785 persons to non-public assistance household food stamp rolls during the nearly two and one-half month strike.[157] This represented more than a 26 percent increase in participation.

---

[152] Transcript of California State Social Welfare Board Meeting, February 27, 1971, p. 17; interviews; and letters.

[153] *Fremont-Newark (California) Argus*, October 2, 1970.

[154] *Ibid.*

[155] Interview, Mr. William E. Rainey, Assistant Director, Alameda County Welfare Department, Oakland, California, August 25, 1971.

[156] Transcript of California State Social Welfare Board Meeting, February 27, 1971, p. 17.

[157] U.S. Department of Agriculture, Food and Nutrition Service.

According to Mr. Rainey, the UAW's Community Service organization worked very closely throughout the strike with the county's welfare agencies. The Community Services Committee coordinated the efforts of the union and welfare department; it handled numerous processing problems for strikers; and it assisted strikers in supplying information needed for welfare relief applications. An example of the latter is shown in Figure 23.

In addition, Mr. Rainey reported that an AFL-CIO Community Services Labor Staff Representative with the United Bay Area Crusade was in constant contact with the Alameda County Welfare Department during the strike. The AFL-CIO representatives had worked very closely with labor groups and welfare agencies for over a decade. Welfare officials talk to labor groups on welfare programs available in California regularly and hold sessions for union counselors in order to train them to screen welfare applications of union members. Although such training classes are not solely for purposes of strikes, it is through this year-round preparation and welfare involvment that unions are prepared to process members for public aid during strikes. In addition, welfare department officials often meet with unions prior to strikes to discuss the availability of welfare benefits.

Mr. Rainey, who has been in welfare services for about thirty-five years, said that he first noticed the use of public aid by strikers right after World War II. The striker used to wait until the strike was nearly over to apply for aid, but now he is not so hesitant about processing for relief. With the liberalization in public benefits, the changing attitude toward going on public relief and the development of organized labor's community service program, strikers now apply for welfare more quickly.

The payment of welfare benefits to strikers worries **Mr.** Rainey. A strike like the General Motors one was a fiscal threat to Alameda County. He believes that if it had gone on longer or if there had been another strike, it could have produced a serious problem for the county. Then, too, the payment of welfare benefits has an effect on a strike. As an example, the Assistant Director said, "UAW members felt with welfare they were not in a position so much worse off than while working. Accordingly, they were willing to stay out until they got what they wanted."

FIGURE 23. *General Motors Strike*
Form Used by Local 1364, UAW,
to Aid Its Members in Obtaining Public Relief
Fremont, California

Date ....

ALAMEDA — COUNTY SOCIAL SERVICE DEPARTMENT

Please be advised that Mr. .... is a member of
this Union. Due to the strike action forced on the United Automobile
Workers of America, by General Motors Corporation, members of the Union
are prevented from working.

The member is not eligible for strike assistance benefits or monies until
October 13, 1970, and will then receive $40.00 per week.

Every member is free to accept any other employment and will be released
from strike duty if necessary.

Very truly yours,

George Stolaroff, Financial Sect'y
U.A.W. Local #1364

James E. Rickman, Chairman Community
Services Committee — UAW Local 1364

GS:hf
opeiu#29

Source: Copy of original in authors' possession.

Los Angeles

The situation was no different in the Los Angeles area where approximately 6,600 members of two UAW locals struck General Motors plants in Van Nuys and Southgate. Soon after the national walkout began, strikers from Local 216 and 645 started applying for food stamps and cash grants. The Chief Administrative Office of the County of Los Angeles reported that a total of 309 employees on strike at General Motors plants and living in Los Angeles County received financial assistance from the AFDC program. The amount of aid provided these recipients totaled $222,848, representing a cost to the county of $36,213.[158]

New Jersey and New York

Strikers at General Motors plants in Linden and Trenton, New Jersey, began applying for financial help from public agencies soon after the strike was called. Non-public assistance food stamp participation jumped more than 16 percent in counties where General Motors strikers resided, as compared to a 5.7 percent rise for the entire state during the same period—September through October 1970.[159] UAW locals worked closely with welfare officials in the administration of aid to union members. As in many locations in Michigan, the union hall became a welfare department processing and assistance center, and union personnel were utilized to support welfare agency efforts to aid General Motors strikers.

In New York, strikers were able to obtain food stamps and public assistance, and after a seven week waiting period they received unemployment benefits as well. General Motors employees who were employed at least 13 weeks before walking off their jobs on September 15 were eligible for up to $75 per week in unemployment insurance. General Motors Corporation estimates that the New York Unemployment Compensation Commission paid about $5,250,000 to its striking employees.[160] Since

---

[158] Letter from Principal Analyst, Chief Administrative Office, Los Angeles County, California, July 2, 1971.

[159] U.S. Department of Agriculture.

[160] George B. Morris, Jr., "Controls or Collective Bargaining—Restraints and Realities," speech delivered before The Conference Board, New York, New York, June 3, 1971.

the unemployment insurance fund in New York is financed through a tax on employers, General Motors was forced to subsidize its own striking workers.

Ohio

Approximately 40,000 employees of Ohio General Motors plants left their jobs in September 1970 to support the UAW's nationwide strike against General Motors. By the middle of October, an official of the Ohio Department of Public Welfare said that one-third of the state's 88 counties had reported receiving applications for food stamps from General Motors strikers.[161] In a November issue of *Business Week,* the director of Ohio's Welfare Department said that the state was "using $10 million in food stamps a month, and the federal agency is having trouble getting that amount of stamps printed and to us."[162]

An article from the *Cleveland Press* reveals several reasons why one particular Ohio General Motors striker decided to accept public aid during the 1970 UAW-GM dispute. Although this striker was reported to have told his wife during a strike six years earlier that he would rather steal than go on relief, his reasons for applying for food stamps this time were:

1) because he refused to let his wife work—strike or no strike;

2) because other auto workers were doing it and they told him he has helped finance the program as a taxpayer;

3) because the Teamsters did it when they were on strike for about 30 days earlier in the year;

4) because a fellow worker told him that a politician was handing out food stamps on the West Side during a political campaign a year or two ago;

5) because it would help him weather the strike against General Motors.[163]

---

[161] *Pontiac Press,* October 14, 1970.

[162] *Business Week,* November 7, 1970, p. 19.

[163] *Cleveland Press,* October 26, 1970.

Pennsylvania

"We have guys eating T-bone steaks now who never ate T-bones before," said the food stamp chairman of UAW Local 544 in an newspaper interview.[164] This article on General Motors strikers at the West Mifflin, Pennsylvania, Fisher Body Plant obtaining food stamps provided the following examples of public aid to strikers in Pennsylvania in the forty-third day of the strike:

> About 75 percent of the 1,300 strike idled workers at Fisher Body have applied for food stamps and most of them are eligible.
> One auto worker, with six children, pays $26 a month for $180 worth of food stamps. Another gets $63 worth of food stamps for $8.50 in cash.
> The one receiving the $180 in food stamps said shopping now is a dilemma because "You don't know what to buy."
> The man on the picket line on Philip Murray Road in front of the plant agreed. "It's not too bad now with the strike benefits and the food stamps." [165]

SUMMARY AND CONCLUSION

The General Motors strike affected all individuals residing in the United States. During a period of swelling public relief rolls, welfare agencies removed at least $30 million from public funds and distributed them to individuals who were without income because they had chosen to strike for higher wages and added benefits. The greatest share of this cost was met by the federal government, since the public relief programs which qualified the largest number of strikers for assistance, Food Stamps and AFDC, are fully or partially financed by the federal government. These two programs are also accountable for the major increases in our soaring welfare costs.

In almost all communities where General Motors plants were on strike, food stamps or surplus commodities provided strikers with the first level of public financial support. Coupled with their union strike benefits, these Department of Agriculture programs eased the economic impact of the long walkout. Although some county welfare agencies may at first have been hesitant about distributing food stamps or commodities to striking work-

---

[164] *Pittsburgh Press*, October 27, 1970.

[165] *Ibid.*

ers, the federal government's policy to aid strikers through the Food Stamp program removed any question regarding the eligibility of individuals involved in a labor dispute. Accordingly, welfare officials around the nation were obligated to provide General Motors strikers with food stamps or commodities, paid for by tax dollars.

In the states where most of the General Motors strikers resided, persons are not disqualified from public assistance because they are involved in a work stoppage. Therefore, public assistance programs provided thousands of General Motors employees with a second level of public support. Once enrolled in a program such as AFDC, many strikers discovered the fringe benefits of being a welfare recipient. Some were able to take care of medical and dental needs for their families. Others found that when economic conditions got bad enough the public would insure that rental or mortgage payments were met and necessary home repairs were accomplished, all at the taxpayer's expense. Still others joined the school lunch program. Although not many strikers are reported to have taken advantage of all these possible benefits available through public assistance, strikers on welfare could not help but recognize the economic protection afforded them.

Unemployment compensation offered General Motors strikers in New York a third level of public support, which helped to relieve some of the economic pressure on New York's welfare budget. In most cases, strikers on public assistance had their accounts with the welfare department adjusted downward when they began receiving unemployment benefits. Instead of the New York State Social Service Department subsidizing General Motors strikers, unemployment insurance financed in part by a tax on General Motors took over the job.

The fact that UAW members in New York received unemployment benefits while on strike against General Motors has encouraged UAW locals throughout the country to strengthen their lobbying efforts to win this privilege for strikers in their states. An officer of a UAW local in Flint said that unemployment insurance benefits for strikers is one of the current goals of his union. He added that it is also his union's goal to obtain uniform public relief benefits for strikers throughout the nation, to include food stamps, public assistance, and unemployment insurance.[166]

---

[166] Interview, Flint, Michigan, March 17, 1971.

Without a doubt the payment of public funds to General Motors strikers had a social and economic impact on our country. The effects were considerable and far reaching. State and local government services were drastically affected. Taxpayers in many states will be paying the bill for some time to come. Welfare agencies near striking General Motors plants will long remember the hundreds of strikers standing at their doors requesting public help. Non-striking welfare recipients will also remember the General Motors employees who were demanding services from county welfare offices and programs designed to help the truly needy and poor of our nation.

Permitting General Motors strikers to obtain financial help from public relief agencies also had an effect on strikers. Many workers who had previously looked upon welfare with distaste voluntarily became welfare clients. "I pay my taxes, too. I'm entitled to something from my money," said one General Motors striker.[167] "They can't starve us out now that we're getting those food stamps," said another striker.[168]

As many General Motors strikers were introduced to food stamps and other public benefits, they became aware of the welfare programs available. They also became knowledgeable of the eligibility requirements for these programs. Some striking workers found that they were qualified for income supplements before they went on strike. Others found that it was not as difficult as they had previously imagined to qualify for food stamps. Consequently, the strike was responsible for introducing more individuals to our nation's welfare programs, as well as providing the welfare system with a host of new clients.

The primary reasons why so many General Motors employees were receiving public aid during the 1970 General Motors strike was because of the encouragement and assistance given by union officials. When these UAW officials were criticized for taking advantage of the public funds available to their striking members, they simply pointed out that the members of the UAW are taxpayers and have continually supported welfare programs through their tax dollars. The president of the UAW, Leonard Woodcock, said that he does not view public aid to strikers as a form of government strike subsidy, and that as long as a striker qualifies for welfare assistance in accordance with all other regulations, he should not be treated any differently from

[167] *U.S. News and World Report*, November 23, 1971, p. 18.

[168] *Pontiac Press*, October 14, 1970.

a nonstriker.[169] In November 1970, when there was concern
by UAW officials that strike benefits might run out, the UAW
president said that once the union could no longer provide weekly benefits that strikers would have to depend completely on
"their own resources and welfare." [170] The argument that public
assistance programs are designed to help people who are temporarily in need, regardless of the reason and UAW members
are taxpayers who are temporarily in need because of the strike
was also made by a UAW official in Lansing, Michigan. "We
feel justified in seeking public assistance," he said.[171] The UAW
succeeded in introducing thousands of American workers to the
welfare rolls at a cost of at least $30 million to the entire nation.

The payment of public benefits to General Motors strikers
seems definitely to have had an effect on the collective bargaining atmosphere. Coupled with union strike funds, public aid
protected General Motors employees from any severe economic
hardship. Although most strikers were not receiving as much
money each week as they would have if working, a significant
proportion of the General Motors strike force was living on
$300 to $350 per month. Under a pay-back agreement with the
UAW, during the strike General Motors continued to pay life
and medical insurance premiums on its employees. Thus, there
was no pressure on strikers in that regard.

The General Motors strike is a good example of the extent
to which public funds have become a vital part of organized
labor's strike assistance program. The fact that the strike
was nationwide and involved over 300,000 workers helped to
publicize this information and bring it to the attention of the
public. Most of our nation's work stoppages, however, are
not national in scope. They do not involve thousands of men and
women, yet they occur every day and in great numbers. As
will be disclosed in the next chapter, many such smaller strikes
are supported by public tax dollars.

---

[169] *Flint Journal,* October 11, 1970.

[170] *U.S. News and World Report,* October 26, 1970, p. 90.

[171] *Lansing State Journal,* October 26, 1970.

CHAPTER VI

The Prevalence of the Practice—
Some Case Illustrations

The use of tax funds to support strikers is not confined to a few key labor disputes. To illustrate further the pervasiveness and prevalence of tax support of strikers, we have included in this chapter a number of cases from various parts of the country. Although none are analyzed in the detail with which the Westinghouse and General Motors cases were discussed, they all confirm the significance of the practice to the taxpayer, and to the institution of collective bargaining.

JOHNS-MANVILLE STRIKE

With the aid of union strike benefits, part-time jobs, working wives, and public relief, approximately 2,500 members of Local 800, United Papermakers and Paperworkers, AFL-CIO, were able to sustain a 157-day strike against the Johns-Manville Products Plant, Manville, New Jersey. This prolonged work stoppage, which began on August 1, 1970 and lasted until January 15, 1971, was highlighted by events such as the workers' refusal at three separate times during the strike to accept a company offer which would have ended the walkout; controversy and turmoil among Local 800 officers; a declaration from the union's international president ordering Local 800 to conduct a secret ballot vote on the company's latest offer; the involvement of members of Students for a Democratic Society (SDS) on behalf of the strikers; and fighting on the picket lines and destruction of Johns-Manville property.

The strike primarily involved Johns-Manville's manufacturing complex in Somerset County, New Jersey, where the company makes roofing, asbestos pipe, packing material, and other home and industrial products. About 200 members of the striking bargaining unit, however, were employees of the corporation's research center in near-by Finderne, New Jersey. About 90 percent of the strikers lived in Somerset County. Because Johns-Manville is the largest employer in Manville and among the top six employers in the county, the more than five-month strike undoubtedly had a depressing economic effect on businesses and local governments throughout the area.

Local 800 apparently had its strike assistance program well developed when the walkout was called. In addition to providing members with strike benefits for doing picket duty (amounting to between $22 to $40 per week), the union was prepared to aid strikers in obtaining public relief funds. Some union officials took an active role in the campaign to qualify members for welfare by acting as liaison between the striker and the county welfare department. Others provided members with information on public aid programs available and arranged appointments with welfare representatives for those strikers desiring aid. The president of Local 800 said, "We encourage all the workers to pick up the food stamps. They have earned them as much as anyone else." [172] Strikers also received assistance from the Somerset County welfare system. An international representative of the UPP sat as a member of the county's welfare board. Before the middle of August strikers were picking up food stamps at their union headquarters,[173] and by the end of that month 350 to 400 Johns-Manville employees, about 14 percent of the strikers, had applied for food stamps.[174]

The impact of the Johns-Manville strike on the county's food stamp program is shown in Figure 24. The data therein, however, are also affected by a strike at RCA, Inc., which began June 2, 1970, and ended 101 days later. This strike involved 1,100 members of Local 438, International Union of Electrical Workers (IUE). The soaring food stamp rolls from June 1970 through February 1971 were partially caused by the increase in public assistance recipients, but the primary reason for the rise was enrollment of Johns-Manville and RCA strikers in the program.[175] The effect of the Johns-Manville strike on the Food Stamp program followed the same pattern as was seen in the

---

[172] *Newark Evening News*, August 12, 1970, p. 26.

[173] *Ibid.*

[174] *Somerset Messenger-Gazette*, September 10, 1970, p. 14.

[175] *Somerset Messenger-Gazette*, November 12, 1970.

FIGURE 24. *Johns-Manville Strike*
Food Stamp Participation
Somerset County, New Jersey
April 1970-April 1971

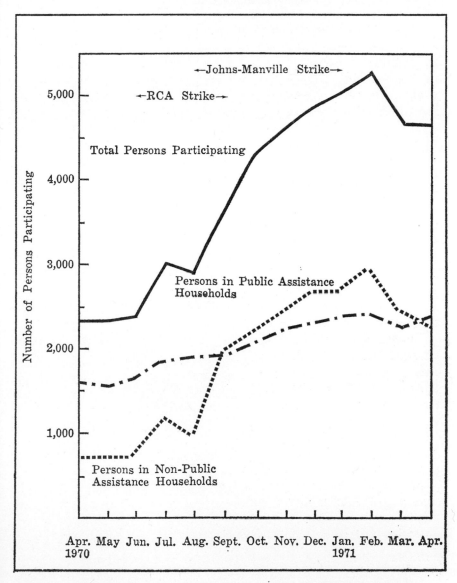

Source: U.S. Department of Agriculture, Food and Nutrition Service.

Note: Dates express monthly averages.

previous cases studied, with the initial rise in food stamp participants taking place in the non-public assistance category where-
as prior to the strike there had been fewer non-public assistance
food stamp recipients than public assistance recipients. By September 1970 this normal situation changed, and it remained
changed until after the strike had been settled.

Figure 24 also depicts the influence of both the RCA and
Johns-Manville strikes on the public assistance household trend.
Substantial increases occurred about thirty days after the start
of each of these labor-management disputes.

Like many of the other county welfare offices contacted, Somerset County did not distinguish between striker and nonstriker
applicants, but estimates were computed and are set forth in
Table 22. We found that 38.2 percent of the Johns-Manville
strikers obtained food stamps at the peak of the strike, considerably less than in the case of other long stoppages. One explanation for this unusually low proportion is the fact that many
Johns-Manville employees apparently left the area for the duration of the strike and sought work elsewhere. A union official
estimated that Johns-Manville permanently lost about 5 percent
of the striking work force, as a result of the strike.[176] A second
explanation is the possibility that some Johns-Manville employees
were eligible for food stamp aid prior to the strike because their
wives were on strike at RCA and the family income fell to a
level which qualified them.

No attempt was made to estimate the number of strikers who
enrolled in AFDC or General Assistance. As indicated above,
however, the strike did have an effect on public assistance rolls.
A clear indication of strikers seeking cash benefits was seen in
the approval of 51 applications for General Assistance in Somerset County during August 1970. This was nearly an 89 percent
jump from the previous month. The same situation occurred in
June 1970 at the beginning of the RCA strike. Here, the increase was nearly 73 percent over May. The average monthly
cash payment to a General Assistance recipient in August was
$115.08, in June it was $107.47.[177] Combined with strike benefits
and food stamps General Assistance could have provided a striker
with a more than $300 a month income.

---

[176] *Plainfield Courier-News*, January 16, 1971, p. 1.

[177] New Jersey Division of Public Welfare.

TABLE 22. *Johns-Manville Strike*
Number of Strikers
Receiving Food Stamps and Financial Aid Provided—Estimated
Somerset County, New Jersey
August 1970-February 1971

Year	Month	Estimated Number of Striker Participants	Percent of Strike Force	Average Bonus Value per Striker	Total Estimated Aid
1970					
	August	350	15.6	$38.20	$ 13,370
	September	525	23.3	48.04	25,221
	October	730	32.4	48.28	35,244
	November	785	34.9	47.72	37,460
	December	840	37.3	48.04	40,354
1971					
	January	860	38.2	46.84	40,282
	February	800	35.6	47.68	38,144
				Total	$230,075

Source: Estimated from data in authors' possession and U.S. Department of Agriculture, Food and Nutrition Service.

AFDC rolls also increased in Somerset County because of the Johns-Manville strike. In January 1971, the director of the county welfare department said that AFDC benefits to Johns-Manville strikers amounted to about $20,000 monthly since October 1970.[178] It was estimated that approximately 100 strikers and their families were obtaining public assistance for food, clothing, and shelter. According to the Somerset County Welfare Department AFDC "provides a food allowance of approximately $1 a day per person, $7 monthly for each individual's clothing, plus an allowance for personal incidentals. Welfare also pays the rent or else the mortgage payment if it is comparable to what rent would be. Welfare negotiates with the mortgage-holder to accept less if it deems the mortgage payment excessive, but at least the interest payments so there will be no foreclosure."[179]

[178] *Somerset Messenger-Gazette,* January 7, 1971.

[179] *Ibid.*

As in other strikes supported by welfare dollars, the payment
of public benefits to strikers had an effect on the collective bargaining atmosphere and on the individual striker. As an example,
a woman who picked up her food stamps at the headquarters of
Local 800 said, "I hate to do this, after working hard for 23
years; it is a shame to live on handouts." [180] Yet, she did accept
public aid and so did many Johns-Manville employees. One such
employee said that with welfare and food stamps, he and his
family were capable of riding out the strike. "We're not hurting
any. I get $40 a week strike benefits and a welfare allotment
that handles the rest of our day-by-day expenses. Of course I
want to see this strike ended. I've got 11 years invested in the
company but I'm in no more of a financial bind now than when
I'm working." This striker's take home pay amounted to about
$85 to $90 a week; he ordinarily made a wage of $3.05 an
hour.[181] Therefore, if working, this employee would have received $367 to $387 during the month of January 1971. On
welfare, his monthly *non-taxable* income was approximately
$380.[182] It would be extraordinary indeed if this situation did
not influence the propensity to settle.

This same Johns-Manville striker emphasized during the strike
that he was willing to stay off his job until the company met
his union's demands, knowing he will have enough money to
meet his mortgage and utility payments, to put food on the table,
and to pay medical bills. He realized that one of the big benefits
of being on welfare was that it qualified his family for Medicaid
benefits, including doctor, dentist, and drug bills. He said that
during the first week of the strike his medical bills "would have
run . . . well over $50 without medicaid." [183]

The Somerset County Welfare Director said that strikers residing in the county are provided welfare aid because under
federal laws it is her duty to assist them. She stated that
strikers throughout the nation are given welfare and her department is concerned only about the basic needs of the striker and
his family, and not the labor-management dispute. She claimed

---

[180] *Newark Evening News*, August 12, 1970, p. 26.

[181] *Somerset Messenger-Gazette*, September 10, 1970, p. 1.

[182] New Jersey Division of Public Welfare.

[183] *Somerset Messenger-Gazette*, September 10, 1970, pp. 1 and 3.

that the welfare department was "not taking sides in the strikes, but we have no right to refuse assistance when it is needed." [184]

Thus the welfare system assumed the responsibility of protecting Johns-Manville strikers from economic need, from the very beginning of the strike to its end strikers recognized that they would be so protected. Some strikers discovered that even after the dispute was settled they would be permitted to continue receiving some form of public relief. In August 1970 the director of Somerset County's food stamp program predicted that many employees would continue to buy stamps after the strike ended. [185] In September 1970 one striker's wife declared, "We plan to continue under food stamps when my husband goes back to work." [186]

The lack of financial pain and pressure on many strikers because they received food stamps, welfare cash grants, medicaid, union strike benefits, or a combination of these financial subsidies had a significant influence on the bargaining atmosphere according to a Johns-Manville representative. He found that without the normal economic stress that is associated with being on strike there was little pressure put on the union bargaining committee for a speedy settlement. To illustrate his point, he told of the difference between the bargaining climate experienced by the company during the strike of 1960 as compared to the more recent work stoppage. In 1960, during a 21-day strike, there existed a great deal of pressure from wives of strikers on union and management officials for a speedy settlement. The wives even marched on the gates of the company demanding settlement.

During the strike a decade later, however, there was little pressure from strikers' wives. "Wives must have found the strike quite tolerable," the management representative said. "They knew because of food stamps and strike benefits that there would be food on the table and basic necessities. They knew just how much money was coming into the household and thus, how much they could spend. Families on public assistance found themselves as well off on strike as when they were working. Many apparently did not care if the strike ever got settled." [187]

---

[184] *Ibid.*

[185] *New Brunswick Home News*, August 25, 1970.

[186] *Somerset Messenger-Gazette*, September 10, 1970, p. 1.

[187] Interview, Manville, New Jersey, October 29, 1971.

Public officials, however, found the strike a great strain. After
it ended on January 15, 1971, the mayor of Manville said, "Hopefully the welfare rolls will now decrease and the additional police
protection that was required will no longer be necessary." [188]
Obviously, the cost to the taxpayer was significant, both in terms
of the funds expended for welfare for strikers, and of the probable lengthening of the strike which undoubtedly resulted from
those payments.

ATLAS CHEMICAL INDUSTRIES, REYNOLDS PLANT STRIKE

Atlas Chemical's powder plant at Tamaqua, Pennsylvania, was
struck by members of Local 8-868, Oil, Chemical and Atomic
Workers International Union (OCAW), at midnight June 2, 1971.
This work stoppage, involving about 850 persons, ended on August 15, when President Nixon instituted the Wage-Price Freeze.
Subsequently, the union and company reached a contract settlement.

The walkout occurred shortly after OCAW had become the
Atlas workers' representative, having unseated District 50 (for-
merly United Mine Workers) in a National Labor Relations
Board election. An Atlas striker pointed out that OCAW was
performing better than his past union, District 50, as to strike
assistance. "OCAW is doing a better job for us because they
provide $15 per week in strike benefits and they inform us of
things we didn't know, such as food stamps." [189] OCAW inte-
grated public benefits into its strike assistance effort, a program
that it had long practiced. The OCAW strike assistance manual
has a chapter on what to know about welfare and how to acquire it.[190] A strike bulletin used by one of OCAW's West Coast
locals is shown in Figure 25. As strikers signed up for picket
duty they were provided information on public relief benefits.
Announcements were made over local radio stations about the
availability of public aid. According to a Schuylkill County welfare official, the union contacted the county welfare department
about two weeks after the strike began, but by then members of
the striking union had already begun to apply for aid.

---

[188] *Plainfield Courier-News*, January 16, 1971, p. 1.

[189] Interview, Tamaqua, Pennsylvania, July 30, 1971.

[190] See Appendix B for a reproduction of this chapter.

FIGURE 25. *Atlas Chemical Strike*
OCAW Strike Assistance Program

LOCAL 1-5

OIL, CHEMICAL & ATOMIC WORKERS INTERNATIONAL UNION

December 31, 1970

Beginning at 10:00 a.m. (this date) OCAW Bargaining Committee will begin meeting with Refinery Management in an effort to reach a contract settlement. It is anticipated that there will be some movement from the current positions of the respective parties in their mutual (we would hope) desire to settle this series of negotiations without any undue difficulties.

However, in the event that an *unanticipated* hangup develops, the following information is offered.

1. Bargaining Unit members have a legal right to participate in sanctioned strike activity.

2. Non Bargaining Unit personnel have been known to collect Unemployment Insurance (upon appeal) if their position statement of record has reflected a refusal to cross a legitimate picket line due to a fear for personal safety.

3. Certain Welfare benefits may be available to qualifying individuals, the information for which will be supplied to "*ALL*" persons requesting same from the Union Welfare Committee.

4. The information contained in #3 above also applies to the Federal Food Stamp program.

5. The Union Welfare Committee can also be utilized to lessen or eliminate pressure from creditors of any description and/or landlords.

6. In the event it becomes necessary, personnel has been selected and assigned to the below listed committees for the express purpose of servicing the requests of "*ALL*" people *approaching* same with specific needs and/or requests:

    (a) Employment (b) Welfare (c) Commissary and (d) Speaker/
    Fund Raising

7. Any letter or verbal threat of intimidation (regardless of source) should be reported to the Welfare Committee for subsequent investigation and recommendation for disposition of same.

8. This information is "*NOT*" presented for the purpose of serving notice of impending strike action, but is intended for the SOLE purpose of giving you some indication of the extensive preparation that has taken place in your behalf in the hope that it will not have to be utilized.

9. The Union Hall at 1515 Market Avenue, San Pablo will be open from 10:00 p.m. to 12:00 m (this date) and ?????? thereafter.

10. The OCAW Negotiating Committee sincerely extends its "BEST WISHES FOR A *HAPPY* NEW YEAR" to each one of you (regardless of personal persuasion).

Source: Leaflet in authors' possession.

There were 191 Atlas strikers on the Schuylkill County food
stamp rolls as of July 23, 1971,[191] or about 32 percent of the
company's labor force living in that county. Because, like other
Pennsylvania county welfare departments, no effort was made
to distinguish striker from nonstriker public assistance applicants the Schuylkill County welfare office could not provide any
information as to the number of Atlas strikers on other forms
of public relief.

KIMBERLY-CLARK CORPORATION STRIKES

Kimberly-Clark, a major paper manufacturing company, suffered a number of strikes during 1970. Two were lengthy and
involved the payment of public aid to striking workers: one at
the business and technical paper mill in Munising, Michigan, in
which the dispute lasted from September 9 to December 7, 1970,
and the other at the coated paper plant in Niagara, Wisconsin,
where the work stoppage extended from September 11, 1970 to
February 8, 1971.[192]

Munising, Michigan

Munising, Alger County, is a relatively isolated community in
the Upper Peninsula of Michigan. The Kimberly-Clark mill is
the sole industrial employer there. Except for a short-lived strike
in 1968, the plant had experienced 64-years of operation without
a major labor-management dispute.[193] The 1970 twelve-week
strike, which involved about 450 members of Local 87, United
Papermakers and Paperworkers, and Local 96, International
Brotherhood of Pulp, Sulphite and Paper Mill Workers, affected
not only the economic health of the area, but also that of Michigan's welfare system.

Like General Motors employees, who went on strike during
the same period, Kimberly-Clark workers were permitted to obtain public aid. A few weeks after the strike began, the Alger
County Department of Social Services notified area newspapers
that under the rules and regulations of the U.S. Department of
Agriculture employees of Kimberly-Clark with large families

---

[191] Interview, Executive Director, Schuylkill County Board of Assistance,
Pottsville, Pennsylvania, July 30, 1971.

[192] Letter from Kimberly-Clark Corporation, March 30, 1971.

[193] *Munising News*, September 9, 1970.

were probably qualified to receive food stamps.[194] By the end of October 1970 the non-public assistance category of the Food Stamp program had climbed by 396 percent.[195] In December 1970, the last month of the strike, participation in the public assistance category was up 128 percent over September and it is estimated that at least 50 percent of the Kimberly-Clark strikers were receiving food stamps.[196]

AFDC-U rolls also soared in Alger County during October, November, and December 1970. Table 23 shows the 355.5 percent increases in participation, from 9 to 41 persons, between September and October, followed by continuing increases during the next two months. After the strike there was a drop in AFDC-U participants from a December high of 114 to 17 in January. It is estimated that more than 12 percent of the strike force, or 55 Kimberly-Clark employees, were obtaining cash assistance from AFDC-U in December 1970. If each of these strikers received the average payment made to an AFDC-U recipient in December, the cost to the taxpayer was about $11,611 in that month alone. When the food stamp cost and other welfare benefit costs are added to this estimated AFDC-U outlay, it is obvious that even a small strike can become a major expense to a county welfare department.

Niagara, Wisconsin

Kimberly-Clark's mill in Niagara is the sole industrial employer of this northeastern Wisconsin community. About 400 of the 680 workers who left their jobs on September 11, 1970 in support of the strike by Local 205, International Brotherhood of Pulp, Sulphite and Paper Mill Workers, live in this village of 2,098 people. Many of the remaining strikers reside in nearby Michigan. This strike, which lasted 150 days, was the first work stoppage at the Niagara mill since it began operations in 1898.[197]

The strike had a direct and obvious impact on the area. The village president reported that, in addition to the $2.5 million mill payroll and purchases, the strike cost the town some $40,000

---

[194] *Marquette Mining Journal*, September 23, 1970.

[195] U.S. Department of Agriculture, Food and Nutrition Service.

[196] Estimated from data obtained from U.S. Department of Agriculture.

[197] *Appleton Post-Crescent*, December 6, 1970, and letter from Kimberly-Clark Corporation, March 30, 1971.

TABLE 23. *Kimberly-Clark Strike*
AFDC-U Participation
Alger County, Michigan
April 1970-March 1971

Year	Month	Persons Participating[a]	Percent Change from First Month of Strike[b]	Average Payment per Case
1970				
	April	5	—44.4	$376.60
	May	4	—55.6	273.75
	June	5	—44.4	269.40
	July	2	—77.8	167.50
	August	4	—55.6	211.00
	September	9	—	251.44
	October	41	355.5	177.68
	November	98	988.9	220.14
	December	114	1,166.7	211.11
1971				
	January	17	88.9	248.82
	February	19	111.1	256.47
	March	23	155.6	259.74

Source: Michigan Department of Social Services.

[a] The Michigan Department of Social Services reported that in October, November, and December 1970 12, 36 and 39 General Motors employees, respectively, were enrolled in Alger County's AFDC program, although all of these strikers were not necessarily participants in the AFDC-U program.

[b] September 1970 was the first month of the Kimberly-Clark strike in Alger County and December 1970 was the last.

in state shared taxes, based on local income taxes.[198] Local businesses lost most of their Christmas sales. Community service
stations reported that gasoline sales were down. School official
decided it was impossible to propose a long-needed building
plan.[199]

A majority of the strikers offset the economic pressures o
the strike with financial assistance from union strike benefit
and food stamps. At that time, Wisconsin did not permit em
ployees involved in a labor dispute to collect public assistance

[198] *Milwaukee Journal*, February 14, 1971.

[199] *Appleton Post-Crescent*, December 6, 1970.

although the state has since changed its policies. Therefore, those Kimberly-Clark strikers living in Wisconsin had to subsist on $28 a week in strike benefits plus federal food stamp aid.[200] The director of the county welfare department refused to allow strikers to obtain food stamps until he received a phone call from a state official telling him he must do so.

According to the *Milwaukee Journal,* "The food stamp program pumped about $85,000 into Niagara and the immediate surrounding area and an estimated $40,000 to $50,000 into surrounding counties" during the strike.[201] Non-public assistance household participation climbed more than 115 percent from September to October 1970.[202] A county welfare official said that 193 Niagara families received food stamps in November whereas food stamps had been unknown there before the strike. Approximately $21,000 in stamps was distributed to these families. In addition, certain children of Kimberly-Clark strikers received free noon meals under the school lunch program.[203]

"Oh, sure, it's hard without the money, but at least we can buy food with food stamps," one striker said near the end of January 1971. "I live on the Michigan side and get A[F]DC so we get along," another striker maintained.[204] This attitude troubled some public figures in Niagara. One was a supervisor of Marinette County and another was a pastor. Charging that there were abuses of food stamp privileges, a county supervisor claimed that people who owned two homes in Niagara were allegedly receiving food stamps and some had drawn their savings out of the credit union so the assets couldn't be found in order to qualify for food stamps."[205] The county welfare director felt, "It's silly, it's wrong for people having equity of $30,000 and on strike to get stamps. The taxpayers are subsidizing the union against management on this program. I don't like it, but we're stuck."[206] Even the wife of one of the strikers

---

[200] *Ibid.*

[201] *Milwaukee Journal,* February 14, 1971.

[202] U.S. Department of Agriculture, Food and Nutrition Service.

[203] *Appleton Post-Crescent,* December 6, 1970.

[204] *Appleton Post-Crescent,* January 30, 1971.

[205] *Niagara News,* January 3, 1971.

[206] *Ibid.*

was disturbed by some of the eligibility requirements for food stamps, which had disqualified her family until the savings they had accumulated fell below $2,000. "People with a new house, a cottage, a car and a snowmobile can get food stamps, though, because they have mortgage payments." [207] She and her husband owned their own home and did not have to meet monthly house payments.

The pastor commented: "Too many people seem too apathetic about the strike. Some people don't seem to care if they get back to work." He was troubled because some young people did not picture the strike as being undesirable, in part because the school eliminated admission fees to home athletic contests as long as the strike lasted. He feared that youngsters were beginning to look on this and the free school lunches as being the good things about a strike.[208]

LEEDS AND NORTHRUP COMPANY STRIKE

On January 29, 1971, the 2,000 members of Local 1350, United Automobile, Aerospace and Agricultural Implement Workers (UAW) struck the Leeds and Northrup Company at North Wales, Pennsylvania. They remained on strike until July 19th of that year.[209] The issues were many and severe, the union having submitted 165 proposals in a new list after working without a contract for about six weeks.[210] It seemed obvious, in retrospect, that the local expected a long walkout. The company, which a few years before had moved its operations out of Philadelphia to North Wales, Montgomery County, was a major employer in this exurban area.

---

[207] *Appleton Post-Crescent*, December 6, 1970.

[208] *Ibid.*

[209] The original draft of this case study was prepared by George T. Mauro, graduate student, Wharton School of Finance and Commerce, University of Pennsylvania, as a research study for a class in Management of Human Resources, November 22, 1971.

[210] The timing of the union's actions is suggestive. In neighboring Bucks County, Local 1354, UAW, struck the Strick Trailer Corporation on January 8, 1971, after working without a contract from October 1970. This coincident sequence of events seems to have had less to do with the bargaining at these two plants than the fact that the UAW's strike of General Motors wasn't settled until mid-November. With the GM strike ultimately costing it in excess of $156 million, it is certainly reasonable to surmise that the International was not about to sanction any other strikes until after all its GM workers were back on the job.

Strike Assistance Program

Local 1350 had a carefully organized strike assistance program which was a well-integrated vehicle for easing the economic burden on the individual striker. Its Community Services Committee, headed by the treasurer, planned and administered the program in coordination with the UAW's Montgomery County Community Action Program Council. Prior to the strike, the committee called upon public and private community welfare agencies to gather information and to solicit assistance. It also acted as a liaison agency between individual members and their creditors, calling upon the contracts it had made with the local community service organizations when necessary. They were very effective, finding that most stores, banks, mortgage holders, utility companies, and the like were sympathetic to the strikers' plight and willing to cooperate. For example, the bank which had the payroll deduction arrangement in the plant, on its own initiative, declared a moratorium on any principal and interest payments due it for the course of the strike.

The available public welfare services were incorporated into the program. The concentration was upon the Food Stamp program, with every member being urged to apply. The Community Services Committee published several newsletters providing detailed information on where and how to apply, and what papers and records to have available. For the members living in Montgomery County, the committee arranged for representatives from the Norristown office of the Department of Public Welfare to come to the union hall to process the applications for certification on the spot. The union took the responsibility for advising their members and scheduling appointments for them to submit their applications. For those living in neighboring Bucks County, which does not participate in the Food Stamp program but distributes surplus commodity foods, the union provided the application forms and advised of the distribution dates.[211]

In addition to these institutional programs, many strikers were able to find part-time or even full-time jobs. This was particularly true as the strike progressed since each member's presence for strike duty was only required for two hours a week. Although the UAW benefit program provides that a striker be-

[211] A representative of the Philadelphia County welfare department met with union members in November 1970, two months before the strike began, to discuss what public benefits would be available if the union decided to strike. Interview, Philadelphia County Board of Assistance, May 26, 1971.

comes ineligible for assistance when his gross weekly income exceeds $50, this rule proved impossible to enforce in practice.

The effectiveness of this multifaceted program seems beyond question. About 1,800 of the 2,000 people on strike actually participated and received union benefit payments. A union official estimated that with this money, food stamps, and income from other jobs or working wives, the average striker might be able to recoup from 60 to 80 percent of his normal income. With the cooperation the union was able to generate among merchants, creditors, and landlords, its membership was well able to meet essential expenses and sustain the economic losses of the long strike.

Use of Welfare Assistance

Public assistance programs were an integral part of this strike. The union was knowledgeable and sophisticated in seeking information and arranging for the cooperation of public welfare service agencies. From the beginning, the Community Services Committee planned for and facilitated the strikers' use of available services. The union, however, kept no formal records of their members' participation in welfare. A local union officer estimated (probably conservatively) that perhaps one-third of the strikers used food stamps, and "very few" used the AFDC or General Assistance programs.[212] The Department of Public Welfare does not differentiate between strikers and any other applicants for assistance, whatever the cause. A supervisor in the Montgomery County office, in Norristown, could not provide any numerical estimates, but said that the impact on case loads was noticeable, and that by May or June the office was receiving a number of applications for the monetary assistance programs.[213]

In the absence of data specific to the strike, the only references available are the county welfare participation statistics. It is extremely difficult to isolate the effect of the strike on these figures, dependent as they are upon the general economic health of the community, the unemployment situation, other strikes, and perhaps other factors which cannot be identified. Nevertheless, a strike idling 2,000 men over a six-month period does have an impact in increasing the number of cases, with perhaps a significantly greater increase at the beginning of the strike.

---

[212] Interview, Doylestown, Pennsylvania, November 5, 1971.

[213] Interview, Norristown, Pennsylvania, November 5, 1971.

Before reviewing the available statistical data, it is appropriate to make some observations about the patterns which could be expected to appear apart from the influence of the strike. According to data provided by the Pennsylvania Department of Public Welfare, participation in the various programs seems to follow an annual cycle. Beginning with a low point in the late summer, perhaps in August, the case load rises steadily through autumn to a high point in mid-winter, typically in February. Beginning in March and April, participation begins to fall again to a summer low, although perhaps still above the preceding year's low point. Thus, the secular trend is upward, but there is a definite cyclical pattern which peaks in February and bottoms out in August.

Other work stoppages in the Philadelphia labor market area,[214] which includes Montgomery County, would also affect public assistance figures. The Leeds and Northrup strike had its greatest impact, however, on but a small proportion of this labor market, Montgomery County and the northern section of Philadelphia County. For the period in question, the Leeds and Northrup strike was the only major labor-management dispute in this area. Although the Strick Trailer strike (Fairless Hills, Bucks County, Pennsylvania) occurred at about the same time and lasted 146 days, it involved only 600 persons, with but half of these persons residing in an area where Leeds and Northrup employees may have lived.[215] In this case it appears that the effects of other strikes can reasonably be expected to have been comparatively minimal.

Unfortunately, at the writing of this case study, public assistance data were only available through May 1971, and food stamp participation data were only available through June 1971. With all these qualifications, an examination of the pertinent figures is nevertheless revealing.

Approximately 1,000 Leeds and Northrup strikers resided in Montgomery County. Table 24 shows the number of persons participating in the county's Food Stamp program from September 1970 through June 1971, and Figure 26 illustrates the impact of

---

[214] The Philadelphia labor market area consists of Bucks, Chester, Delaware, Montgomery and Philadelphia Counties in Pennsylvania and Burlington. Camden and Gloucester Counties in New Jersey.

[215] Interview, Management Representative, May 25, 1971. The authors were informed that Strick Trailer strikers were receiving public aid.

TABLE 24. *Leeds and Northrup Strike*
Food Stamp Participation
Montgomery County, Pennsylvania
September 1970–June 1971

| Year | Month | Persons Participating | | | Percent Change from Previous Month | Percent Difference from First Month of Strike |
		Public Assistance	Non-Public Assistance	Total		
1970	September	2,869	2,072	4,941	25.7	—10.2
	October	3,161	1,560	4,721	—4.5	—14.2
	November	3,443	1,523	4,966	5.2	—9.8
	December	3,710	1,706	5,416	9.1	—1.6
1971	January	3,924	1,580	5,504	1.6	—
	February	4,361	2,374	6,735	22.4	22.4
	March	4,730	3,095	7,825	16.2	42.2
	April	5,092	3,235	8,327	6.4	51.3
	May	5,457	3,271	8,728	4.8	58.6
	June	5,608	3,570	9,178	5.2	66.8

Source: U.S. Department of Agriculture, Food and Nutrition Service.

Note: January 1971 was the first month of the Leeds and Northrup strike and July 1971 was the last, but data were available only through June.

FIGURE 26. *Leeds and Northrup Strike*
Food Stamp Participation
Montgomery County, Pennsylvania
September 1970-June 1971

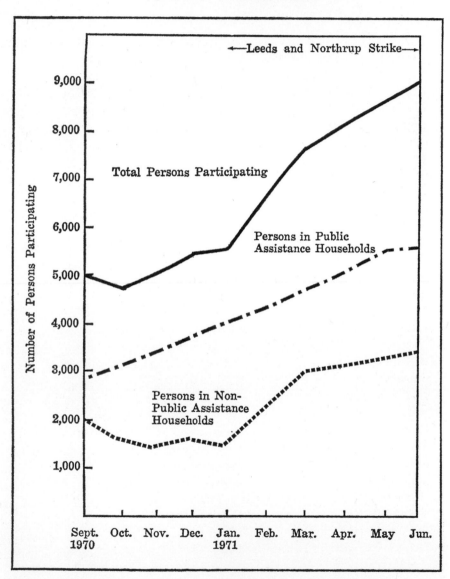

Source: Department of Agriculture, Food and Nutrition Service.

Note: The Leeds and Northrup Strike extended to July 1971, but data were available only through June.

the strike on food stamp rolls. Since the strikers are not likely to have immediately qualified for cash benefits, their participation should be reflected, at least initially, in the non-public assistance category. Focusing on these figures alone, there is a dramatic increase in February over the relatively stable level of the preceding four months. Figure 26 graphically portrays the effect of the strike on the program by illustrating the impact on food stamp participation during the period January through June 1971.

Normal seasonal patterns would suggest that February ought to mark a high point, with at least a leveling off, if not a decline, in March. In the present case, the March figures are substantially higher than those in February. Although not representing as great a percentage increase, the change in the number of participating households was almost as great in March as it was in February, well above the numerical change between any two preceding months.

Some 800 of the striking employees lived in Philadelphia County, with the overwhelming majority concentrated in the two northernmost welfare districts in the city. About 450 lived in the Hill District and 295 in the North District.[216] If the strike were to have any noticeable effect in Philadelphia, it would be in these two districts. Table 25 details Food Stamp program participation from September 1970 through April 1971. The trend seems to be the same as it was in Montgomery County; generally upward throughout the period. Here again, there is very little indication of the seasonal peak in February, but it does show up in March in the North District.

Turning to the data on the other two public aid programs which would apply, AFDC-U and General Assistance, the picture is less clear. The welfare official interviewed indicated that the strikers did not begin to use these programs in any great numbers until May and June 1971.[217] Yet the figures in Table 26 show a considerable increase in the number of persons receiving AFDC-U in February, March, and April. The absolute numbers involved are so small that any generalization must be suspect; however, it can be observed that there is nothing here to contradict the trend observed in the Food Stamp data. The General Assistance caseload

---

216 Interview, North Wales, September 23, 1971.

217 Interview, Norristown, Pennsylvania, November 5, 1971.

TABLE 25. *Leeds and Northrup Strike*
Food Stamp Participation
Hill and North Districts, Philadelphia County, Pennsylvania
September 1970-April 1971

| | | Persons Participating | | | | | |
| | | Public Assistance | | Non-Public Assistance | | Total | |
Year	Month	Hill	North	Hill	North	Hill	North
1970							
	September	1,534	3,152	254	1,004	1,788	4,156
	October	2,152	3,509	394	1,103	2,546	4,612
	November	2,013	3,614	436	1,174	2,449	4,788
	December	2,346	3,940	470	1,356	2,816	5,296
1971							
	January	2,342	4,073	549	1,381	2,891	5,454
	February	2,521	4,178	599	1,317	3,120	5,495
	March	2,749	4,547	774	1,722	3,523	6,269
	April	2,786	4,613	754	1,840	3,540	6,453

Source: Department of Public Welfare, Commonwealth of Pennsylvania.

Note: January 1971 was the first month of the strike and July 1971 was the last, but data were available only through April.

reflects a steady increase over the entire period, as Table 26 shows. Although there are no sudden increases, neither is there any evidence of the beginning of the normally anticipated summer downturn. Figures 27 and 28 present data for these two programs in a graph comparing the period under consideration with that a year earlier.

TABLE 26. *Leeds and Northrup Strike*
AFDC-U and General Assistance Participation
Montgomery County, Pennsylvania
September 1970-May 1971

| Year | Month | Number of Persons | |
		AFDC-U	General Assistance
1970			
	September	14	779
	October	14	804
	November	14	884
	December	14	1,046
1971			
	January	10	1,081
	February	16	1,172
	March	25	1,276
	April	29	1,358
	May	29	1,406

Source: Department of Public Welfare, Commonwealth of Pennsylvania.

FIGURE 27. *Leeds and Northrup Strike*
AFDC-U Participation
Montgomery County, Pennsylvania
September 1969-May 1970 and September 1970-May 1971

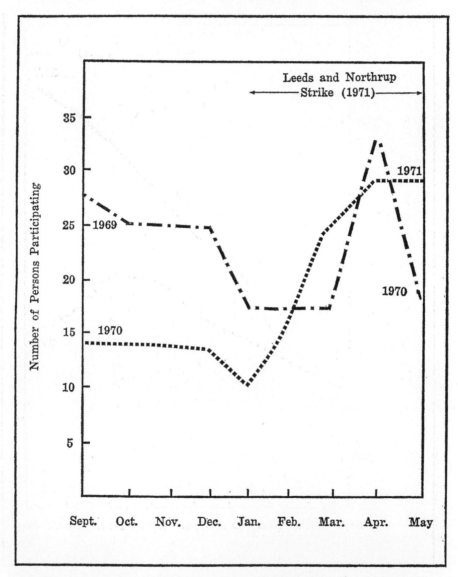

Source: Department of Public Welfare, Commonwealth of Pennsylvania.

Note: The Leeds and Northrup strike extended to July 1971, but AFDC-U data were available only through May.

FIGURE 28. *Leeds and Northrup Strike*
General Assistance Participation
Montgomery County, Pennsylvania
September 1969-May 1970 and September 1970-May 1971

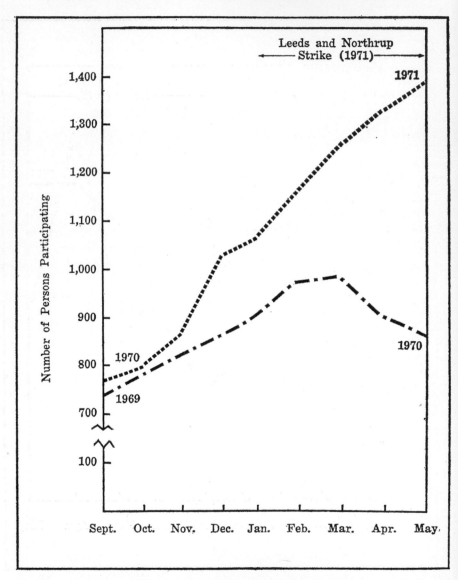

Source: Commonwealth of Pennsylvania, Department of Public Welfare.

Note: The Leeds and Northrup strike extended to July 1971, but data
were available only through May.

Just as there are no exact measures of the impact of the Leeds and Northrup strike on Pennsylvania public assistance programs, there is no rule by which to gauge the impact welfare had upon the strike. The interviews presented in the next few pages will provide a picture of how an official of Local 1350, a management representative of Leeds and Northrup, and a Montgomery County welfare official viewed the effects of providing welfare to strikers.

Union Viewpoint

Interviewer: Were you satisfied with the cooperation you received from welfare officials?

Union Official: Generally yes. Most agencies were very helpful. The people in Norristown were really outstanding. They sent a team out here to process the initial certification of our members as they came through to pick up their benefit checks. Our people who live in Philadelphia or the other counties had to go in to their local welfare offices. We had no reports that they encountered any difficulties.

Interviewer: Was this strike the first time your union has used a significant amount of public aid to assist striking workers?

Union Official: Yes. Of course this was the first strike since the UAW became the bargaining agent. We were certified in 1967, when we replaced an independent local. There had been a short strike back in 1962, but that was before many of these programs were available.

Interviewer: Would your membership have been able to cope with the strike without some sort of public assistance?

Union Official: That's a sensitive question. Certainly the food stamps were a very big help. They kept some food on the table for the wife and kids. I suppose you could say that the food stamps balanced out the lack of the UAW emergency assistance program.

Interviewer: Should changes be made in welfare laws as to eligibility requirements?

Union Official: No, I don't think so. Of course I would love to see strikers receive unemployment benefits, but that would never happen. There would be such a public clamor against it that it would be impossible to do.

Interviewer: What is the attitude of your union members toward the welfare program? Do you think that their experience as participants affected their attitudes?

Union Official: We were happy to be able to participate in the program. We have an above average membership; they're mainly upper middle class. Welfare is foreign to their outlook, but their need dictates that they use the program. They were reluctant to begin, but once they got the food stamps and used them, they liked it well enough. The strike is an unusual situation. I don't think there were any long lasting attitude changes toward welfare in general.

Interviewer: What is your reaction to efforts to make strikers ineligible for welfare benefits?

Union Official: No way . . . union members are not second class citizens. We are entitled to the benefits because we are in need.

Interviewer: What effect do welfare payments have on the collective bargaining process?

Union Official: I don't think they had any effect in this strike. The length of our strike indicates that it was an unusual situation. I don't think you can make a general statement; every case is different.

Interviewer: Do you view aid to striking workers as a form of government intervention in labor negotiations?

Union Official:	It could be a two-edged sword. The aid enables you to say out on strike longer. In the long run, this might hurt the union. Without the assistance you couldn't take such a hard line. Both sides, the company and the union, might be more businesslike about the negotiations. Since the individual member is getting some help and has food on the table, he isn't hurting as much and he doesn't pressure the bargaining committee. Even so, the union member is hurt by his loss of income. He might be able to recoup maybe 60 percent to 80 percent through all the programs available, but he can never recover the difference he loses. The assistance just allows the member to survive.

I can't be too forceful in saying we're entitled to it. For 99 percent of our lives we work and contribute to these programs. When we use them, we're not getting something we don't deserve. After all, if government money can go down ratholes all over the world, certainly we should be entitled to a share of it.

Management Viewpoint

Interviewer:	What, if any, effect did welfare payments to the strikers have upon the strike?
Management Official:	There is no doubt that welfare payments to our strikers prolonged the strike. In addition, some strikers were able to find work. The food stamp program kept food on the table and part-time or full-time jobs or welfare kept money in their pockets. Without welfare the strikers would have been in dire financial condition. Many people wanted to get back to work. However, they could stay out with welfare without being seriously hurt financially.
Interviewer:	What effect do you think welfare payments to strikers have on collective bargaining?

Management Official: There did not appear to be any economic
                        pressures on the strikers. Considering there
                        were so many older workers who were not
                        behind the UAW, why didn't they and oth-
                        ers put pressure on the union's bargaining
                        committee to obtain a settlement? The
                        younger workers did not take the strike that
                        seriously, and the protests and pressures
                        just didn't get off the ground. With the $30-
                        $40 a week in strike benefits plus welfare
                        aid, there just wasn't any severe economic
                        pressures associated with the strike.

Interviewer: Do you think the strikers' willingness to
                        use welfare reflects a change in the com-
                        munity's attitude about public assistance?

Management Official: The situation reflects an attitude which ap-
                        pears common among many people today, a
                        concept of society toward welfare. The con-
                        cept is that welfare is a right. If the op-
                        portunity arises to take it, take it regardless
                        of the circumstances, if you're on strike or
                        not, or if there is any real need or not.

Welfare Agency Viewpoint

Interviewer: Which of your services are available to
                        strikers?

Welfare Official: We would treat a striker just as we would
                        any other unemployed worker. He would be
                        eligible for all of the programs after his
                        first payless week. In perhaps 80 percent
                        of our striker caseload, they apply only for
                        food stamps. Often, however, the longer the
                        strike lasts, the more they use the other
                        programs. For instance, in the Leeds &
                        Northrup strike, we began to have strikers
                        applying for monetary assistance by May
                        and June.

Interviewer: Have you had contact with unions as such to
                        explain the programs to the leadership or
                        the members?

Welfare Official: We have made our staff available to service striker applications at the site. We are normally asked to go to the union site—the unions know of the program and generally call in advance of the strike. We appreciate the notice so we can prepare. We have a limited staff, but we try to help. Usually we can give our standard handouts to the union and they put out the details to their membership.

Interviewer: Do you have any feeling for what proportion of your caseload is made up of strikers, or how much you've paid in monetary benefits to strikers?

Welfare Official: That depends upon the number on strike and where they live. I couldn't really say. We do keep track of the number of strikes we get involved in. There were 15 between January 1 and August 31, and perhaps 6 since then.

Interviewer: What effect do you think welfare payments to strikers have on collective bargaining?

Welfare Official: I think many strikes depend upon food stamps. The leaders can get up and say: "Vote yes—we'll get food stamps." We have often spoken to union members when they weren't even considering strikes. The welfare assistance takes the pressure off the strikers. They are still eating and managing to get by somehow. The mortgage company won't foreclose, so all they really need is the food.

Interviewer: Do you think strikers are now more receptive to and willing to use welfare?

Welfare Official: Yes, there is no hesitation about using food stamps. There is still some feeling about accepting public assistance. For public assistance, they have to sign a lien on their property. There is still some stigma attached.

Interviewer: Has there been any effect on community
                        attitudes toward welfare and welfare re-
                        cipients?

Welfare Official: More people are becoming aware of the
                        benefits available, and as awareness in-
                        creases, the stigma is decreasing. Now wel-
                        fare is considered a right, and people are
                        comfortable in asking for aid. Even when
                        they're working, many people use welfare
                        as a supplementary income. In fact, people
                        can be very demanding—anyone can apply
                        and it's often difficult to tell someone that
                        he is not eligible. I think the case this sum-
                        mer where teachers were drawing welfare
                        during their summer vacations indicates
                        how community attitudes have changed.

Interviewer: As a matter of policy, do you think it is
                        right for strikers to be eligible for benefits?

Welfare Official: Yes; I think as long as there is need, we
                        should help. Sometimes I can't reconcile the
                        regulations, though. For instance, during
                        the wage-price freeze, the President asked
                        that unions not go on strike. Yet, when
                        they did strike illegally, they were still eli-
                        gible for welfare. I know the benefits ena-
                        ble strikers to be comfortable and allow
                        them to stay out longer, so I can see man-
                        agement's point of view. But I know how
                        bad the economy is, and I agree with the
                        reasons why people go out on strike. As
                        long as things are so bad, and people have
                        to strike, they should get help. I guess may-
                        be I feel this way because I'm involved
                        mainly with the unions and strikers and I
                        can see their side.

Summary

In the absence of any significant pressure from its members,
the union can afford to take a harder line during negotiations.
The effect was to alter the collective bargaining process and
the environment in which it took place. Without welfare aid

to its members, Local 1350 would have had to take a more businesslike attitude toward negotiations.

It is likely that the Leeds & Northrup strike would have occurred, and it might have been a long one, regardless of the availability of public aid. Although welfare may not have been central to the strike decision, it was certainly a factor in hardening the union's position and enabling it to better endure a long strike.

CALIFORNIA AND HAWAIIAN SUGAR COMPANY STRIKE

A strike of production and maintenance workers (Sugar Workers, Local 1) occurred at the Crockett, California refinery of the California and Hawaiian Sugar Company on June 1, 1970.[218] The union membership narrowly rejected (440 "no" votes, 431 "yes") a contract settlement proposed by their negotiating committee and accepted by the company. The striking union members already were earning an average of $7,564 per year, including a fixed annual Christmas bonus. In addition, they were provided employee benefits including a pension plan, health and welfare plan, company paid life insurance, premium pay for shift work and overtime, etc. The value of these benefits was $2,525 per year for the average employee. Thus, the average combined total of wages and employee benefits was $10,089.

In striking, the union membership rejected wage increases of 10 percent the first year, and 5 percent plus up to 3 percent in cost-of-living adjustments in each of the second and third years of a three-year contract. Increased shift work premiums as well as a company-paid dental plan for employees and dependents were also part of the rejected proposal. In the third year of the new contract, the total value of wages and benefits for the average employee would have been $12,987 per year.

In spite of the level of pre-strike wages and the size of the rejected offer, the business agent of the striking union stated publicly in the fifth week of the strike that about 60 percent of the workers were receiving some form of welfare or food stamps,

---

[218] The original draft for this case study was prepared by Mr. Donald T. Hanson, Industrial Relations Manager, California and Hawaiian Sugar Company. Mr. Hanson presented this case history before the California State Social Welfare Board on February 27, 1971, at which time the Board was conducting one of its two public hearings on the issue of public aid to strikers.

including those who required such assistance before the strike and those who qualified for aid when the strike began. Although Social Service offices will not divulge statistics on welfare benefits being drawn by strikers, at a meeting of the County Board of Supervisors one of the Board's members reported that 52 striking employees had qualified for welfare benefits in the third week of the strike. He reported that of this number, 31 were buying homes, 49 owned automobiles (11 had two or more automobiles), and 28 had savings accounts.

In Contra Costa County, home of the C and H Sugar Refinery, a member of the Board of Supervisors asked the County Social Services Director to report on eligibility requirements for strikers receiving welfare, because such situations were disrupting labor negotiations. The supervisor reported that he had heard reports that sugar refinery employees were "bragging" about how easy it was to obtain welfare benefits. This same supervisor said he had personally received a number of phone calls from union members at C and H Sugar Company who wanted to get back to their jobs, complaining that some others of the strikers were bragging about their welfare benefits and were not in any hurry to go back to work. The supervisor expressed concern that welfare benefits were prolonging the strike at Crockett.

The Social Services Director responded that workers on "bona fide strikes" are entitled to receive welfare payments, if they qualify, and they can receive food stamps without showing that they are involved in a "bona fide strike." He went on to say that if a strike is in effect involving workers of a particular trade, it is sometimes looked upon as meaning that no job is available and therefore the applicant is considered as complying with the rule that he be available for employment.

The Contra Costa County Policy and Procedure Manual on welfare benefits states, "All *liquid* assets shall be considered in determining eligibility based on need." At the time the strike started on June 1, 1970, 958 (80 percent) of the striking union were members, with savings, in the company-sponsored Federal Credit Union. Yet during the 17-week strike, the company received only five telephone calls from welfare offices investigating applicants' eligibility for benefits.

Regarding food stamps, the Director of Social Services reported, "Eligibility rules for food stamps are in no way related to whether or not a person is involved in a labor dispute. Persons who are not receiving welfare assistance can qualify for food stamps regardless of the status of their employment." He concluded his report by stating, "The State Department of Welfare should establish better guidelines for use in determining the eligibility of strikers for assistance."

Reports indicated that food stamps were more than abundantly available. One striker had more food stamps than his family could use, so he sold the stamps to buy liquor. A local grocery store owner reported some of his customers who were receiving food stamps were eating expensive steaks and chops every day during the strike. Strikers were receiving so many food stamps that their freezers were being filled with steaks and roasts that would feed their families for months after the strike. During an extended negotiating meeting in San Francisco, one of the officers of the union used food stamps to buy groceries for dinner for the entire union negotiating committee.

On at least two occasions the union members were instructed at membership meetings on the availability of welfare benefits. They were encouraged to apply for these benefits.

It is reasonably clear that the ready availability of welfare benefits and food stamps prolonged this strike. Membership pressure on union leaders to reach a settlement seemed reduced because the strike was subsidized by welfare benefits. This strike was apparently so well subsidized by welfare benefits that the union's strike fund went unspent during the 17-week strike. Prior to this strike, the longest strike by this union lasted only six weeks. Although the employer improved his offer a month after the strike started, the union negotiating committee refused to submit the improved offer to the membership for a vote and union members did not show any great interest in voting on it then—or even later when the strike was two months old, despite a wage and benefit loss to the average union member totaling $1,950 at that time.

NEW YORK TELEPHONE STRIKE

The seven-month strike of 23 New York Communications Workers of America (CWA) locals began on July 14, 1971, as part of a nationwide CWA walkout. When the national union signed a three-year contract on August 14, 1971 for its approximately 400,000 members, the New York State contingent, consisting of about 38,000 workers, decided to continue the strike.[219]

---

[219] Victor Riesel, *Inside Labor* (Publishers-Hall Syndicate), January 12, 1972.

The presidents of CWA locals in New York announced that they rejected the whole package "because it did not fulfill the needs of the New York Telephone people." [220] The strike lasted until February 16, 1972 at which time the New York Communications Workers ratified a settlement on terms that represented "only a nominal improvement over those originally available. . . ." [221]

In order to achieve these minimal gains New York telephone strikers had to give up over $90 million in gross wages.[222] They cost their own union an estimated $11 million in emergency strike benefits,[223] and they remained off their jobs in opposition to the wishes of the CWA's international officers. The question is how were these strikers able to resist a settlement for seven months in the face of so many pressures, especially the economic pressures associated with a prolonged strike.

The answers for these more than 38,000 unionists were New York State's unemployment insurance, public assistance, and Food Stamp programs. Each of these public relief programs came to the striker's aid, protecting him and his family from severe economic loss.

The program which undoubtedly provided the greatest monetary support to striking telephone workers was unemployment insurance. Seven weeks after the walkout began, most strikers were able to draw up to $75 per week in benefits, putting the employer in a position of subsidizing his own strike, since the employer pays the taxes that finance the New York unemployment program.[224] A *New York Times* editorial described the situation as follows:

> The New York Telephone Co. had $41 million credited to its insurance reserve account when the first strike benefits were paid last September. By the end of last week [February 11, 1972] every dollar in the account had been drained and the company was $500,000 in the red in its payments into the fund. . . .
> To replenish its unemployment insurance account, the telephone company's taxes—geared to the volume of joblessness it throws on the fund—will go up from $3 million in 1971 to $11.6 million this year and $12.7 million next year. In a real sense,

---

[220] *Daily Labor Report*, No. 26 (February 4, 1972), p. AA-6.

[221] Editorial, *New York Times*, February 18, 1972, p. 32.

[222] Riesel, *loc. cit.*

[223] *New York Times*, February 18, 1972.

[224] *Ibid.*

the money will come not from the Bell System but from telephone users, who will now find the higher costs in wages and taxes reflected in the company's rate base.[225]

WEYERHAEUSER COMPANY NORTHWEST PULP AND PAPERBOARD STRIKE

On May 6, 1971, about 2,300 members of the Association of Western Pulp and Paper Workers struck four of Weyerhaeuser Company's pulp and paperboard operations in Oregon and Washington.[226] The walkout lasted until August 17, 1971.

The union apparently is not financially strong and could not provide strike benefits to its members, but by securing loans from other unions, extremely needy members were provided some cash assistance. The Weyerhaeuser Company found that food stamps or surplus food commodities played a major role in helping their striking employees to sustain the work stoppage. Although it was difficult to obtain any information from county welfare departments about Weyerhaeuser strikers obtaining public benefits, it was estimated at one plant location that at least 30 percent of the strikers were using food stamps.[227] The county in which its Longview, Washington, mill is located (Cowlitz) experienced a 66.8 percent increase in non-public assistance food stamp participation between the end of April and the end of June 1971.[228] When compared to a 1.5 percent fall for Washington as a whole during the same period,[229] when food stamp rolls generally decline, it is very probable that the large increase in food stamp participation in the Longview area was due to Weyerhaeuser strikers.

CONCLUDING REMARKS

The case studies presented in this chapter represent additional examples of labor-management disputes where organized labor has been successful in mobilizing public funds to subsidize their

---

[225] *Ibid.*

[226] Interview, Weyerhaeuser Company, Tacoma, Washington, September 2, 1971.

[227] Interview, September 2, 1971.

[228] U.S. Department of Agriculture, Food and Nutrition Service.

[229] *Ibid.*

FIGURE 29.
Public Aid to Strikers
Selected News and Related Articles

Garbage Strikers on Relief

Martinez—Welfare payments are helping Contra Costa County [California] garbage collectors weather their strike, it was disclosed today. . . .

George Gordon, attorney for the struck 12 scavenger companies, said what it amounts to is that the taxpayers are subsidizing the strike.

"We have definite information that some of these striking employees are getting welfare and moonlighting at the same time," he said. He said there were at least 25 cases, some in this county and some in Alameda County where many of the strikers live. *San Francisco Examiner,* April 25, 1968.

Striker Welfare Rule Sought

Martinez—The Contra Costa County Board of Supervisors yesterday called on state officials to clarify regulations surrounding welfare assistance to striking union members.

County Welfare Director Robert E. Jornlin was instructed to draft a resolution requesting clarification after he told supervisors that existing rules are insufficient. . . .

He said that his department authorized welfare aid for striking AC Transit district employees but turned down World Airways mechanics who had walked out in sympathy with striking Teamsters.

Supervisor James E. Moriarity, Lafayette, asked for clarification from the State after noting that he had been told by union leaders that the fact that striking employees can get welfare slows down negotiations. . . . *Oakland Tribune,* June 24, 1970.

County Welfare Problem

Fairfield—The Board of Supervisors yesterday made an emergency appropriation of $128,088 from the general fund to cover increased welfare costs in Solano County [California].

For the second straight year the supervisors had to take the unprecedented step of covering an overrun in welfare aid payments. . . . The board was advised by the County Counsel Milton Goldinger the county was bound by law to provide the money for the aid. . . . During the morning session Scofield reported that 51 county residents were collecting welfare payments while on strike at the C&H Sugar Refinery. He said it was wrong that the taxpayer has to pay the bill. . . .

FIGURE 29.—continued

Scofield told the Board that of the 51 strikers who are collecting benefits from Solano County, 49 were driving late model cars, and that 31 were buying homes. *Vallejo Times Record,* June 24, 1970.

300 Laborers Picket Union To Protest Dues

Philadelphia—About 300 members of Local 332, Laborers Union, AFL-CIO, today picketed their union headquarters on Ridge av. near 13th st.

They said they were seeking a moratorium on the payment of union dues for the duration of a strike of more than 12,000 laborers against the construction industry.

The men complained their demands for a freeze on dues have gone unheeded. The strike began May 1.

Ray Poorman, a spokesman for the pickets, said the majority of the strikers have been forced to go on relief as a result of the strike.

He said that the men find it a hardship to use their Department of Public Assistance money for the payment of union dues. *Philadelphia Evening Bulletin,* June 1, 1970.

Strikers Brace For Long Fight At Midvale

Nicetown [Pennsylvania]—"We're not going to back down," said Edward Dizalo. . ., as he stood with a group of pickets outside the firm [Midvale-Heppenstall Company] at Wissahickon and Midvale aves.

"I think it's going to be a long one [strike]," he said. "Some of the fellows are already on relief and some are receiving food stamps."

William Hall, a press driver, said he was forced to go on relief and receives $69 every two weeks.

"It's not much," said Hall, who is single. "But I intend to stay out as long as I have to." *Philadelphia Evening Bulletin,* October 13, 1971.

West Virginia Hard Hit By Long Coal Strike

There is also a price for the taxpayer. Over 15,000 West Virginia families were added to the Food Stamp program for this month. This swelled the state's Food Stamp rolls by 20%. Last week, the state's welfare department distributed $1.7 million in food stamps to the miners' families. The federal government pays for the program, which enables recipients to exchange stamps for food. *Wall Street Journal,* November 11, 1971.

FIGURE 29.—continued

At Maytag, Public Relief Funds Also Asked

Newton, IA.—Jasper County Attorney Dennis Chalupa contends that if he hadn't fought "tooth and nail," Maytag Co. employes would have used Iowa relief funds earlier this year to support themselves while on strike.

As it was, the United Auto Workers (UAW) union members had plenty of government help—including surplus commodities and food stamps—during their 150-day strike against the washing machine manufacturer.

There are similar stories across Iowa—in Sioux City, Clinton, Davenport and Des Moines—and the nation of organized labor striving to use public assistance programs to take care of strikers.

Over the bargaining table during the 150-day strike here, union negotiators said calmly that they could hold out forever because of food stamps.

In one month, the number of households in Jasper County getting food stamps jumped from 169 to 502. *Des Moines Sunday Register*, November 28, 1971.

Federal Food Stamps Go To ARCO Strikers

Philadelphia—Union officials said yesterday that most of the workers who are striking the Atlantic-Richfield Co. are receiving federal food stamps.

Joseph E. Thompson, Jr., president of the Atlantic Independent Union, said union officials assisted the workers in applying for the stamps. He said many strikers also are receiving welfare payments, and some have found jobs to tide them over during the walkout. *Philadelphia Sunday Bulletin*, January 30, 1972.

Impact of Chicago Teamsters Strike

The teamsters strike nearly wrecked the food stamp program in Cook County. Food stamp officials processed applications of strikers at union headquarters. Union members assisted county officials in preparing applications for the strikers and ATP [authorization-to-purchase] cards were manually issued. The USDA Inspector General is presently investigating large losses of ATP cards which occurred during this operation. House Committee on Agriculture, "Field Investigation on the Operation of the Food Stamp Act," December 8, 1970, p. 9.

FIGURE 30. *Public Aid to West Coast Dock Strikers*

Benefits Subsidize Strikers, Increase Taxpayer's Burden

Liberal government benefits are insulating longshoremen as the devastating dock strike nears its 90th day. While the economy and taxpayers suffer, strikers are qualifying for tax-supported welfare grants and food stamps. This places the government in the awkward position of subsidizing one party to a dispute.

By studying the net pay of longshoremen and comparing it with the welfare and food stamp benefits available to strikers, the California Chamber of Commerce discovered that 33 percent of the longshoremen work about 1,000 hours per year, earn $6,000 or less and could bring home, while on strike, government benefits up to 77 percent of their normal take home pay of about $435 per month; 28 percent work about 800 hours per year, earn $4600 or less and could bring home while on strike government benefits worth up to 97 percent of their normal take home pay of about $348 per month; and 19 percent work about 425 hours per year, earn under $2260 and could bring home while on strike government benefits worth up to 192 percent of their normal take home pay of $188 per month.

Some longshoremen are eligible for government benefits valued at nearly double the amount they would normally bring home if they were working. For example, the maximum gross pay of such a longshoreman is $188 per month. His only standard deductions are $1.88 for state disability insurance and $10.00 for social security, with no federal or state income tax to pay, providing a net of $176. On welfare, however, he can receive up to $338 in welfare and food stamp assistance—a 192 percent increase in income compared to his net pay while working.

Other facts discovered through Chamber research show that a married longshoreman with two children averages $655 per month in take home pay. While on strike, he can receive up to $280 per month in welfare grants under the Aid to Families with Dependent Children with Unemployed Fathers (AFDC-U) and food stamps valued at $58 in cash. This totals about 52 percent of his net pay.

In addition to welfare and food stamps, once the longshoreman is on welfare, he and his family are automatically entitled to Medi-Cal benefits. Medi-Cal benefits are now worth approximately $1100 per year, or $91 per month for a family of four.

Meanwhile, as the dock strike continues, California's $700 million world trade volume per month and its dependent 400,000 jobs have been placed in serious jeopardy. Other trading nations have moved in to capture markets, causing untold future losses.

FIGURE 30.—continued

Practically every business in California is feeling the financial hardship of the strike. The hardest hit is the already burdened agriculture industry. Nearly $4 million was lost in the month of July, alone, in alfalfa and tallow; 100,000 tons of rice worth $7.5 million was kept from delivery; 80,000 tons of safflower was left in storage, and an anticipated $55 million in corn and milo threatened.

The dock strike indirectly adds another cost to business. Although strikers are ineligible to receive unemployment insurance in California, non-striking workers laid off because of the strike are eligible for unemployment insurance payments which are financed entirely by employers. Layoffs are necessary by many businesses in California due to the strike. For example, C & H Sugar Refinery Company laid off 1,000 out of 1,300 workers because of the strike. One ship repair firm reported laying off 440 of its 500 employees.

Meanwhile, welfare and food stamp offices along the coast report increases in striker's applications for benefits. San Francisco welfare officials report an increase of up to 15 percent in food stamp cases alone because of strikers in their area.

The economy of California suffers while ironically taxpayers continue to subsidize the cause of the suffering—strikes.

Source: *Pacific Business Bulletin,* California Chamber of Commerce, Vol. 61, No. 18 (September 27, 1971), p. 1.

FIGURE 31. *Food Stamps to Strikers*
Extracts from U.S. Department of Agriculture
Monthly Reports

September 1967: Twenty-seven states and the District of Columbia reported gains. Participation rose 22% in Michigan, which added 16,000 persons to the program. Of these, 12,510 were in Wayne County where the strike against Ford Motor Company made many idled workers eligible.

October 1967: A substantial portion of Michigan's gains, estimated at 13,100 persons, was localized in the Wayne County area (Detroit) where striking Ford Motor Company workers remained eligible for program participation.

December 1967: Striking workers at the John Deere Machine Company helped swell the food stamp ranks in Iowa.

February 1968: Ohio reported the largest increase in participation with a gain of 16,192 persons, principally as the result of several strikes.

March 1968: Since January, there has been a 45% participation increase in Shelby County, Tennessee, primarily as a result of the sanitation strike.

March 1969: West Virginia added 15,012 persons due to a strike by coal miners. Pennsylvania gained 11,465 persons, mainly in Washington and Philadelphia Counties. The increase in Washington County resulted from a strike at the McGraw-Edison Company.

April 1969: Michigan added 12,726 persons with more than half in four new projects and the remainder mostly the result of a power company strike in the counties of Eastern Michigan.

November 1969: The Midwest Region gained 8,144 participants, with a net gain of 2,798 in Wisconsin—Milwaukee County, added 3,002 due to the General Electric Company strike. . . . The Northeast Region reported a net gain of 7,638 principally due to the General Electric Company strike increasing participation in Allegheny, Erie, and Philadelphia Counties, Pennsylvania.

April 1970: St. Louis City, Missouri, reported 46,866 participants, an all time high—primarily due to strikes by the Teamsters Union and Kroger employees.

May 1970: Cook County, the largest project in the Program this month, accounted for 69% of Illinois' 70,000 participation gain—attributed almost

FIGURE 31.—continued

---

entirely to the Teamster's strike. The county's non-assistance participation showed the greatest effect with an increase of 962% over last month.

July 1970: A miner's strike in Southern West Virginia was the principal factor for an estimated increase of 136,000 persons.

October 1970: The largest participation increase of 296,462 occurred in Michigan, with the counties of Macomb, Genesee, and Oakland accounting for 61%. The important factor here and in the state of Pennsylvania with a 43,107 increase, was the General Motors strike.

December 1970: New York, Michigan, and Ohio, states with a large participation, reported participation decreases. The Michigan and Ohio drops are related to the General Motors settlement.

January 1972: The January participation of 11,112,049 shows almost 72,000 less people than last month's 11,183,712. This decrease resulted from the end of the miner's strike, with some 96,000 persons in West Virginia no longer needing Food Stamps.

Source: U.S. Department of Agriculture, Food and Nutrition Service, *Food Stamp Program Statistical Summary of Operations*, various issues, Washington, D.C.

cause. They by no means exhaust the number of strikes which have involved the use of food stamps, AFDC, General Assistance, unemployment insurance or other forms of tax-financed public aid to support strikers. Additional instances are briefly noted from news reports summarized from around the country in Figure 29. A Chamber of Commerce report on the impact of welfare in the recent West Coast Longshoremen's strike is shown in Figure 30. For several years, U.S. Department of Agriculture monthly summaries of Food Stamp distribution programs have noted the influence of strikes on program participation. Excerpts from these reports are shown in Figure 31.

Together, these case reports and supporting documents are representative of the many ways the American taxpayer has assumed a significant share of the cost of prolonged work stoppages, and especially a substantial proportion of the cost of labor's strike assistance program.

PART THREE

Analysis, Conclusions, and Recommendations

Comparison of Costs and Benefits, Examination of the Legal and Moral Bases for Eligibility, and Proposals for Change

CHAPTER VII

Cost Estimates and Possible Benefits

The previous chapters have demonstrated that public support for strikers has been made available in ever larger amounts and that the practice has become pervasive. In this chapter, we shall attempt to estimate the costs of providing this tax support and to determine what offsetting benefits may accrue from the practice. For this purpose, we shall utilize the cost-benefit comparisons, insofar as practicable.

COST-BENEFIT COMPARISONS

For many years, cost-benefit analyses have been performed to analyze whether some specific project, for example a deeper channel in a river, or a new highway, is a worthwhile undertaking.[230] In pure form, cost-benefit analysis consists of monetizing and discounting over the life of the project all possible incremental benefits to all parties who might be affected by it, and dividing this by the initial and discounted continuing costs, again over the life of the project.[231] These costs are usually in dollars, and so do not have to be monetized. The benefits are often social benefits which require careful analysis to reduce to dollar terms. The viewpoint from which the costs and benefits are to be measured is usually the societal one where government funds are involved. If the resultant ratio of benefits divided by costs is greater than one, the subject may be considered useful; and if the ratio is greater than that for alternative projects available, it can be considered the best use of funds available.

---

[230] The authors have had considerable experience with the application of this technique to port and river development projects on the eastern seaboard and have also supervised projects involving the application of the technique to ghetto and minority business development problems.

[231] Carl S. Strokes, *Managerial Economics* (New York: Random House, 1969), pp. 181-187.

Unfortunately, although cost-benefit analysis is an attractive procedure, it cannot be fully performed on welfare for strikers. One problem is that at this particular point in time the extent of several indirect and imputed costs cannot be estimated adequately because the statistical base is not great enough. A second problem is that many of the human costs—for example the loss of self-respect which may accompany going on welfare—are non-monetizable. There are other difficulties as well, and taken all together they are sufficient to void the validity of any attempt at a precise cost-benefit analysis. Nevertheless, we feel it important for at least a cost-benefit *comparison* to be undertaken. On the cost side, which will be covered first, we shall consider direct dollar costs, indirect dollar costs, imputed costs, and other effects on the total welfare system and the economy. Then we shall turn our attention to the benefits of public support of strikers.

Dollar Costs

When a dollar of welfare money is given to a striker that dollar, of course, is a dollar of cost. Therefore, the first factor which should be included is the total of direct public support expenditures. As we have defined "public support," this includes all payments made to striker recipients under AFDC, General and Emergency Assistance, food stamps, unemployment insurance, and all other smaller programs which we have discussed in previous chapters. Because strikers are seldom identified as such when they are recipients under these programs and therefore cannot often be separated out of the overall statistics collected, we can only estimate the total direct payment impact.

To make the estimate, we shall project, by simple regression analysis, the numbers of persons who will participate in strikes of various durations for some near-future year and estimate for each striker the likelihood that he will participate in a public support program and the amount of benefits he will receive. We say "for some near-future year," rather than "for 1972" or "for 1973" so that we can eliminate the effect on these statistics of the temporary wage-price freeze which occurred during the last half of 1971 and which may create oscillating conditions of labor dispute activity. The analysis, in other words, provides an estimated figure applicable to the first "normal" year when the freeze or wage and price controls have no significant effect and established patterns of labor disputes are followed. As a matter of notational convenience, we shall call that year "1973."

A simple regression performed on data available from the Department of Labor indicates that about three million persons will participate in strikes of various duration during "1973." On the basis of our analysis, we shall assume that approximately one-fifth of these strikers would be on strike for less than four days, which, it can reasonably be assumed, is too short a time for them to apply for or to obtain any type of public support. About one-half would be on strike for four days to a month, and some proportion of these would, no doubt, receive food stamps for which there is no waiting period, but none would receive AFDC and few, General Assistance. The figures extended by similar logic, are presented as Table 27. The proportion of strikers who would be expected to receive food stamps (60 percent), AFDC (15 percent) and General Assistance (2 percent) are based on the proportions of strikers who actually did receive such payments in the major strikes of 1970 and 1971 which we have discussed in previous chapters. As the knowledge of welfare use spreads and more and more strikers overcome their inhibitions and aversions to going on relief, these proportions would be expected to increase, but we believe that the numbers presented are fair-to-conservative estimates of the near-term future.

Total anticipated public support payments require some assumptions concerning average monthly payments per case. These are shown in the notes to Table 28, where the total anticipated payments under these three programs are estimated at nearly $304 million for 1973. It should be noted that two important items are not included in these calculations: payment overruns and unemployment insurance.

Although welfare regulations are quite precise about waiting periods and other factors affecting the timing of the initialization of payments, they are usually silent concerning termination. Naturally, if a welfare office is alert, it will insure that no payments are made after the strike is settled.[232] Nevertheless—and we have pointed these cases out in earlier chapters—payments do continue for more than one full month beyond the end of the month in which the strike was terminated. Although this is a

---

[232] There are some strange exceptions. In the Westinghouse case study we mentioned one. Pennsylvania has a ruling directing welfare offices to pay at least one additional welfare allotment to strikers after they have returned to work and have received one pay check.

TABLE 27.   *Estimated Striker Participation in Public Support Programs*
Major Programs
1973

	All 1973	Length of Strike				
		Less than 4 Days	4-30 Days	31-60 Days	61-90 Days	Over 90 Days
Workers idled by strikes (thousands)[a]	3,000	681	1,428	498	165	228
Percent[b]	100.0	22.7	47.6	16.6	5.5	7.6
Number of group who will receive food stamps[c]	(60%)	409	857	299	99	137
Number of group who will receive AFDC[c]	(15%)	102	214	75	25	34
Number of group who will receive General Assistance[c]	(2%)	14	29	10	3	5
Months of benefits[d]						
Food Stamps		—	1	2	3	5
AFDC		—	—	1	2	4
General Assistance		—	—	1	2	4

Source: Derived from U.S. Bureau of Labor Statistics, *Handbook of Labor Statistics, 1969*, BLS Bulletin 1930; and *Monthly Labor Review*, Vol. 94, No. 8 (August 1971), Table 32.

[a] Excludes lockouts. Estimated by regression analysis using 1958-1970 as base.

[b] Percentage breakdown based on historical data.

[c] These numbers are necessarily approximate. They are based on projection of actual experiences in strike situations in 1970 and 1971 and are considered by the authors to be conservative.

[d] Based on waiting-time requirements of the programs. Does not contemplate emergency payments during first month under AFDC or GA or any payment continuation beyond end of the month in which the strike terminates.

TABLE 28.   *Estimated Public Support Costs for Strikers*
Major Programs
1973

Program	Total Monthly Equivalent Payments [a]	Average Monthly Payment per Case	Total Payments for Year
Food Stamps	$2,437,000	$ 98.00 [b]	$238,826,000
Aid to Families with Dependent Children	261,000	240.00 [c]	62,640,000
General Public Assistance	36,000	67.00 [d]	2,412,000

Source: Calculated as noted below.

Note: Total payments for year, three major programs—$303,878,000.

[a] Derived from Table 27.

[b] The federally contributed portion of food stamp coupon allotments increased substantially in July 1971. This figure represents the bonus available to a family with two children and an income of $50 to $60 per month. U.S. Department of Agriculture, "Food Stamp Program," *Federal Register*, Vol. XXXVI, No. 146, Part II, p. 14118.

[c] This figure is the average payment per family under the AFDC-U (unemployed parent segment) during fiscal year 1971. U.S. Department of Health, Education and Welfare, Social and Rehabilitation Services, *NCSS Report A-2*, Table 7 (individual months).

[d] This figure is the average payment per recipient during fiscal year 1971 in 18 major cities for which figures are maintained. U.S. Department of Health, Education and Welfare, Social and Rehabilitation Service, *NCSS Report A-2*, Table 13 (individual months).

very real cost factor, we are unable, at this time, to document it sufficiently to estimate the general trend and so are forced to neglect it here.

Similarly, we must neglect unemployment insurance costs, although for different reasons. Unemployment insurance is ordinarily paid to strikers only in New York and Rhode Island, and on the railroads. For the two states, a waiting period of seven to eight weeks is involved. The total amount paid in any one year depends very much on whether some large union engages in a very long strike in a covered situation. If it does, the costs can be great. As described in Chapter VI, when twenty-two locals of the Communications Workers of America—38,000 persons

—went on strike, it cost the New York telephone company more than $41 million in unemployment insurance payments—an extremely large amount.[233] But, unfortunately, statistics are no help in predicting individual events such as the recurrence of an equally large and long strike in a covered situation next year. Thus, although recognizing that large amounts may possibly be involved, we shall not include them here. What we shall include are estimates of certain indirect costs associated with the direct payments noted above.

Indirect Costs

Our next step, then, is to determine the reasonable indirect costs associated with the direct dollar distributions. We shall consider as reasonable those indirect costs which result from processing and distribution of the direct costs—administrative costs of the specific programs—and the costs of additional benefits available only to those who are recipients under one of the programs already available to strikers. The most significant of these is the Medicaid program. We shall *not* consider as reasonable any indirect costs which are more remote. For example, although a case could be made for allocating some proportion of the costs of supporting the U.S. Internal Revenue Service and other tax collection agencies for collecting taxes to provide funds distributed by the welfare agencies, or of the U.S. Bureau of Labor Statistics or of many other facilities related to strikes or welfare in a service capacity, we feel these costs are too remote from the direct benefits.

Administrative costs vary greatly from program to program, and generally depend on the amount of time which must be devoted to each case. This, in turn, depends on two factors: the checking, verifying, and other paperwork required by the program, and the length of time an individual recipient stays on it. Thus, it should be expected that the AFDC program would have higher administrative costs than would, for example, Aid to the Blind—and this is the case. Similarly, strikers who usually have more resources which must be verified and who participate in welfare programs for only short periods of time, should be expected to require more administrative time in proportion to the benefits distributed than the average case.

Table 29 shows the range of administrative costs experienced by the state of California over a recent five-year period. The

---

[233] *New York Times*, February 18, 1972, p. 32.

TABLE 29. *Administrative Costs
Associated with Various Public Support Programs
California, 1963-1968*

| Program | Administrative Costs per Dollar of Total Assistance Expenditure | | | | | |
	1963-1964	1964-1965	1965-1966	1966-1967	1967-1968	Average
General Relief	$0.31	$0.30	$0.35	$0.32	$0.25	$0.31
AFDC	0.18	0.20	0.21	0.21	0.25	0.21
Aid to Disabled	0.18	0.18	0.17	0.17	0.19	0.18
Aid to Blind	0.13	0.11	0.10	0.09	0.12	0.11
Surplus Food	0.09	0.08	0.09	0.09	0.08	0.08
Old Age Security	0.08	0.08	0.09	0.09	0.06	0.08
Food Stamps	n.a.	n.a.	n.a.	n.a.	0.04	(0.04)
School Lunch	0.04	0.03	0.02	0.03	0.04	0.03
All Programs	$0.15	$0.16	$0.17	$0.18	$0.20	$0.17

Source: Calculated from California Legislature, Subcommittee of General Research, *A Study of Welfare Expenditures*, California Legislature, Vol. 21, No. 15, Senate, 1969, pp. 225-230.

usually neglected administrative costs are here seen to be as much as one dollar for every three actually distributed in assistance, which is indeed rather significant. The heavily used AFDC program requires a dollar of administration for each five of assistance. Although for reasons already mentioned, strikers probably require greater administrative costs than indicated, and although the overall trend in administrative costs is upward, we have used the average figures indicated from Table 29 to produce a total estimated administrative expense of $23.5 million.

The other indirect costs which we should consider are those arising from add-on benefits for which one becomes eligible if participating in one of the major welfare programs. A person receiving Aid to Families with Dependent Children support, in addition to being qualified automatically for food stamps if desired, may also receive Medicaid and qualify for mortgage payment or special rent support, emergency assistance, and the School Lunch program. All of these benefits are available, but the amount of benefit which any individual may derive from them varies.

Medicaid is a vendor payment program, as explained in Chapter I. Payments under it are at the discretion of the recipient of medical services. For a striker and his family, benefits received might be nothing at all, or could amount to several hundred dollars a month. As a broad estimate, we shall assume each striker on AFDC-U or General Assistance receives benefits of $50 a month. This is in keeping with the scanty statistical evidence available.

Data concerning striker use of emergency assistance, mortgage payment support, and School Lunch programs are extremely difficult to isolate, much less generalize about. In Cuyahoga County, Ohio (Cleveland) in one strike, for example, almost 50 percent as many vouchers were authorized for rent and mortgage payments for strikers as were vouchers for food stamps.[234] Although we do not believe that this proportion holds true in the general case, we are impressed by the fact that it must be happening with some regularity, and feel that an average of $25 per AFDC striker a month would not be overstating the case.

The School Lunch program benefits seems to be about $.40 per lunch. A striker with two school-age children during the school year could thus receive benefits of $16 per month. Not all schools have this program, and not all AFDC strikers will use it. We, therefore, estimate that the average indirect benefits here amount to $8 per month.

There may well be other indirect social welfare support functions from which strikers on welfare could derive valuable benefits, but we shall use only the above for estimating total indirect dollar costs. These total $83 per month.

Total of Direct and Indirect Costs

Following the methodology presented in Table 27, these identified indirect costs would amount to just under $25 million over a year's time ($24.65 million). Including these costs in the total, direct and indirect dollar costs of public assistance to strikers is estimated to exceed $329 million a year—almost a million dollars a day—for the average year of the near future.

---

[234] "Labor Strikes, Public Pays," Labor Information Memo No. 4, Transportation Association of America (undated), p. 11.

Imputed Costs

The projection or estimation of the direct and indirect identifiable dollar costs of public support for strikers by no means exhausts the list. Just as the taxpayer ultimately shoulders the burden of government spending through higher taxes or inflation, the consumer ultimately must pay for wage raises in excess of productivity gains through higher prices or inflation. We are not here making the case that all strikes result in inflationary wage settlements. But it would be a denial of the empirical facts presented in previous chapters to maintain that welfare support for strikers has no effect either on the length of strikes or on the terms of their settlement. If the back-to-work pressures from individual union members and their wives (which are what frequently lead to settlement) are reduced—and testimony included in our earlier chapters as well as our earlier theoretical analysis says they are—then the conclusion is inescapable that at least some strikes are either lengthened or made more costly by public support. Consumers and taxpayers must eventually shoulder these costs. Unfortunately, the existence of such imputed costs can be demonstrated by examples, but cannot be neatly monetized or generalized. Years of statistical collections would be required before the many exogenous factors which determine strike length and settlement terms could be sufficiently stabilized to allow analysis of the effect of this one item.

Even excluding any consideration of welfare or public support costs, strikes are fiercely expensive exercises. Companies lose profits, workers lose wages, governments lose taxes, local businessmen lose sales. Suppliers to the struck company lose business and retailers of the company's products lose sales. Transportation companies are often affected, and even the unions to which the strikers belong dispense massive amounts of funds if they pay strike benefits. Some of these costs are recoverable or partially offset; others are not. All have second order or multiplier effects, and a massive strike against a huge company soon affects the economy generally. Without tracing this chain very far or concerning ourselves with the multiplier effects, it can be demonstrated that the 1970 General Motors strike involved high imputed costs: it cost the company an estimated $5.2 million per day in lost profits, the work force $10.3 million per day in lost wages, and various levels of government $16.7 million per day in lost taxes. The union's daily bill for strike benefits and insurance was almost $2 million.[235] (This last is a transfer payment from a compensatory fund created by the strikers and paid to strikers, and therefore is excluded from estimations of total cost of the strike from the societal view.[236])

What these figures demonstrate is that if the strike was lengthened by a single day as a result of public support for the strikers, the cost of that day was more than $32 million. And, on the other hand, if instead of making the strike one day longer, welfare benefits contributed to making the settlement one cent more expensive, then the cost over the life of the three-year contract would exceed $29 million to General Motors alone, and perhaps more than $100 million if extended to all autoworkers whose wages would tend to reflect the settlement at General Motors.

Although these costs are substantial—running as they do to perhaps hundreds of millions of dollars—and could be statistically extended to cover, for example, the cost of extending the average strike during 1973 by one day, we cannot estimate the total imputable to welfare support for strikers with any statistical validity. As mentioned, empirical study and collective bargaining theory tell us that welfare support makes strikes either longer or costlier, but it does not tell us by how much. Unlike unemployment insurance payments which, although similarly unquantifiable, we could ignore, we cannot ignore these imputed welfare support costs and maintain any validity in a cost-benefit analysis. It is for this reason that we must be content with comparisons of cost and benefits rather than analysis of them.

Cost Summary

Based on the experiences provided by major strikes since 1969 and projecting them into the near-term future, direct and indirect dollar costs of providing welfare support to strikers will exceed $329 million a year. This figure does not include the costs of prolonging strikes, influencing higher wage settlements, or of

---

[235] *U.S. News and World Report*, October 26, 1970, p. 90.

[236] This is not to say that the unions did not pay out this amount or that the payments had no effect on the length of the strike. For as we argued in Chapter V, the impending installment payment due on insurance premiums is held by many to be one of the principal causes of the strike terminating when it did. The union's strike fund was almost depleted, and many felt it was the international union officials rather than the individual workers who were anxious to end the stoppage.

spreading unemployment which will increase in proportion as strikers are out longer because of public support. It does not include the possible cost in self-respect or self-esteem to many workers induced to give up their independence and accept welfare. It does not include the costs to the country of an inflation fueled both by spending on public support for strikers and also by the costlier strike settlements which will probably be their result. It does not include the potential harm which may be done to the system of free collective bargaining which is the basis of our labor policy. What benefits have accrued to whom in return for these costs?

Benefits

The benefits arising from public support for strikers accrue principally to two groups: the strikers and their families, and the unions of which the strikers are members.[237] Depending on his particular circumstances, the direct dollar benefits to a striker can be significant. As soon as the strike begins and his income stops, a striker who meets the eligibility requirements (set forth in Appendix A) may receive food stamps which provide a bonus of from $32 to $180 or more (depending on family size). If he is receiving no strike benefits, and has two children, the figure would be $108. If he has strike benefits of $120 a month, this might be reduced to as low as $77.

After a four-week waiting period, he would become eligible in most of the major industrial states for Aid to Families with Dependent Children (also covered in Appendix A). The amount of benefits again depends on family size, where he lives, how much he pays for housing, and a number of other factors. During fiscal 1971, the average payment per family under the AFDC-U program was $240; and this figure should be representative. If the striker were receiving strike benefits from his union, this amount would be reduced by some but not all of the union strike benefits, and the bonus premium from food stamps should also decrease. Even so, total monthly income from welfare alone or from welfare and union benefits should be approximately $300.

---

[237] Some benefits also may accrue to local shopkeepers. Public support may reduce their economic losses during the strike, but because it may also cause the strike to last longer and therefore provide for a net reduction of striker spending over time, these benefits may actually be negative.

When qualified for AFDC (or General Assistance, emergency relief, or others), the striker could also come in for the other benefits which were noted earlier in this chapter. It should be remembered that there we estimated the average value of the fringe benefits—Medicaid, mortgage payment support, and the School Lunch program—to be almost $83 per month.

Taken all together, a striker who plays all of his options in an average way (not necessarily mulcting them) should be able to realize some $350 worth of benefits a month from working the welfare system rather than his job. All of these benefits are tax free.

To see the potential benefits to the unions here, we must only consider that if the strike benefits are removed, welfare benefits rise accordingly and make up a large part of the difference. Eliminating a dollar of union strike benefits lowers his total striker support by only about twelve cents, and consideration of the tax differences would reduce this even further. Because of this, we may expect most unions to consider, as some have, halting strike benefits to members receiving welfare, thus making the governmental treasuries of the country the union strike funds.

Now $350 a month translates directly to an equivalent hourly wage of $2.02, but one would have to work at a considerably higher wage rate to arrive at this figure for take-home pay. It is not subject to federal, state, and city taxes, social security, disability insurance, or union dues. For the average worker, being on strike and receiving average returns on welfare in terms of 1971 standards is far superior to working at the minimum wage and comes within a few cents an hour of the 1971 annual average take-home pay in all private U.S. employment. (The annual average wage in all private U.S. employment in 1971 was $3.43. Taxes and other deductions would average approximately 24 percent, leaving a take-home pay of $2.61.))

In some industrial strikes involving workers averaging more than $4.00 per hour, we have found cases where benefits from welfare have totaled 80 percent of prestrike wages for workers with large families, without even considering the "fringe benefits." [238]

---

[238] This was true in Los Angeles County, California, for example, during the General Motors strike. This situation is noted in Chapter V, above.

BENEFITS AND COSTS COMPARED

Welfare benefits are transfer payments. To the extent that they are financed by general revenues, they are simply a redistribution of wealth. A dollar taken from A and given to B is a cost to A and an equivalent benefit to B. So from a societal view the transaction cancels itself out.

In a strict sense, this applies to strikers, for welfare payments to them are costs to the taxpayers but equivalent benefits to the strikers. Following this line of argument, the net cost of welfare for strikers would consist only of the imputed cost of longer or costlier strikes and whatever incremental indirect costs which could be attributable to strikers compared with other recipient populations. The basic argument, however, is flawed.

Before a transfer payment transaction can be considered to balance in any but a technical, accounting sense, the recipient, B, must be able to summon justification for the benefits for the receipt of which he is calling upon A to incur costs. Thus we do not consider it a costless or balanced transaction if X takes, at the point of a gun, the contents of the wallet of Y, even though from a societal viewpoint a simple transfer payment has occurred.

The benefits which a striker receives from welfare must come from somewhere unless we make the totally unrealistic assumption that the resources of this nation and its people are unlimited. Either these welfare costs for strikers must be taken away from other welfare recipients (which would be true if welfare funds were a controlled budget item, which they are not), or they must be provided by reducing appropriations to other government services or by raising the necessary funds by levies on the taxpayers, or by increasing the budget deficit. The real costs of supporting strikers with tax money—in the parlance of economics, the "opportunity costs"—involves the value of what is given up by society so that strikers may receive benefits paid for by taxpayers. So we must ask, are the benefits accruing to a small group (strikers) sufficiently great that society should put aside other programs or benefits in order to provide them? This calls for an analysis of the moral and legal arguments adduced to justify such payments, which is the subject of our next chapter.

CHAPTER VIII

Do Strikers Have a "Right" to Welfare?

Much of the discussion regarding welfare and other tax supported payments to strikers centers around the question of whether strikers have some type of a "right" to welfare. This in turn raises the question of the nature of right, as it is defined in both moral and legal terms. This chapter discusses these two aspects of "rights" as they apply to public support for strikers.

THE MORAL "RIGHT" TO WELFARE—
THE PRO-ARGUMENTS CONSIDERED

Arguments of unions and others supporting the continuation of providing welfare and other tax supported benefits to strikers emphasize five points:

1. Need should be the sole criterion, regardless of cause.

2. Union members are taxpayers and therefore are entitled to the benefits of tax supported programs.

3. It would be outrageous to permit children to starve just because their breadwinning parent is on strike.

4. Companies receive subsidies from the government even during strikes; therefore, it is only fair that unions and union members be likewise favored.

5. Tax supported payments to strikers reduce the peril of violence and disruption.

These arguments are all found in the interviews with, and quotations from, union officials and partisans which have been set forth in detail. They are repeated in handbooks, strike manuals, etc., many of which have been previously cited.[239] All have been put forward numerous times in speeches and articles

---

[239] See Appendix B for further examples.

by Leo Perlis, Director of Community Services, AFL-CIO. In a widely publicized letter, he pointed out that the taxpayers' dollars are used to support persons and their families who live in other countries, who are criminals in prisons, or who are enemy prisoners of war. (The need-regardless-of-cause argument.) It then states:

> Even if some bitter-end union haters want to starve strikers into submission, how can they justify starving their wives and children?
>
> If providing needy strikers with food stamps is tantamount to subsidizing a strike against a company—then letting new contracts or failing to cancel old contracts while the strike is in effect is tantamount to subsidizing the company's position.
>
> In the final analysis—all strikes eventually end. The question is does management want its employees back seething with hatred and contempt for attempting to starve its employees into submission. Or does management want a more pleasant relationship based upon human consideration and moral conduct?
>
> We need *not apologize,* but we *can justify* our strike assistance program to needy people whose need may have been caused by an act of God, an act of nature, an act of management or an act of labor. Who is to determine the cause of need?
>
> Here the sole criterion is need.[240]

Let us look at each of these arguments.

Taxpayers' Rights

The idea that because one pays taxes he is entitled to specific benefits from government is one that is often cited by various persons and groups in support of their demands for government largess of one kind or another. So it is that union spokesmen proclaim, as a right separate from that which arises from need, that strikers, as taxpayers, contribute to welfare programs when they are working and therefore should be entitled to receive benefits from them when they are not. This, however, is simply a misinterpretation of the role of taxation.

The only right which can be said to accrue specifically to taxpayers is the right to pay taxes. The individual has no claim to indemnification or to any specific return from his taxes save the value of the benefits he receives as a citizen from the actions of government as, for example, in providing for the common defense or in maintaining a public school system. Any

---

[240] Leo Perlis, letter addressed to "Dear Sir and Brother," October 16, 1970. Emphasis in original.

childless payer of school taxes will be happy to attest to the lack of specific return from his tax dollars. Likewise, the person who owns no automobiles pays taxes that are used for highways and the one who fears to ride in airplanes sees his tax money contribute to the building and maintenance of airports. Even the taxpayers who would have welfare abolished in its entirety cannot prevent their tax money from being used toward meeting the seemingly ever-increasing welfare load. In fact, there is no insurance component to general taxes and no rights or claims to services are generated by paying them. Their payment remains a duty rather than the purchase of deferred future individual benefits.

Starving Children

The image of starving strikers and, even more poignantly, the image of their starving wives and children has been recurringly drawn in the history of labor relations. It becomes increasingly unconvincing as the general level of affluence in the labor force continues to skyrocket. Union members are the elite of the labor force. Within union ranks, $6,000 a year is considered almost poverty-level, $10,000 a year is common, and $15,000 a year is not all that rare. The timing of legal strikes is well known in advance of their commencement, and the duration of strikes is at least dependent on the collective, voluntary actions of the strikers themselves. Under these circumstances, a person would have to be positively clever as well as friendless and improvident to starve. It is not our intention here to sound flippant. But it does seem that the pattern of industrial sociology which to any degree admitted the possibility of starvation of striking workers has been gone, quite fortunately, for thirty years.

A word should also be said about the lesser argument also raised here—that denial of welfare benefits to strikers will pose an undue burden (although perhaps not starvation) on strikers or their unions. This argument, too, deserves little credence. Denial of welfare is not deprivation of an existing right. Although some forms of public support have been available to some strikers since the early 1930's, the overwhelming majority of the millions of workers who have participated in tens of thousands of strikes since that time have done so without welfare support. Certainly, no reasonable person would argue that during this period the collective bargaining system was overwhelmingly unbalanced toward the management side. Nor would any sane person argue that the general lack of public support payments during this period infringed the right to strike. The right to strike does not imply nor necessitate any rights to subsidization during such strikes.

Company Subsidies

Another recurring idea that has been forwarded by the unions to justify their pursuit and use of public funds for strikers is that government contracts with struck companies are not terminated and occasionally new contracts are let during the strike. This, it is said, is a form of government subsidy to the companies, and if the companies can have subsidies, so can the strikers.

Because there is no way of knowing exactly what types of contracts are referred to here, we shall have to deal with generalized situations. There are four possibilities. First, production under an existing contract might be continued during a strike, using managerial and supervisory personnel. There would seem to be nothing to argue with here. The government is neither obtaining nor providing any sort of subsidy, provided quality levels remain unchanged. Both sides, during a labor dispute, can use such self-help at their disposal to lessen the impact of the strike. Strikers can continue working by finding other, temporary jobs if they can; managements can continue production by using supervisory help if they can. If companies were to continue to receive payments on a production contract, even though production had ceased and deliveries were not being made, then this would be a situation analogous to strikers receiving public support payments and we would argue against continuation of such practices. It is doubtful, however, that this is the case.

Second, orders under an existing contract might be filled during a strike from inventory. If labor were paid for its services for producing the items in inventory, it can have no argument with those items being sold during the strike any more than management could argue with strikers spending money that they had saved in anticipation of the strike, or eating cans of soup stored on pantry shelves since before the strike started. In labor disputes, both sides are free to take action in anticipation of the strike which will lessen its impact when it arrives. No subsidies or unfair advantages are involved.

Third, performance might be curtailed during a strike without voiding a contract which is to be resumed after the strike terminates, or fourth, a new contract might be awarded during the strike for implementation after the strike terminates. The arguments in both cases are the same. To view either case as a government subsidy to the company is to see the company as an entity separate from the people who are comprised by it. After the strike is over, the company will profit from the contract, but so, of course, will the workers of the company.

Another and somewhat related idea that is occasionally raised is that of tax benefits which are said to accrue to companies during strikes. This, too, is said to be a government subsidy of companies. Since the maximum corporate tax rate is 50 percent, it is said that the tax mechanism saves companies about half the cost of maintaining their overhead and fixed expenses during a strike. This reasoning deteriorates rapidly when it is realized that the total net benefit to a corporation (or a person: strikers also have similar benefits since they pay no taxes on wages they are not earning) are exactly one-half as great as the total net loss. To look at it another way, by the same logic a company could save more of the costs of the strike and thus receive even greater benefits through the tax mechanism if the tax rate were 60 percent instead of 50 percent, and would save all of the costs and thus receive a truly splendid benefit if the tax rate were 100 percent. This does not seem to be the sort of government subsidy for which businessmen would generally strive.

A final analogous argument is that corporations are the beneficiaries of many government programs which aid their profits: tariffs, depletion allowances, government information and research, etc. So they are, but some of these are advocated by unions as well, for example, tariffs as protective of jobs. Such benefits are hardly unique. Employees and unions likewise receive the benefits of many laws and government actions: minimum wages, maximum hours, rights to bargain collectively, civil rights, etc. Such laws are not suspended during strikes; indeed at such times they often serve to enhance union power and to aid in securing settlements desired by unions. Hence this argument in support of welfare payments to strikers does not bear careful scrutiny.

Industrial Peace

How does welfare support of strikers affect the mood of the work force during the strike and the conditions of industrial peace after it? The contention seems to be that if tax supported payments to strikers are provided, there will be a reduction in the manifest bitterness during the strike and improved moral after it. There seems to be little empirical evidence to support such reasoning. The Chicago Teamsters strike in 1970, the New York Telephone strike of 1971-72, the Westinghouse strike covered in Chapter IV, and the Johns-Manville strike reported in Chapter VI are all examples of strikes marred by more than ordinary violence, but also characterized by the use of public support funds for strikers. We are also unaware of any evidence pointing to a different work force mood after strike terminations in publicly supported strikes from that which occurs when such support is absent, nor have, to our knowledge, those utilizing this argument put forth any facts in support of it.

WELFARE RIGHTS

As has been seen, most of the arguments raised by the unions for public support of strikers are easily overcome. The one which remains is that strikers have a right to welfare because during strikes they are in need, and welfare is provided to those in need, regardless of the cause of their need. The counterarguments are formed around two points. First, welfare is provided to those in need only if they fall within the definitions established by each program. There is no constitutional requirement that need be redressed, no constitutional right to welfare. Second, in establishing the eligibility definitions for each welfare program, the *cause* of need as well as its seriousness has usually been taken into account by the legislators or administrators responsible. Welfare or relief is seldom provided regardless of the cause of need.

Need as the Sole Criterion

If, as is maintained, welfare relief is a right based solely upon the criterion of need, then it is important to know what sort of a right it is and what level of economic deprivation qualifies as "need." The courts have insisted that laws be fairly administered with due process and with equitable treatment of those similarly situated. But no constitutional right to welfare based on an overriding and consistent definition of need regardless of pertinent legislation has been recognized under the Equal Protection clause. Thus, the United States Supreme Court, in discussing a Maryland statute, unanimously determined:

> In the area of economics and social welfare, a State does not violate the Equal Protection Clause merely because the classifications made by its laws are imperfect. If the classification has some "reasonable basis," it does not offend the Constitution simply because the classification "is not made with mathematical nicety or because in practice it results in some inequality."
> . . .
> We do not decide today that the Maryland regulation is wise, that it best fulfills the relevant social and economic objectives that Maryland might ideally espouse, or that a more just and humane system could not be devised. Conflicting claims of morality and intelligence are raised by opponents and proponents of almost every measure, certainly including the one before us. But the intractable economic, social, and even philosophical problems presented by public welfare assistance are not the business of this Court. The Constitution may impose certain procedural safeguards upon systems of welfare administration, *Goldberg* v. *Kelly*, 397 U.S. 254 (1970). But the Constitution does not empower this Court to second-guess state officials charged with the difficult responsibility of allocating limited public welfare funds among the myriad of potential recipients.[241]

It is quite clear from the court's opinion that there is no constitutional right to welfare and that each program, or in some cases each state, may decide for itself what level of need will be provided with welfare support under what circumstances. In fact, no two welfare programs are likely to define need exactly the same and even within one program, the term may mean quite different things or be interpreted in various ways in various political jurisdictions. State unemployment compensation laws and welfare laws define "unemployment" quite differently. A striker may be immediately eligible for food stamps but be required to wait a minimum period for AFDC, regardless of his "need."

Need is subject to other qualifications. A person must often demonstrate his need by good faith attempts to obtain work, or by proving that his need occurred from noncontrollable rather than controllable causes. Again, each law or program differs in defining these matters and, in turn, various jurisdictions differ in their requirements under the same or similar laws.

---

[241] *Dandridge* v. *Williams*, 397 U.S. 472 (1970), at 485 and 487 (citations omitted).

We conclude, therefore, that the cause of need *is* important to determining if welfare will be available and that the need itself is neither a consistent nor a sole criterion of welfare support. What rights, then, do strikers have to welfare? The answer is found in the legal and administrative history of the programs in recent years.

THE LEGAL RIGHT TO WELFARE

We have already noted that there is no constitutional right to welfare. The United States Supreme Court in *Dandridge* v. *Williams,* quoted above, unanimously sustained this view. Recently, the question was reviewed again before a three-man U.S. District Court convened because a constitutional question was raised about the State of Maryland's refusal to provide AFDC-U benefits to strikers. Citing *Dandridge* and other pertinent cases, the Court declared:

> Dealing first with the constitutional challenge relating to labor disputes, this Court is of the opinion that rational bases exist for Maryland's decision denying AFDC-E [sic] benefits to children of fathers who are out of work because of labor disputes, just as there are rational reasons for the opposite view which has been adopted by most of the states. Thus, the equal protection challenge to Maryland's denial of benefits to such fathers must be rejected.[242]

After further discussion, this same Court concluded: "Accordingly, the constitutional challenge stated by plaintiffs is rejected, *in toto.*" [243]

Absent a Constitutional right to welfare, there still remain other legal grounds, including one constitutional one, for determining what right to tax supported payments to strikers exists: federal preemption, congressional action and/or intent, and administrative action. These are discussed briefly below.

The Preemption Issue

Where federal and state statutes, or administrative actions relating thereto, conflict, the Supremacy Clause of the Constitution, Article VI, provides that the federal statute shall be controlling and "preempt" the field, unless Congress otherwise di-

---

[242] *Francis* v. *Davidson,* U.S. D.C. Md., January 28, 1972. Mimeographed copy, at 22.

[243] *Id.* at 24.

rects. In a series of rulings commencing in 1950, the courts ruled numerous state laws inoperative in interstate commerce because they interfered with the right to strike guaranteed by the federal Taft-Hartley Act.[244] Thus state laws insisting that employees take a vote before striking,[245] that they submit disputes to compulsory arbitration instead of striking,[246] that they submit to fact-finding procedures prior to striking,[247] or that they refrain from striking if the state seized the facilities in which they were employed [248] were all found to conflict with the Taft-Hartley Act, and therefore not operative within that law's jurisdiction. The United States Supreme Court has further ruled (the *Garmon* doctrine) that state courts lack jurisdiction to regulate union conduct that is potentially subject to exclusive federal regulation under the Taft-Hartley Act, except where such conduct is merely a peripheral concern of that Act, or involves maintenance of domestic peace that is subject to state jurisdiction in absence of clearly expressed congressional direction to the contrary.[249]

On the other hand, where no congressional jurisdiction has been taken, or where it has been expressly ceded to the states, these are not preemption issues. Thus hospitals and their employees are excluded from the coverage of the Taft-Hartley Act, and states may regulate their labor disputes.[250] Similarly Section 14(b) of the Taft-Hartley Act specifically cedes the right to states to regulate compulsory union agreements, and nineteen states have enacted "right-to-work" laws.

---

[244] These laws are analyzed in Herbert R. Northrup, *Compulsory Arbitration and Government Intervention in Labor Disputes* (Washington: Labor Policy Association, Inc., 1966), pp. 141-152, 215-300.

[245] *International Union, UAW* v. *O'Brien*, 339 U.S. 454 (1950); see also *Automobile Workers* v. *Finklenberg*, 53 N.W. 2d 128 (1952).

[246] *Amalgamated Association* v. *Wisconsin Employment Relations Board*, 340 U.S. 383 (1951); see also *Marshall* v. *Schricker*, Cir. Ct., Vandenburgh Co., Ind. (1951), 20 LC #66372; and *Henderson* v. *Florida, ex rel. Lee*, 65 SO. 2d 22 (1953).

[247] *Grand Rapids City Coach Lines* v. *Howlett*, 137 F. Supp. 667 (1966); *General Electric Co.* v. *Callahan*, 294 F.2d 60 (1962); and *Oil, Chemical and Atomic Workers* v. *Arkansas Louisiana Gas Co.*, 320 F.2d 62 (1964).

[248] *Division 1287, Street Employees* v. *Missouri*, 374 U.S. 74 (1963).

[249] *San Diego Building Trades Council* v. *Garmon*, 359 U.S. 236 (1959).

[250] An early case on this point involved Minnesota's law requiring compulsory arbitration of disputes between hospitals and certain of their employees. *Fairview Hospital Ass'n* v. *Public Board*, 241 Minn. 523 (1954).

The preemption issue applied to tax supported benefits to strikers was raised by a division of International Telephone and Telegraph Company in Massachusetts in 1970 in *ITT* v. *Minter*.[251] ITT claimed, in the words of the Court of Appeals, First Circuit, that the

> . . . Commissioner of the Massachusetts Department of Public Welfare is wrongfully intruding in a labor dispute by making available welfare benefits to strikers who otherwise qualify under Massachusetts statutes providing for General Welfare and Aid to Families with Dependent Children. . . . [and] that such state action alters the relative economic strength of the parties, thus entering a field preempted by the national policy guaranteeing free collective bargaining in violation of the Supremacy Clause of the Constitution.[252]

The court denied ITT's application for an injunction expressing doubt that significant frustration of national collective bargaining policy had occurred:

> . . . Where Congress has not clearly manifested its purpose to exclude state action which takes the form of exercise of its historic police powers, such state action will not be invalidated under the Supremacy Clause "in the absence of persuasive reasons," or unless the administration of the state law "palpably infringes" upon the federal policy.[253]

Yet, as noted in the foreword of this book, this court was extremely troubled by the issue because of the lack of evidence presented. It stated that

> The very novelty of the issue posed . . . places it outside the focus of San Diego Building Trades v. Garmon, its ancestors and progeny.
> What we therefore confront is the question of applying the Supremacy Clause to a non-Garmon situation, where the asserted conflict is not an invasion by the state into an area of conduct regulated by a national instrumentality but a tangential frustration of the national policy objective of unfettered collective bargaining by state economic sustenance of some of the individuals who participate in federally protective, concerted activity.[254]

---

[251] *ITT* v. *Minter*, 435 F.2d 989 (1st Cir., 1970); cert. den., 420 U.S. 933 (1971).

[252] 435 F.2d 989, 76 L.R.R.M. at 2205.

[253] *Id.*, 76 L.R.R.M. at 2206-07 (citations omitted).

[254] *Id.*, 76 L.R.R.M. at 2206 (citation omitted).

To invalidate state action, the court felt it would need much information:

> . . . A court would first have to determine the quantum of impact on collective bargaining stemming from the granting of welfare benefits to strikers. If this is found substantial a court would then have to weigh the impact on the state of declaring needy strikers and their families ineligible for welfare against the extent to which making them eligible stripped state government of its neutrality in a labor-management dispute.
> . . . Under such an approach, a court would be interested in how many states permit strikers to receive welfare; whether or not strikes tend to be of longer duration where welfare is received; any studies or expert testimony evaluating the impact of eligibility for benefits on the strikers' resolve; a comparison between strike benefits and welfare benefits; the impact of the requirement that welfare recipients accept suitable employment; how many strikers actually do receive welfare benefits; and a host of other factors. In addition, the state's legitimate interests must also be considered: its interests in minimizing hardship to the families of strikers who have no other resources than the weekly pay check, its concern in avoiding conditions that could lead to violence, its interest in forestalling economic stagnation in local communities, etc.[255]

Finally, this court questioned whether the courts should resolve this issue:

> This very catalogue of data relevant to a macrocosmic weighing, which a court, if called upon, would have to undertake, indicates the preferable forum to be Congress. Congress would be particularly appropriate in resolving this issue.[256]

As a result of the *ITT* case, the preemption issue was raised in a number of other cases with evidence presented, or available, to supply answers to the questions raised in the opinion of the First Circuit. Such evidence has, however, not been given weight, but rather the decision in *ITT* has been held depositive of the matter.[257] As the matter stands now, therefore, the right of strikers to receive tax supported benefits is neither one that is

---

[255] *Id.*, 76 L.R.R.M. at 2207.

[256] *Id.*

[257] See, e.g., *Francis* v. *Davidson*, U.S. D.C. Md., January 28, 1972; *Lascaris* v. *Wyman*, 79 L.R.R.M. 2535 (1972); *Super Tire Engineering Co.* v. *McCorkle*, Civil Action 853-71, U.S. D.C. N.J., June 24, 1971. Some of these cases are discussed in Robert W. Clark III, "Walfare for Strikers: *ITT* v. *Minter*," *University of Chiacog Law Review*, Vol. XXXIX (Fall 1971, prepublication copy), pp. 79-114.

a constitutional right based upon the Equal Protection Clause nor is it a benefit that can be denied as violative of the Supremacy Clause.

Congressional Action and Administrative Regulation

Tax supported benefits to strikers thus derive solely from congressional action and/or intent, and administrative regulations that have been issued pursuant thereto. The issue, as noted in Chapter III, was not duly considered when the Social Security Act became law in 1935, but the administrators quickly took advantage of their discretion to provide welfare to strikers during the New Deal period, both prior to the passage of the Social Security Act, and thereafter. State welfare administrators took their cue from these precedents and generally provided aid to strikers thereafter.

Likewise the Social Security Act placed no restrictions on providing unemployment compensation to strikers. The Nixon Administration recommended legislation which would have prohibited states from granting unemployment compensation to strikers in 1969, but Congress declined so to act.[258] The Nixon Administration's attempt to end unemployment compensation to striking railroad workers has also been unsuccessful.[259]

Although Congress has made no explicit provision to pay food stamps to strikers, it did several times reject attempts to make strikers ineligible for such benefits.[260] The U.S. Department of Agriculture's regulations now provide that strikers are specifically eligible.[261]

The greatest controversy in recent years has been over the eligibility of strikers whose families receive Aid to Families with Dependent Children (AFDC-U). Aside from the already discussed constitutional issues, the question has been raised in the courts whether, pursuant to existing law and regulations, such aid may be denied strikers; the consistent answer of the courts is that it cannot *except by change of law or regulation.*[262] The bases for these court opinions are found in the legislation creat-

---

[258] Clark, *op. cit.,* p. 80, n.10.

[259] *Ibid.*

[260] *Ibid.*

[261] *Ibid.,* p. 81, n.14.

[262] See *Lascaris* v. *Wyman,* 79 L.R.R.M. 2535 (1972); and *Francis* v. *Davidson,* D.C. Md., January 28, 1972.

ing the "unemployed father" option of AFDC and in the regulations established by the Secretary of Health, Education and Welfare adopted pursuant to that legislation.

The original 1961 legislation creating the unemployed father option left the definition of unemployment to those states deciding to bring their laws under that option.[263] In 1968, however, the law was amended to provide, among other things, that unemployment would be "determined in accordance with standards presented by the Secretary [of Health, Education and Welfare]." The states were thus not left with any discretion to define unemployment. The Secretary then ruled that "If a State wishes to provide AFDC for children of unemployed fathers, the State plan . . . must . . . [i]nclude a definition of an unemployed father . . . [and] shall include any father who is employed less than 30 hours a week. . . ."[264]

The definition of unemployed thus quoted provides no exception for strikers, those discharged for misconduct, or others. The Secretary can change this ruling to exclude such persons or others, based on reasonable rules reasonably arrived at. Until he does, however, or until Congress alters the law, strikers are eligible for AFDC-U after the thirty-day waiting period imposed by law. At present, congressional intent as to the inclusion of strikers is not clear. The ranking Republican on the House Ways and Means Committee, Representative Byrnes, emphasized on several occasions that the Committee had gone to great lengths so that the benefits of AFDC-U would not go "to people who in a sense may be more or less voluntarily unemployed and who are refusing work," and he stated that the bill would "assure that aid would only go to children of the involuntarily unemployed." [265] During the debate, however, in answer to a question by Representative Dominick, Chairman Mills of the House Ways and Means Committee stated that states could, if they wished, grant AFDC benefits to strikers.[266] According to *Francis* v. *Davidson,* the most recent court decision, states which desire to deny strikers the right to receive such payments cannot lawfully do so.[267]

---

[263] The history of this legislation is well reviewed in *Francis* v. *Davidson.*

[264] *Id.* at 6.

[265] 107 Congressional Record 3528, daily ed., March 10, 1961.

[266] *Id.* at 3526.

[267] U.S. D.C. Md., January 28, 1972, at 33.

THE SPIRIT OF THE LAW

From the legal and administrative analysis above we can see that the rights which strikers have to welfare are administrative rights. These are highly qualified and subject to change. Strikers often obtained coverage in specific programs by accident of definition, by the inability of the drafters of legislation to draw objective eligibility requirements which excluded them but allowed the truly deserving, or by the legislators not forseeing that the question of striker eligibility might arise.

Examples abound in the various welfare programs of conditions and restrictions supporting the contention that the relief provided was intended for those who, through no fault of their own, are unable—rather than unwilling—to help themselves. Strikers, who often *are* able to help themselves during their work stoppages, and who are in a condition of need through their own voluntary actions, do not meet this condition. They are therefore outside of the *spirit* of many of the programs even though they may be covered by the letter of them.

The question remains whether legislative or administrative bodies responsible for establishing the conditions of eligibility should be asked to alter this situation. This question can be answered by a judgment as to whether the benefits to the society are worth the costs, and is dealt with in our final chapter.

CHAPTER IX

Conclusions and Recommendations

The purpose of this study has been to determine (1) the extent to which strikers utilize tax supported funds; and (2) the impact of such utilization on the American collective bargaining system, and particularly on the propensity to strike, the duration of strikes, and the terms of strike settlement. In addition, we have analyzed and discussed other questions flowing from these major inquiries and raised in the *ITT* v. *Minter*[268] opinion, such as the social implications of denying benefits to strikers. Here we set forth our conclusions and recommendations.

WIDE USE OF WELFARE BY STRIKERS

It is the inescapable conclusion of this study that public welfare support is widely available to strikers, that its use is already substantial, and that its use is growing rapidly. The three major forms of public support which have been investigated— Food Stamps, public assistance (AFDC, General Assistance, and Emergency Relief), and Unemployment Compensation—are each subject to different availability and conditions of use. These have been extensively detailed in earlier chapters, and will not be summarized here. But it has been apparent to the authors, during the year that this study has been underway, that the availability of public support is increasing. During this period, the Congress has declined to make strikers ineligible for the Food Stamp program and the regulations of the U.S. Department of Agriculture have been amended to make strikers specifically eligible; and judicial interpretations have removed the roadblocks which had previously prevented strikers from receiving public assistance support in some states.

At the time of writing, the early spring of 1972, strike activity in the country was at a much lower level than is typical

---

[268] 435 F.2d 989 (1st Cir., 1970); *cert. denied*, 420 U.S. 933 (1971).

because of the initial impact of the wage and price stabilization system. It is likely, however, that the depression in the number of strikes will be temporary even if the wage-price stabilization system continues. When strike activity does return to its traditional pattern, a greater use of tax supported programs by strikers seems certain, in part because the stigma of being on welfare has been reduced through program changes and overcome through the personal experience of many strikers with the public support system, and also because knowledge of the availability of benefits and procedures for applying for them spreads with experience. These factors may push total assistance costs far above the $329 million yearly (exclusive of unemployment compensation) which were estimated in Chapter VII. Moreover, it should again be emphasized that these direct costs are only a fraction of the total impact of tax supported benefits for strikers.

IMPACT ON COLLECTIVE BARGAINING AND STRIKES

As was pointed out in Chapter II, collective bargaining largely depends for its survival on a viable strike mechanism to insure that to both sides of a labor dispute the costs of disagreement, as reckoned at the negotiating table, are greater than the costs of agreement. The evidence presented by our empirical studies appears to demonstrate that tax supported benefits to strikers have already had a substantial impact on strikes and strike settlements, even though our statistical base is neither as large nor as refined as would be required to quantify our conclusions.

Although the evidence presented in the previous chapters indicates that it is probably unlikely that many persons go on strike in order to receive welfare benefits,[269] it must nevertheless be concluded that one of the effects of the availability of public support for strikers on strikes themselves is to increase the propensity of unions to undertake strikes, and to increase the probability that they will be longer, costlier, or both. If union officials know that the public, rather than the union treasury, will be responsible for the economic security of their members while on strike, and if such public benefits preclude a political reaction of union members and their wives against the economic

---

[269] Cases were noted, however, of persons who decided *to remain* on welfare after strikes were over.

losses stemming from a strike, then obviously strikes can be undertaken more lightly.

The overwhelming weight of opinions unearthed by our studies, including those of strikers, union officials, and management personnel, was that the payment of tax supported benefits to strikers, by greatly reducing the economic pressures on those strikers, substantially diminished the back pressures from union members to settle and thereby made strikes last longer. Moreover, it seemed clear in the cases studied that strike settlements were made more costly as managements, realizing what was occurring, paid more dearly to end the dispute.

How much in additional sums have been or will be added to wage settlements (and prices) because management regards it futile to risk a strike where strikers are supported by government funds is of course impossible to estimate. When strikes are supported by welfare, food stamps, unemployment compensation, or some combination of these benefits, it does seem quite clear that the strike cannot effectively, in Dr. George W. Taylor's words, "serve as the motive power which induces a modification of extreme positions and then a meeting of minds." [270] Rather, the union is put close to the position where "there is everything to gain and nothing to lose by trying to get one's unusual demands approved without cost." [271] Such an inequitable situation, if continued, or worsened as we predict, will undoubtedly result in demands for drastic changes in our industrial relations system.

SOCIAL IMPLICATIONS

It is the general public which must shoulder the burden of paying several times over for the use of public funds by strikers. The impact on the public consists of the direct costs of support payments to the strikers and their administrative expenses, and the costs of the more frequent strikes, or longer strikes and/or higher settlements. In view of the inflationary pressures already extant, one must assume that such additional costs cannot be offset by gains in productivity. The result then, in addition to providing increased disruptions to the economic system, is higher prices—meaning, of course, inflation.

---

[270] George W. Taylor, "Is Compulsory Arbitration Inevitable?" *Proceedings of the First Annual Metting, Industrial Relations Research Association,* 1948, p. 64.

[271] *Ibid.*

The impact on the general public is one of the social implications of welfare payments to strikers which the First Circuit Court neglected to ask in *ITT* v. *Minter*. The questions which it did ask concern the impact or implications of *denying* benefits to strikers in terms of the impact on the families of strikers, on the level of violence associated with strikes, and on economic stagnation in local communities. It should be pointed out that, at the time the questions were asked (and even now), receiving welfare benefits during strikes was not a tradition in American labor relations. The court's questions arose because of the novelty of the situation, and therefore were stated in terms of denying benefits to strikers, rather than in terms of continued payment. The distinction is most important, and results in some of the First Circuit questions answering themselves. Denial of welfare benefits to strikers will cause no hardships to the families of strikers which those families have not traditionally borne themselves and mitigated to the best of their abilities in the past. In this regard, the authors agree with the conclusions reached by the California State Social Welfare Board:

> The Board is safe in assuming that prior to the trade dispute, there existed a normal intact family unit where there was continuous and regular employment for a period of time, the continuity of which is broken by the trade dispute. The Board has not been shown facts or any evidence that serious deprivation would exist in the families of persons engaged in a trade dispute. Further, in that the termination date of a union contract is usually known far in advance, and contractual negotiations usually begin early, it is hoped that families will take the necessary economic precautions in advance to reduce the effect of unemployment by virtue of possible trade dispute.
> Certainly, as a matter of policy, the economic impact of trade disputes on the families of strikers should not become an area of public responsibility.[272]

By similar logic, denial of welfare benefits will not impose on local communities a burden of economic stagnation greater than that which the communities had grown to expect during strikes, and hopefully to prepare themselves against. And certainly, if one of the goals is to reduce the economic stagnation of communities which result from strikes, then a far better way to achieve that goal would be to insure that strikes would be infrequent and as short as circumstances permit—conditions which

---

[272] (California) State Welfare Board, "Position Statement, Issue: Aid to Strikers," (mimeo, March 1971), p. 11.

are directly opposite to the expected and found results of paying publicly supported benefits to workers while they are out on strike.

The last social impact question deals with avoiding conditions that could lead to violence during strikes. Superficially, it seems reasonable to assume that strikes would be less bitter when the striking workers were supported by public funds, and even though this smacks of social blackmail, it is a fact which should be considered. In the investigations for this study, however, no pattern of violence different from that traditionally associated with a particular industry or company was discovered in those situations where the workers were receiving public support. It must therefore be concluded that, at least to date, this factor has not proved to be important.

SUMMARY OF CONCLUSIONS

In summary, the conclusions of this study are that paying welfare benefits to strikers is an unwarranted imposition on the public treasury and the private good. Organized labor's relative bargaining power before public support was certainly great enough to be influential. The additional power which $329 million per year in direct benefits can buy may well upset the relative bargaining positions of unions and managements so greatly that the fundamental structure of collective bargaining will be seriously threatened. The general public must pay the costs, not only directly through higher taxes and higher prices, but also indirectly through greater disruption to the economic system and through inflation. The benefits accrue to a relatively small group which did not really need them in the past, and does not need them now.

PROPOSALS FOR CHANGE

The question thus remains whether there is any reason why the economy and the collective bargaining system should be thus subjected to strain. Paying welfare benefits to strikers, like all such welfare questions, is up to the society to decide. It is perhaps important to point out here that although one of the basic questions which must be answered by all economic systems is the priorities which are to be placed on resource distribution, the science of economics is unable to supply the answer. Establishing spending priorities is a societal and political question rather than an economic one. The best that economics can do is to point out the costs or implications of one course of action as compared with another. It is within our function, however, to point out that those priorities are drifting into a new ordering.

Welfare for strikers was not deliberately created under any of the three major welfare support programs. Even under the Food Stamp program, where exclusion of strikers was specifically rejected by the Congress, they were not initially intended for inclusion, but fell within the law by Congress, in essence, sanctioning a practice that had already developed. Nevertheless, it is clear that specific congressional action will now be required to remove strikers from this eligibility position.

In the public assistance areas (General Assistance, Aid to Families with Dependent Children, and others), strikers were not initially considered for inclusion, but recent court interpretations of perhaps vague eligibility requirements have sanctified the already existing use of these programs by strikers in some states and apparently required it in others where the basic programs exist. Clearcut administrative decisions by the Secretary of Health, Education and Welfare could eliminate this eligibility without additional legislation.

Unemployment Compensation was not initially intended to embrace strikers. Only three of the fifty-three programs (counting the railroad program) do so directly although others have experimented with it in the past, and several states provide benefits if the strike is ruled a lockout or if the affected employees are not held to be directly involved. Several state legislatures are under almost constant pressure to include strikers. Although the Congress could require that strikers be made ineligible as President Nixon has requested, this is largely a matter to be left up to the state legislatures, with the exception of the railroad program, which is a federal program and would require specific federal legislation to change.[273]

The problems associated with striker support through the welfare system, although still developing, are clearcut. The means for solving them are available, but to do so requires administrative and/or political resolve. It is our recommendation, based

---

[273] The rationale for a separate railroad program is in itself questionable and could well be eliminated entirely.

on the analyses of this study, that such resolve be made. There are, however, many different directions which it could take.

Welfare Reform

One way to handle the question is through welfare reform now before Congress. H.R. 1 provides some potential for improvement, but leave many loopholes for continued striker support.[274] The legislation sets up two family programs: (1) Opportunities for Families Program, and (2) Family Assistance Plan. Persons available for work would be required to register for employment and training under the Opportunities program; those eligible families with no member available would receive benefits under the Assistance program.

Under H.R. 1, benefits would not be paid persons who refuse training "without good cause." Although jobs at struck plants could be declined without ending benefits, it would not seem that the law contemplates giving strikers training and paying them allowances. The bill does, however, provide for voluntary registration and does not preclude strikers from volunteering for training and thus obtaining training allowances to support them during strikes if they can be otherwise eligible. A similar device was utilized under existing U.S. Department of Labor manpower training programs by General Motors workers during the 1970 strike.[275]

The eligibility requirements of the Assistance Program set forth in H.R. 1 would definitely be a step in the right direction. The bill provides that "all income except that excluded would be used to reduce benefits otherwise payable." [276] It figures benefits on the basis of estimates of quartely income made on the basis of the preceding quarter's income. Unlike most welfare recipients, strikers are persons with high yearly incomes who, during strikes, temporarily give up that income. The AFDC-U program provides them with benefits on the basis of one month's income level. The provisions of the Family Assistance Plan would help

---

[274] This analysis is based upon U.S. House of Representatives, 92nd Congress, 1st Sess., *Social Security Amendments of 1971. Report of the Committee on Ways and Means on H.R. 1, To Amend the Social Security Act. . . .* Union Calendar No. 86, House Report No. 92-231 (Washington: Government Printing Office, 1971).

[275] See Appendix A.

[276] *Report on H.R. 1, op. cit.,* p. 31.

in correcting this misuse by spreading the base for calculating income over a longer period, so that averaged income of strikers would probably not fall below the eligibility standard line for at least a number of weeks after the strike started.

Undoubtedly, a waiting period requirement would help to curtail payments to strikers in many cases, because there are many more short strikes than long ones. Unfortunately, there are also some dysfunctional effects of waiting periods, as has been found to be the case with the six or seven weeks waiting periods required by the two states that pay unemployment compensation to strikers. The promise of payments to begin at some specified future time strengthens the resolve of strikers approaching the deadline to hold out until they begin. Thus such a waiting period might well have the effect of increasing the number of long strikes, or at least of extending the duration of some strikes.

Another shortcoming of H.R. 1 is the exclusions which it provides. Thus the first $720 per year earned income (above some other minor exclusions) plus one-third of the remainder are excluded in figuring resources. So is "assistance based on need received from public or private agencies except veterans' pensions." Maximum exclusions for a family of four could not exceed $3,000. Although a family would be ineligible for benefits with resources in excess of $1,500, a reasonably priced home, assets necessary to self-support (an automobile), and certain insurance policies would not be include in figuring the $1,500.[277] Under these definitions, we believe that some strikers might be eligible and others, by manipulating savings accounts, etc., as they have allegedly done in strikes which we examined, could maneuver themselves into eligibility.

H.R. 1 provides that no one eligible for benefits under its programs would also be eligible for food stamps. On the other hand, there is nothing contained in H.R. 1 which would prevent strikers not eligible for Opportunities or Assistance benefits from continuing to be eligible for food stamps.

Since Medicaid, mortgage and rent support, and other such benefits are now made available to those on welfare (AFDC), H.R. 1, to the extent that it made it difficult for strikers to receive welfare benefits, would have a like effect on any such benefits associated with AFDC. On the other hand, states could

---

[277] *Ibid.*, p. 32.

still give emergency assistance, general assistance, etc., to
strikers.

We conclude, therefore, that the Nixon Administration's welfare reform bill, as amended by the House of Representatives
Ways and Means Committee, would reduce striker eligibility
for welfare payments but continue to leave a considerable range
of possibilities for tax supported benefits to be paid to strikers.

Repayment Provision

A method to discourage (rather than to end) the payment of
publicly supported benefits to strikers has been urged by Mr.
Robert W. Clark III.[278] Noting that federal regulations in current welfare programs implicitly allow states to enact repayment provisions for welfare, and that several states actually
have such provisions (although they are seldom used and usually
enforce repayment by claims against property or assets rather
than income), Clark recommends that these provisions be modified and extended by the states:

> If obligations were levied on the temporarily unemployed, who
> have a high earnings potential, substantial repayment would be
> achieved without burdening those who have the least incentive
> to leave the welfare rolls. Repayment would also be more ef-
> ficient than at present if it were taken from the recipient's in-
> come rather than his assets. In the absence of federal welfare
> reform, then, the states should require that a recipient of either
> AFDC-U or General Assistance benefits whose long-term income
> is reduced because of participation in a labor dispute or whose
> reemployment is imminent repay the state out of his subsequent
> income if that income remains above the welfare level for a sub-
> stantial period.[279]

Clark feels that this method would protect laborers in the
organizing stage, where they are least able to endure a long
strike, and reduce benefits to laborers whose bargaining position
is better established. "The problem of striker eligibility is thus
reduced to the question of where to set the standard of income
above which strikers will be denied welfare benefits or required
to repay benefits received."

---

[278] Robert W. Clark III, "Welfare for Strikers: *ITT* v. *Minter,*" *University
of Chicago Law Review,* Vol. XXXIX (Fall 1971 prepublication copy), pp.
112-113.

[279] *Ibid.,* p. 113.

Although this method has attractions and does reduce the problems of having to define such vague terms as "good cause" or "voluntary unemployment," a new problem arises from the need to set a particular standard to differentiate between the interests of aiding low income families and the interests of preserving the present framework of collective bargaining. The administration of such a requirement would most certainly be subject to severe political pressures. Additionally, this method fails to divorce the welfare system from the collective bargaining system, which is, after all, the goal that we believe should be sought.

Congressional and/or Administrative Exclusion

There are undoubtedly many methods by which publicly supported benefits might be denied strikers, or at least made more difficult to obtain. Yet most of these ways seem indirect and would only establish temporary stumbling blocks, rather than permanent barriers to this use of public dollars. We propose that Congress, state governments, and appropriate administrative officials simply declare strikers ineligible for any tax supported benefits. We recommend that the Secretary of Health, Education and Welfare establish regulations or Congress enact legislation prohibiting the distribution of federal monies in the form of AFDC-U and other public aid benefits to workers involved in a work stoppage; that Congress take appropriate action to prohibit striking workers from obtaining food stamps or surplus food commodities; that Congress and/or state legislatures enact legislation which would prohibit states from granting unemployment compensation to strikers; and that state governments enact laws which would make strikers ineligible for public welfare benefits under the control of state welfare agencies.

We believe that the above recommendations are in the general interest and that any hardship which might result is fully within the capacity of organized labor to care for. The empirical evidence set forth in this volume points to this. It must also be recognized that modern labor unions are big business. Trade unions today have large payrolls; administer major pension and welfare funds; maintain major investments in stocks, bonds, and property; are occasionally struck and picketed by their own office and staff workers; and in a great many respects share in the problems and are versant in the managerial techniques of big business. Through the brotherhood of labor, the administrative power and financial expertise of large unions can be made available to newly organized groups, such as has been done for the United Farm Workers Organizing Committee headed by Cesar Chavez. There would, therefore, seem to be no reason why big labor cannot establish and administer a strike benefit system which meets their members' needs.

We recognize that tremendous funds are required to support strikes, especially companywide or industrywide strikes. We also recognize that enormous union "war chests" are needed, not because of worker poverty, but because of worker affluence. As George Meany, President of the AFL-CIO, noted in a recent interview:

> There is a growing feeling that strikes of people getting $7500 a year or more just don't make sense. You see, years ago you put people on strike who were making 50 cents an hour. That's all you had to make up: 50 cents an hour. You could go begging and you could get food; you could keep them going.
>
> But now the workers have a little home, they may have a couple of kids going to college. You put them on strike, they're overboard within a week.[280]

If, as seems apparent, the intensified union demands for public support for strikers arises from the strange conditions that workers have become too affluent to be satisfied with the levels of strike support which their unions previously supplied, it is entirely fair to ask those workers to devote some portion of their higher wages to purchase strike insurance. If organized labor, however, believes that it would be an unfair imposition upon its membership to raise dues sufficiently to provide strike assistance at the levels demanded by its increasingly affluent membership, and to support union goals, then we recommend that one of the oldest forms of economic security be employed— insurance. The need levels of individual union members vary with their family sizes, life styles, etc. Most, however, are well versed in the idea of providing individual economic security for themselves through automobile insurance, life insurance, fire insurance, medical insurance, etc. There is no reason why organized labor could not explore with private insurance companies the possibilities of establishing strike insurance programs, perhaps leaving to individual union members the option of buying above a maximum level varying degrees of economic protection.

---

[280] *U.S. News and World Report*, February 21, 1972, p. 28.

The insurance industry should have no difficulty in devising a strike insurance system which does provide sufficient protection without making the payments themselves an incentive to strike or to remain on strike. A number of industries have established such plans in order to improve individual companies' resistance to union demands.[281] A union strike insurance plan would be a similar, legitimate self-help arrangement. Union strike funds, under this system, could then be reserved for emergency cases or for new entrants to the unions, and to insure that these funds provided no disincentive to the insurance system, could even be distributed as loans, if that is the desire.

Whether unions accept our strike insurance suggestion is not the important question. Rather, it is whether Congress and state legislatures will take the steps that are necessary to free welfare programs—and the taxpaying public—from the burden of supporting strikers. And more importantly, if they will untangle collective bargaining from the welfare system which, if not done, could drastically reduce, or possibly end, the usefulness of the American system of collective bargaining.

---

[281] See, e.g., John S. Hirsch, Jr., "Strike Insurance and Collective Bargaining," *Industrial and Labor Relations Review*, Vol. XXII (January 1969), pp. 243-248.

APPENDIX

A. *Major Assistance Programs*

B. *Union Strike Assistance Documents*

Appendix A

MAJOR ASSISTANCE PROGRAMS
AVAILABLE TO STRIKERS

FOOD STAMPS

Food stamps are coupons which are sold to households whose incomes and assets are below certain guidelines issued by the U.S. Department of Agriculture (USDA). Food stamps are sold at a discount, with the two variables controlling the cost being family size and monthly net income. The stamps are redeemed at face value by designated, participating retail food stores which may in turn redeem them from their wholesaler or a commercial bank. The stamps are usable to buy food or food products for human consumption except alcoholic beverages, tobacco, and certain imported foods. Food retailers are not remunerated for their administrative burden in handling food stamps, but participate in the program in the hopes of increasing sales and improving cash flows through reducing the number of credit accounts carried.

Administration

The Food Stamp program is administered by the Food Stamp Division of the Food and Nutrition Service (FNS) of the USDA. The Food Stamp Division has regional staffs in five geographical areas which supervise several hundred USDA employees designated as "officers-in-charge" of the various "project areas" into which the country is divided. These officers-in-charge deal principally with supervising the functioning of the program, handling the relationships with participating banks and stores and enforcing the regulations with respect to accountability in issuance and redemption of the stamps. They have no official authority over certification of eligible stamp users or actual dispersing of the stamps, which is within the province of the Department of Health, Education and Welfare.

The appropriate state welfare agency is responsible for the operation of the Food Stamp program at the project area level.

This responsibility includes the establishment of certification and issuance procedures. Although the state welfare agency may not delegate its control of the certification process, it can contract to have stamps issued by another agency, for example banks.[1]

History

The use of special script for advantageous food purchases by selected buyers is not new. A food stamp plan was undertaken in 1939 as part of the general experimentation during the New Deal. The purpose of that plan was to increase consumer food purchasing power and to direct purchasing towards nutritional foods while insuring that the federal subsidy was actually used to increase food consumption rather than for other purposes. Unstated, but nevertheless important, was the concurrent factor of clearing the embarassing food surpluses without allowing agricultural prices to drop to levels ruinous to the farmers.

Two colors of stamps were involved in the program: orange stamps were sold at face value and could be used for any purchases; blue stamps were given free in proportion to one-half the amount of orange stamps purchased, but could be used only for designated surplus foods. Surplus food lists (which included quite a large number of items in 1939) were distributed monthly to participating grocers, who could redeem the stamps they took in from the Department of Agriculture or their wholesaler so long as they maintained adequate records.

Some safeguards against misuse existed. Participation was generally limited to persons on work relief, unemployment relief, or general or specific assistance, and participants were required to buy orange stamps in amounts equal to their usual food expenditures ($1 to $1.50 per person per week in 1939). Controls existed on issuance and handling of the stamps, making change and so forth. Nevertheless, misuses did occur, the most common form being that purchasers would buy those surplus items which they would have purchased in any case with the eligible blue stamps, which would free additional orange stamps for purchase of non-surplus items. Additionally, the usual problems of fraud were in evidence and at least some retailers added brokering in stamps to their normal business.

Complications arose in the administration of the program from these causes and from others, and it was finally recognized that

---

[1] Control Systems Research, Inc., *The Food Stamp Program and How It Works*, Vol. 1, No. 2 (February 1971), p. 11.

the program was insufficient to overcome the natural imbalance between what commodities happened to be surplus and those which people wanted to buy. Even though specifications of the program and eligibility standards were modified from time to time, the basic imbalance of the program remained until employment and demand skyrocketed as a result of participation in World War II. The war essentially eliminated both major reasons for food stamps simultaneously. They were dropped in the spring of 1943.

In the forty-six months of its operation, the food stamp program served almost twelve million persons in 1,741 counties and 88 cities at a cost to the federal government of over $260 million. Year-to-year operations between 1938 and 1942 are shown in Table A-1. As is typical of such programs, the cost per participant increased each year (except the final, incomplete one), rising from $2.43 in 1938 to $29.21 in 1941. The change between 1940 and 1941 was the most dramatic: program costs increased by 35 percent even though the number of participants declined by 4 percent.

Also typical of such programs, only a fraction of the total number of potentially eligible participants utilized the program. It has been estimated that had the plan been available to all families receiving general welfare or other assistance during 1939-1943, the cost of the federal contribution would have been about $400 million a year, almost six times the average monthly costs actually incurred.

TABLE A-1. *Food Stamp Program, 1939-1943*

Fiscal Year	Number of Persons (thousands)	Federal Gov't Costs (thousands)	Cost per Participant
1938	51	$ 124	$ 2.43
1939	1,488	16,414	11.03
1940	3,969	82,820	20.87
1941	3,821	111,616	29.21
1942	2,600	49,129	18.90

Source: Dale M. Hoover, *Food for the Hungry*, National Planning Association, Planning Pamphlet No. 126 (Washington: The Association, 1969), p. 25.

Following the termination of the original food stamp program, this aspect of the welfare system was left to the direct commodity distribution plan until January 21, 1961, when President Kennedy in his Executive Order No. 1 directed the Secretary of Agriculture to increase the amounts and variety of foods being distributed to low-income families. By March of the same year the Secretary had responded with plans to resurrect a food stamp plan, and a number of pilot areas were designated to evaluate if stamps provided an effective means of expanding farm markets and improving food consumption and nutrition in low-income households.

During a five-month period in 1961, eight pilot projects were in operation, attracting an average of 138,000 persons per month, (although about as many in the same areas preferred to continue using the direct commodity distributions). Average monthly stamp utilization was about $2.8 million, of which slightly more than $1 million was the direct federal subsidy. Administrative costs on the federal level were quite high, but it was recognized that a significant portion of them could be attributed to start-up problems, and expectations were that federal administrative costs would not exceed 4 percent of total program costs once established. (To date, an accurate prediction.)

In the eight project areas, retail food store sales increased by an average, seasonally adjusted 8.4 percent (an increase which should have been no great surprise) and surveys showed that higher proportions of expensive (and nutritious) foods were consumed. The project was therefore considered a success, and its increased utilization was recommended. By August 1964, the pilot program was operating forty-three project areas in twenty-two states, and over 350,000 persons were participating in it. The federally supplied bonus value of the coupons was up to $2.2 million a month, and those involved were happy with the results which had been achieved. At the end of the month, President Johnson made the program permanent by signing into law the Food Stamp Act (Public Law 88-525).

Principles

The Food Stamp Act authorized the Secretary of Agriculture to administer and bear most of the costs of a program designed to increase the buying power of needy persons or families. In participating communities, low income persons could buy, for a small amount, stamps worth a larger amount when presented at the local food store, the difference to be made up by the federal government. The amount paid for the stamps would depend on the family size and economic status of the purchaser. Local administration and certification of purchasers would be a state and local responsibility. Food stamp programs would be set up in communities only if requested, but where they were established they would replace existing programs for free distribution of federal surplus foods. President Johnson felt that food stamps would improve the diets of the needy, and that the program was designed "to protect those who are specially vulnerable to the ravages of poverty."

Benefits

Food Stamps is a federal program, and the benefits from it are now uniform nationally. (There had been originally some regional differences, but these were eliminated and the overall bonuses were raised in late 1969.) Program eligibility, which had previously been handled on a state or local level and therefore subject to some variation for participation, was standardized and benefit levels were again modified in mid-1971.

Table A-2 shows the benefits which are available to families of various sizes and income levels. For example, a man with a wife and four children and a monthly net income of $300, if certified eligible (by the procedures to be discussed in the next section) could purchase $148.00 of stamps for $85.00. The federal government makes up the $63.00 difference. If his income is lower or his family larger, he qualifies for a larger subsidy. It should be noted that all income figures are in terms of *net* monthly income.

Table A-2 shows benefit levels for households of up to eight persons. For larger households with net incomes of up to about $600 a month, the purchase requirements are the same as for the eight-person households, and the monthly coupon allotment is increased by $16.00 for each person over eight. For higher income levels, a formula exists which is available from the local welfare office.

Eligibility

Determination and certification of eligibility for food stamps was a matter until recently left to the discretion of the states by the Food Stamp Act. With the exception of households which

TABLE A-2. *Food Stamp Program
Coupon Allotment by Selected
Household Size, and Purchase Requirements
by Household Size and Net Income to Maximum Allowable Level*

Total Monthly Net Income [a]	Purchase Requirement by Number of Persons in Household and Coupon Allotment [b]				
	1	2	4	6	8
	$32.00	$60.00	$108.00	$148.00	$180.00
$ 0	$ 0	$ 0	$ 0	$ 0	$ 0
20	1	1	0	0	0
40	6	7	7	8	8
60	10	12	13	14	16
80	14	18	19	21	22
100	18	23	25	27	29
120	22	29	31	34	36
140	25	34	37	40	42
160	26	36	41	43	45
180		42	47	49	51
200		48	53	55	57
250			71	73	75
300			83	85	87
350			95	97	99
400				115	117
500				139	144
600					171
Maximum allowable monthly income	$170	$222	$360	$493	$600

Source: U.S. Department of Agriculture, Food and Nutrition Service in
Fed. Reg. Vol. XXXVI, No. 146, Part II (July 29, 1971), p. 14118.

[a] Selected sizes.

[b] Selected incomes are representative rather than continuous. Alternative
income levels within the intervals selected may or may not have different
purchase requirements.

were already receiving welfare assistance and were thereby automatically eligible, standards set by the states merely had to be consistent with those used in other federally aided public assistance programs. This allowed considerable leeway. As recently as June 1970, the maximum allowable net monthly income for a family of four varied from a low of $180 in South Carolina to a high of $360 in New Jersey. The average of all of the states' programs was $283. Amendments to the Food Stamp Act in July 1971 applied, for the first time, a uniform national income standard of eligibility for participation by households which were not already receiving public assistance (and therefore automatically eligible) to be no less than indicated by income poverty guidelines issued by the Secretary of Agriculture. As these are now set by the Department of Agriculture, a family of four may still be eligible if monthly income is as high as $360, the same as the highest allowable net monthly income of any of the state plans under the old program. The maximums for other representative family sizes are shown in Table A-2.

The income limitation is not as restrictive as it at first appears, because it deals only with net income. Total gross income is reduced in two ways. First, some forms of income are excluded. Second, certain deductions are made from non-excluded income. Among types of income excluded are the following:

1. Income earned by a child residing with the household who is a student under the age of eighteen.

2. Non-monetary gains (such as the free use of a house).

3. Non-recurring payments (such as inheritances, sale of property, gifts, income tax refunds).

4. Ten percent of employment income up to a maximum of $30 per household per month.

From this level of income, the following deductions are then made:

1. Mandatory deductions:

    a. Local, state, and federal income taxes.

    b. Social Security taxes.

    c. Union dues.

2. Shelter deductions:

   a. Shelter costs in excess of 30 percent of income after exclusion and the mandatory deductions above but before the exclusion of other deductions.[2]

3. Hardship deductions:

   a. Medical expenses in excess of $10 per month.

   b. Unreimbursed disaster or casualty losses.

   c. Child care or other payments when necessary for a household member to accept or continue employment.

   d. Educational expenses for tuition and mandatory school fees, even if covered by scholarships, grants, loans, fellowships, or veterans' benefits.

Taking into account these exclusions and deductions, the typical wage-earner with wife and two children can actually command a somewhat greater income level than the ceiling figures might lead one to believe. The maximum monthly wage allowed for eligibility is $360. For the standard 170-hour work month, this is equivalent to an hourly wage rate of $2.12. But assuming only the $30 exclusion and a modest set of mandatory, shelter, and hardship deductions, a wage rate of perhaps $3.50 to $3.75 would still qualify, exclusive of money earned by the children. These wage rates correspond to annual income levels of $7,140 to $7,650. (It is based on these figures and taking into account the asset limitations below that we have estimated in the body of the study potential eligibility of perhaps 25 percent of the country's population in the Food Stamp program.)

In addition to the income limitations there are a few other conditions which must be met. The first of these is an asset limit. As with income, prior to 1971, asset limitations varied from state to state. Now it is standardized at $1,500 for each household of total liquid and non-liquid resources. Again, however, there are certain important exclusions which make this limitation less rigorous than it appears.

Liquid resources include cash on hand, checking and savings accounts, savings bonds, and stocks and bonds. Non-liquid re-

---

[2] Shelter costs include actual rent paid plus utility costs—heat, cooking fuel, lighting, water heating, and water rent—or the maximum public assistance allowance for these utilities. For home ownership, shelter allowance includes prorated taxes, ground rent, mortgage interest, fire insurance amortization, and utility costs.

sources include buildings, land and other real or personal property. Excluded, however, are the following items: the home, automobile, household goods, cash value of life insurance, personal effects, income-producing property, and property (such as another car, tools, or machinery) needed for employment.

Another condition is work registration. Every able-bodied person between 18 and 65, including specifically persons on strike and excluding only mothers of dependent children, students, or persons working at least thirty hours per week, must register for employment and show good faith in being willing to accept suitable work. ("Suitable work" is not defined, but examples of work not considered suitable are given. These include certain formulations of minimum wages, conditions of employment such as risk, experience required, distance from the resident's home or work, a requirement for joining or refraining from joining labor organizations, and "work offered at a site subject to a strike or lockout at the time of the offer.") The 1971 regulations also include, for the first time, a specific reference to the eligibility of strikers: "No household shall be denied participation in the program solely on grounds that a member of the household is not working because of a strike or lockout at his usual place of employment."

Use

After the Food Stamp program was made permanent in 1964, its use spread rapidly. During the final year of the test, or pilot, program in fiscal 1964, more than 350,000 persons participated in forty-three areas of twenty-two states. They received bonus coupons valued at $28.6 million. By the end of fiscal year 1970, the program was operating in 1,747 project areas in forty-five states and the District of Columbia, and nearly 6.5 million people were participating. The value of the bonus coupons was upwards of $600 million.

The magnitude of the increase in usage apparently took many, including the original drafters of the Food Stamp Act, by surprise. For example, in 1970, the Food Stamp program contained appropriations authorizations of $170 million for July 1 through December 31, 1970. However, this was soon seen to be grossly insufficient to meet actual demand, and the Second Supplemental Appropriations Act of 1970 (H.R. 17399; Public Law 91-305, July 6, 1970) appropriated an additional $300 million for the program. But even this was too little, and the figure was subse-

quently increased to $600 million in a continuing resolution
(H.J. Res. 1388; Public Law 91-454, October 1970). The time
horizon was expanded one month, to January 31, 1971, but total
appropriations authorized expanded by $600 million to $770 million for the seven-month period.

Evidence from participation in the food stamp program in
cities where it has operated for a number of years indicates
that usage will continue to skyrocket even after the geographical
expansion terminates. In nine cities selected to represent a cross-
section of the country, food stamp usage as reflected in the value
of the cash bonuses distributed increased by an average factor
of almost four between January and July 1970. In Baltimore,
for example, food stamp bonuses were $339,481 in January 1970
and $1,124,498 by July.

Overall usage, by number of participants and value of bonus
coupons, is shown in Table A-3.

AID TO FAMILIES WITH DEPENDENT CHILDREN AND TO FAMILIES WITH DEPENDENT CHILDREN OF UNEMPLOYED PARENTS

Aid to Families with Dependent Children (AFDC) is a public
assistance program which provides money payments and social
services to certain categories of dependent children and their
families held to be needy. The federal government participates
in payments to needy families until the youngest child is age 18
(or age 21 if in school). Original provisions of the Social Security Act of 1935 (which established the program) made grants
to states for children (only) whose dependency was based on
the death or incapacity of a parent or the continued absence of
the parent from home. Coverage was extended to include benefits
for the parent or other person caring for the child in 1951. In
1961 the program was expanded to include intact family units
with children whose need arose from unemployment of a parent
and in 1968, Congress amended the statute and replaced the
word "parent" with the word "father." [3]

Administration

AFDC is a federal-state program. The Social Security Act of
1935 authorized federal participation in money payments to needy

___
[3] The use of "states" in this appendix is meant to include the fifty states
plus the District of Columbia, Guam, Puerto Rico, and the Virgin Islands.

TABLE A-3. *Food Stamp Program*
Summary of Operations
1962–1971

Fiscal Year	Projects in Program	States in Program	Monthly Average No. of Persons Participating	Annual Value of Coupons		Average Monthly Bonus per Person
				Total (000)	Bonus (000)	
1962	8	8	142,817	$ 35,202	$ 13,153	$ 7.67
1963	42	21	225,602	49,876	18,640	6.88
1964	43	22	366,816	73,485	28,644	6.51
1965	110	29	424,652	85,472	32,505	6.38
1966	324	41	864,344	174,232	64,813	6.25
1967	838	42	1,447,105	296,106	105,550	6.08
1968	1,027	44	2,211,224	451,801	173,142	6.52
1969	1,489	44	2,878,113	603,351	228,819	6.62
1970	1,747	46	6,470,000[a]	1,089,811	549,649	7.08 [a]
1971	2,022	49	9,375,568[a]	2,703,200	1,517,561	13.49 [a]

Source: U.S. Department of Agriculture, Food and Nutrition Service, *Food Stamp Program Statistical Summary of Operations*, various issues.

[a] Preliminary data.

dependent children. It provided for matching grants to states for programs operating under approved state plans. The choice of participating rests with the individual states. Currently, all jurisdictions have federally approved plans of AFDC, and twenty-four states have additionally adopted the unemployed father provisions.

States are responsible for developing and administering their own public assistance programs (including AFDC) within the guidelines and boundaries established by the federal government. These requirements include such stipulations as the following:

1. The plan must be statewide in character and operated by a single agency within the state.

2. Applicants must pass a means test.

3. States cannot apply residency, age, or citizenship conditions beyond those represented by federal law.

4. Appeal procedures must exist.

Within these requirements, the states have considerable latitude in determining how their programs will be organized and administered. (We shall cover some of those relevant differences below.)

Federal administrative authority for AFDC is in the hands of the Department of Health, Education and Welfare—more specifically, the Social and Rehabilitation Service. This Bureau maintains a field staff which examines state operations, advises on technical matters, conducts reviews, carries on supervisory functions, etc. Departments of public welfare exist in all of the states and these supervise the over 3,000 local departments of welfare operated either by counties or local communities, or as local offices of a state agency.

Both program costs and administrative costs are shared by the federal and state governments, and usually by local government as well. These costs are almost invariably financed from general revenue.

History

Through the nineteenth century and the first thirty years of the twentieth, a variety of public programs for the relief of the poor grew up in states and localities. Some of this was work-house, sheltered workshop, or orphanage relief, some was "outdoor relief" where relief was carried to the homes of the poor, and some was "categorical" relief, under which programs were established to provide special assistance to certain groups such as children of widows or veterans.

Among the first of these were local "mothers' pension acts." These and other efforts to provide assistance to children were given impetus by the White House Conference on the Care of Dependent Children called by President Theodore Roosevelt in 1909. This conference recommended that children "who are without support of the normal breadwinner should, as a rule, be kept with their parents, such aid being given as may be necessary to maintain suitable homes for the rearing of the children." [4]

The first state laws of this nature were passed by Illinois (the Fund to Parents Act) and Missouri, in 1911, and appear to have been patterned on the workmen's compensation laws which were appearing at about the same time. Within two years, twenty states had such laws, and by 1934 they existed in all states except Georgia and South Carolina.

As is always the case with new social legislation, there was great controversy associated with their adoption, and their provisions and administration varied widely from state to state. Most were administered on the county level, but some were by juvenile courts, some by special county boards, some by departments of public welfare, and some by the state poor law authorities. In 1931, monthly grants varied from a low of $4.33 in Arkansas to a high of $69.31 in Massachusetts.[5] In practically all cases, grants were made upon need determined on the basis of an investigation, and certain moral safeguards surrounded the legislation. In the usual case, the mother had to be a widow or the wife of a husband permanently incapacitated by mental or physical disability or of a husband sentenced to a penal institution for one or more years "or of a husband deserting her continuously for one year or more during which all legal remedies to compel him to support his family had been exhausted." [6]

---

[4] White House Conference, 1909, *Proceedings of the Conference on the Case of Dependent Children*, held at Washington, D.C., January 1909. Reported in Charles I. Schottland, *The Social Security Program in the United States* (New York: Appleton-Century-Crofts, 1963), p. 95.

[5] Arthur P. Miles, *An Introduction to Public Welfare* (Boston: D. C. Heath and Company, 1949).

[6] *Ibid.* Chapter 637 (Wisconsin), *Laws of 1915*, p. 204.

Most of the state programs were unable to stand up to the impact of the Depression. By 1933, many counties had suspended or discontinued aid, and many of those which continued could do so only by shifting federal unemployment relief funds into them. In late 1934 a total of only about 190,000 families were participating in some sort of dependent children program. This program was one to be incorporated in the Social Security Act of 1935.

The Social Security Act broke the prior pattern of local responsibility for relief. It authorized federal participation in public assistance money payments to three categories of the needy—the aged, the blind, and dependent children. (Other categories of need have been established by subsequent amendments.) The Aid to Dependent Children (ADC) section of the Act had been approved by the time the first payments were made, in February 1936.

Since its passage, the Social Security Act has been amended every two or three years. The degree of federal participation has been the most frequent subject of change, but the nature of the coverage has also been modified. The ADC program was occasionally changed in this way. Prior to 1951, the needs of a parent or relative caring for a dependent child were not included for federal funding purposes. This was changed to allow payments to one relative with whom the child resided in 1951.

In May 1961, on a temporary basis, federal grants were made available to states wishing to extend their programs to include children deprived of care due to the unemployment of the father. This program was optional with the states, and the definition of "unemployment" was left to the states. The following year, these temporary provisions were extended until 1967, providing for federal matching in assistance to both parents. At this time, the name of the program was changed to "Aid to Families with Dependent Children" (AFDC) to reflect emphasis on the family unit. This provision was again extended in 1967 for one year. The following year it was made permanent. Also in 1968, two important provisions were added to AFDC-U. One called for the Secretary of Health, Education and Welfare to prescribe the definition of unemployment rather than leaving it up to the states. (This has not yet been done in a way which assures uniformity of application.) Another prohibited payments to a family on the basis of a father's unemployment for any week in which the father receives unemployment compensation.

Operations

The AFDC program has universal state coverage. The last state plan to be approved was Nevada's in 1955. AFDC is the largest of the federally aided public assistance programs in terms of the number of recipients. The AFDC-U program is not yet universal. As of March 1971, its provisions were in effect in about one-half of the states, as listed in Table A-4.

AFDC Benefits

The Social Security Act requires that an individual's income and resources must be considered in determining his needs, but does not specify a standard or level of living to be used by the states in administering their programs. Each state, therefore,

TABLE A-4. *Aid to Families with Dependent Children*
of Unemployed Fathers
States Participating
February 1972

Provision in effect—24 states:

California	Illinois	Nebraska	Rhode Island
Colorado	Kansas	New York	Utah
Delaware	Maryland	Ohio	Vermont
D. C.	Massachusetts	Oklahoma	Washington
Guam	Michigan	Oregon	West Virginia
Hawaii	Minnesota	Pennsylvania	Wisconsin

Provision not in effect but plan material submitted—1 state: Arizona

Provision not in effect but legislation either
enacted or in process—5 states:

Connecticut	Virginia
Florida	Wyoming
Montana	

Provision dropped from program during 1971—3 states:

Maine
Missouri
New Jersey

Source: U.S. Department of Health, Education and Welfare, Program Characteristics Branch. Telephone interview, February 15, 1972.

defines the income level used to determine who "needy persons" are and the amounts of assistance they are to receive. The income necessary to meet a defined package of "basic needs" in the largest urban or highest cost area within the state is designated the "full standard." Income levels below this amount (if other conditions mentioned in the next section are met) determine financial eligibility.[7]

Each state also establishes a "payment standard" which may be (and often is) the same as the full standard. This is the amount from which income available for basic needs is subtracted to determine the amount of assistance to which a recipient is entitled. For specific assistance groups, however, the largest amount the state will pay for basic needs may be less than the payment standard because of state law or agency regulations. For an individual or family with no other income, this is the total payment which will be made for basic needs. Some characteristic figures are shown in Table A-5. For recipient families of other sizes and with one or two needy adult family members there are formulas in all states which vary the amount of benefits provided. Not only the amounts paid but also the formulas differ in each state and we shall not attempt to summarize them here. The amounts actually paid under both AFDC and AFDC-U are what is important, and this information is shown in Tables A-5 through A-8.

Eligibility

The AFDC program, like others under the Social Security Act, is basically a federally aided state program. The conditions for eligibility are under guidelines established by the Department of Health, Education and Welfare, but do show considerable variation from state to state. The following are general characteristics and provisions in effect June 1, 1970.[8]

---

[7] The "full standard" is mandatory only for AFDC applicants with earned income who have not received assistance in any one of the four preceding months. In other cases, the "payment standard" is used. U.S. Department of Health, Education and Welfare, Social and Rehabilitation Service, *OAA and AFDC: Standards for Basic Needs for Specified Types of Assistance Groups, March 1971*, NCSS Report D-2, March 1971.

[8] U.S. Department of Health, Education and Welfare, *Compilations Based on Characteristics of State Public Assistance Plans: General Provisions in Effect June 1, 1970* (Summary of Jurisdictions, Agencies, and Programs.) This compilation includes the 50 states, the District of Columbia, Guam, Puerto Rico, and the Virgin Islands. For convenience, all are referred to as "states." Our compilations are therefore based on 54 states.

TABLE A-5. *Aid to Families with Dependent Children Monthly Benefit Amounts for Basic Needs under Full Standard and Payment Standard, and Largest Amount Paid for Basic Needs for a Family Consisting of Four Recipients March 1971*

State	Full Standard		Payment Standard		Largest Amount Paid	
Three Highest States						
1.	Alaska	$400	Alaska	$400	Alaska	$375
2.	Maine	349	Maine	349	Mass.	349
3.	Mass.	349	Mass.	349	N. J.	347
Three Lowest States						
1.	N. Car.	$184	W. Va.	$138	Miss.	$ 60
2.	S. Car.	198	N. Car.	158	Ala.	81
3.	N. Mex.	203	Texas	179	S. Car.	103
Average all states		$280		$262		$219

Source: U.S. Department of Health, Education and Welfare, NCSS Report D-2, March 1971.

To be eligible for AFDC, one must first have a family containing at least one dependent child. The federal statutes define a dependent child as one under the age of 18, or age 18 to 21 if in school or taking vocational training. Seventeen states, however, also specify with varying exceptions that children 16 to 17 must also be attending school. All of the states except two also require a recipient to be a resident of the state at the time of application. However, since the 1969 Supreme Court decision in *Shapiro* v. *Thompson*, no durational requirement can be imposed. A "resident" is a person living in the state voluntarily with the intention of making his home there. Nineteen states provide for payments made on behalf of an unborn child. Only one state (Texas) requires a recipient to be a citizen of the United States.

A "dependent child" is more than one who meets the residency requirements and is under a specified age. The federal statutes define a dependent child as one who has been deprived of parental support or care by reason of the death, continued absence from home, physical or mental incapacity of a parent or unemployment of the father who is living at home, in a foster home or certain private child-care institutions. The plans of all of the states follow the federal definition with variations. "Continued absence from home" must be for longer than a specified waiting period when involving desertion, abandonment, or separation (although not necessarily imprisonment or military service) in seven states. Nine states similarly set a time for which "incapacity of a parent" must be expected to continue before granting eligibility. Finally, as we have already seen, only twenty-four states provide aid to children of unemployed fathers. A number of states also place restrictions on living with relatives of greater distance, and twenty have attempted definitions of and restrictions on the "suitability" of the home.

As with the Food Stamp program or other public assistance programs based on need, to participate in the program one must show a defined financial need. The federal requirement on the state plans is simply that they define the level of need they will support, that they disregard earnings of children under 14, earnings of full or part-time students, and that for other individuals included in the assistance group, the first $30 of total monthly earnings plus one-third of the remainder be disregarded. Individual states provide further income exclusions, either in lump sum or because it is earned by a child or set aside for future education. If the remainder, after these exclusions, is such that it does not provide a "standard of living compatible with decency and health" or some other such general provision (defined as the "full standard" or "payment standard"), all states except two will provide aid. Of the other two states, one (Oklahoma) sets a specific limit ($310 per month per family) and one (Michigan) specifies a budget deficit ($4 of family requirements in excess of net income).

The state plans also impose limitations on non-home real property, personal property, and financial assets. These range from a low of $150 for the primary recipient and $50 for each additional family member in Illinois to a high of $1,800 for the primary recipient and $3,000 for the entire family in Texas. There are so many variations in between that it is very difficult to tabulate these limitations. (For example, some state plans mention that limitations exist on specific types of assets, but neglect to specify what the limitations are.) In general, they run $500 to $800 per recipient and $1,000 to $1,500 per family. These limitations are somewhat more restrictive than those for food stamps in most states. About half the states' plans also have provisions prohibiting the transfer or assignment of property without adequate consideration prior to application for public assistance, but this condition is only as good as the administrative mechanism designed to verify it.

Finally, the states' plans for assistance eligibility sometimes contain additional special restrictive provisions. Twenty-three states, for example, require that an employable parent must not refuse available employment if suitable plans can be made for the care of children. (This is a separate condition from AFDC-U or the federally required referral to the Work Incentive Program, and refers primarily to mothers.) Two states require that conferences on the matter of employment be held with the recipients, fifteen states require that incapacitated parents must not refuse remedial medical treatment or vocational rehabilitation, and three states require that children over 16 not attending school be referred to WIN for job training and employment. These, then, are the major provisions of the state plans affecting program eligibility.

Use

Use of the AFDC and AFDC-U programs are shown in Tables A-6 through A-8. In Table A-6 can be seen the dramatic increase in program utilization in recent years, not only in levels of expenditures, but also in rate of use. Table A-7 shows the month-to-month growth in both AFDC and AFDC-U, and calls attention to the higher average monthly payment per family in AFDC-U which is mostly a result of the larger family size found in this program (5.1 persons per family for AFDC-U compared with 3.8 in AFDC). Table A-8 shows the use of AFDC-U in a single month by persons in those states which offer the program. It also shows the wide difference in average family benefits, which range from a low of $131 in West Virginia to a high of $307 in Pennsylvania and $358 in Hawaii.

TABLE A-6. *Aid to Families with Dependent Children and Aid to Families with Dependent Children of Unemployed Parents Recipients and Expenditures 1936-1971*

Fiscal Year	AFDC			AFDC-U
	Avg. Monthly No. recipients (000,000)	Rate[a]	Expenditure for assistance (000,000)	Expenditure for assistance (000,000)
1936	n.a.	n.a.	$ 43	n.a.
1938	n.a.	n.a.	84	n.a.
1940	n.a.	n.a.	123	n.a.
1942	n.a.	n.a.	157	n.a.
1944	n.a.	n.a.	136	n.a.
1946	n.a.	n.a.	173	n.a.
1948	n.a.	n.a.	326	n.a.
1950	n.a.	n.a.	520	n.a.
1952	n.a.	n.a.	547	n.a.
1954	n.a.	n.a.	561	n.a.
1956	n.a.	n.a.	639	n.a.
1958	n.a.	n.a.	815	n.a.
1960	n.a.	n.a.	1,021	n.a.
1962	n.a.	n.a.	1,339	n.a.
1964	n.a.	n.a.	1,537	$109
1965	4.2	45	1,589	125
1966	4.4	47	1,734	154
1967	4.7	52	2,043	146
1968	5.3	58	2,536	177
1969	6.1	68	3,142	192
1970	7.4	85	4,074	n.a.
1971[b]	9.4	n.a.	5,658	413.3

Source: U.S. Department of Health, Education and Welfare, Social Security Administration, *Social Welfare Expenditures Under Public Programs in the United States, 1929-1966*, Research Report No. 25, Office of Research and Statistics; Social and Rehabilitation Service, *Trends in AFDC, 1965-1970*, NCSS Report H-4, National Center for Social Statistics; *id., Public Assistance Statistics* (monthly), NCSS Report A-2, National Center for Social Statistics, compiled from individual monthly reports 1971; and *id., Annual Report*, 1964-1969.

[a] Child AFDC recipients per 1,000 children under 18 in population.

[b] Subject to revision.

TABLE A-7. *Aid to Families with Dependent Children and Aid to Families with Dependent Children of Unemployed Parents Recipients and Expenditures July 1970-June 1971*

Month	Number of Families (000)		Number of Recipients (000)		Payments to Recipients (000,000)		Average per family	
	AFDC	AFDC-U	AFDC	AFDC-U	AFDC	AFDC-U	AFDC	AFDC-U
July 1970	2,206	101	8,445	534	$403.4	$24.8	$183	$246
August	2,269	105	8,659	592	419.9	25.8	185	246
September	2,332	109	8,873	563	443.8	26.6	188	243
October	2,400	119	9,104	608	451.1	28.6	188	240
November	2,475	140	9,390	712	453.9	32.6	183	233
December	2,552	157	9,657	796	484.3	35.9	187	227
January 1971	2,587	155	9,773	779	482.4	37.6	186	243
February	2,634	163	9,952	827	484.6	40.1	184	246
March	2,705	173	10,166	868	511.8	41.6	187	240
April	2,726	171	10,227	861	505.4	41.0	185	240
May	2,740	164	10,212	827	503.5	39.4	184	240
June	2,747	158	10,224	794	511.4	39.3	183	247
Monthly average	2,531	143	9,557	730	471.3	34.4	185	241

Source: U.S. Department of Health, Education and Welfare, Social and Rehabilitation Service, *Public Assistance Statistics* (monthly), NCSS Report A-2, National Center for Social Statistics. Compiled from individual monthly reports, all subject to revision.

UNEMPLOYMENT COMPENSATION

Unemployment Compensation (or "insurance") is part of the broad spectrum of social insurance programs, and provides cash benefits to regularly employed members of the labor force who become involuntarily unemployed and who are able and willing to accept suitable jobs. Although unemployment compensation was established by the Social Security Act of 1935, the federal government does not exert great influence over either the administration or the funding of the program. Funding is not raised from general revenues, but rather from a tax imposed on employers.

Administration

Unemployment Compensation is primarily a state-administered program. The federal act provided an incentive to the states to establish their own unemployment insurance plans by imposing a federal tax, 90 percent of which could be offset by employer taxes paid under state laws meeting certain general standards. The tax, of 3.0 percent on the first $3,000 of annual wages of

TABLE A-8. *Aid to Families with Dependent Children*
of Unemployed Parents
Recipients and Expenditures by State
June 1971

State	Number of Families	Payments to Recipients (000)	Average per Family
California	61,900	$14,194	$230
Colorado	2,100	569	266
Delaware	170	31	178
D.C.	540	107	198
Hawaii	710	255	358
Illinois	15,000	4,257	284
Kansas	910	233	256
Maine a	870	183	210
Maryland	640	131	204
Massachusetts	2,300	910	255
Michigan	9,300	2,829	304
Minnesota	1,000	325	316
Missouri a	620	106	173
Nebraska	220	44	202
New Jersey a	15,500	3,940	254
New York	18,900	5,229	277
Ohio	8,500	1,800	212
Oklahoma	360	73	201
Oregon	3,600	683	192
Pennsylvania	3,400	1,044	307
Rhode Island	820	193	236
Utah	1,800	440	247
Vermont	430	131	303
Washington	4,900	1,118	230
West Virginia	3,800	496	131

Source: U.S. Department of Health, Education and Welfare, Social and
    Rehabilitation Service, NCSS Report A-2, *Public Assistance Sta-*
    tistics June 1971, Table 8, Subject to revision.

a These states have subsequently dropped the program.

b Includes special grants not included in average per family.

an employee, was originally imposed on all employers having eight or more employees in covered employment in twenty weeks of the year. All of these conditions have by now changed, but the principles remain the same.

All of the states have approved unemployment insurance programs, and because it is a state program, there is wide variation among the states with respect to specific provisions. Employers who are subject to these programs pay their state tax and receive credit against their federal tax. The remaining federal tax (about 0.4 percent of the covered payroll) is used by the federal government for federal and state administration (including the operation of public employment offices) and to bolster the reserves of the state programs. The state taxes are deposited in the unemployment trust fund in the federal treasury, and from these funds the states make weekly payments to unemployed persons covered by the state laws. Separate accounts are maintained for each state.

The state agencies which administer this program are generally either part of the state department of labor or an independent department or board. They operate through approximately 2,000 local employment offices which not only handle the unemployment claims but provide job-finding and other services. Federal functions are mostly handled by the Department of Labor, although the Treasury Department maintains and invests the trust fund.

History

The development of unemployment compensation was closely alligned with that of workmen's compensation, the idea being that there is no great difference between being unable to work because of injury or being unable to work because of unemployment. John R. Commons, Professor of Economics at the University of Wisconsin, is generally credited with implementing this movement, and his state passed the first such unemployment bill in 1932. Unlike any previous systems, the Wisconsin act provided that contributions were to be paid solely by employers. The economic theory of the law was based on Professor Commons's belief that industry should be penalized for what he considered the chief cause of unemployment—overexpansion of credit in boom times. Thus he assumed that the risks of unemployment are comparable to those of work accidents and both are a part of overhead. Bills reflecting this attitude were introduced to the Wisconsin legislature in 1921, 1923, 1925, and 1929. In 1932, a bill was finally passed which modified few of the professor's ideas.

This bill established a compulsory state unemployment reserve to be financed by a tax on employers (2.2 percent on wages up to $3,000). It paid benefits of $10 per week for ten weeks after a two-week waiting period. The bill was hotly contested by managements, who claimed that the existence of these taxes would make the state's output uncompetitive and would make the state unattractive as a place for new companies to locate. As a result of these pressures, unemployment insurance plans spread slowly, and by 1935, only four additional states had passed such laws, none of which were yet effective. To escape the Wisconsin plan, some employers left the state, but it did them little good. The federal Social Security Act, in 1935, largely followed the Wisconsin plan, only increasing the taxes and raising the benefits.

In the years since 1935, there have been a great many changes in the federal unemployment compensation laws and literally thousands of them on the state level. The only one which we shall deal with in this section was the modification, in 1939, which took railroad employees out of coverage under the regular state plans and established for them a separate unemployment compensation system. The reasons for this change involved the difficulties of establishing equitable payments to employees working across state lines and the difficulties encountered by the railroads in having to make reports in every one of the states in which they were doing business. These difficulties are no longer relevant, but the separate program remains. It requires higher taxes on a higher base pay than is the rule under the state plans, and pays higher benefits for a longer period of time with no waiting period delay. Most importantly, from our viewpoint, it has since 1953 allowed benefits to strikers and nonstrikers idled during labor disputes by their refusal to cross picket lines of other unions.

Other program developments since 1935 have dealt principally with changes in coverage and modifications in the scope and level of benefits. Separate federal unemployment programs now exist for exservicemen and federal civilian employees.

Operations

The Social Security Act did not establish or make mandatory unemployment compensation laws. The Act constituted enabling legislation allowing the states to do so, imposing a tax structure which greately encouraged them to do so, and establishing minimum conditions for their programs if they participated. Each state determines specific qualifications for benefits (e.g., allowable reasons for job separation), specific interpretation of terms (e.g., "able to work," "available for work"), and other conditions such as allowable earnings when unemployed.

The federal act does stipulate situations where a state cannot deny aid to an otherwise eligible applicant, particularly if he refuses to accept new work because (1) the job opening is available because of a strike or lockout, (2) the wages or conditions are substantially less favorable than those prevailing for similar work in the locality, or (3) the job requires an individual to join, resign from, or refrain from joining a bona fide labor organization.

When a worker is unemployed, he reports to the local employment office, where, if the office cannot place him in a suitable job, he may file a claim for benefits. These are paid to the worker on a weekly basis in an amount and for a period determined by state law. Generally, the amount is about 50 percent of past earnings, subject to a maximum.

Subject to these federal requirements, the states have considerable discretion in deciding who shall be covered, the amount and duration of benefits, the taxes to be paid, and the procedures to be used for handling claims. For example, a state may include in its own program a provision whereby an employer with low unemployment history may pay a lower tax, or it may adopt a standard tax rate which is different (higher) than the federal rate of 2.7 percent.

Coverage

Unemployment insurance is provided for only covered employment. This relates primarily to industrial and commercial workers in private industry. The federal act excludes from coverage agricultural workers, domestics, certain casual labor, employees in some governmental and nonprofit organizations, the self-employed, and employees in firms of fewer than four workers in twenty weeks in a year. Railroad workers are also excluded, but have their own separate program. Many of the state plans, however, do not exclude all of those excluded by the federal act. For example, about half the states begin coverage on employers with only a single worker, and several state plans cover domestics or agricultural workers. Nevertheless, about 80 percent of the employed wage and salary workers of the country are covered, including practically all of the members of organized labor who could be involved in a strike.

Eligibility

Eligibility conditions, like all other aspects of the individual state provisions, vary greatly, but there are usually these four:

1. The period of unemployment must be longer than some waiting period (usually one week).

2. The claimant must have qualified for benefits by having worked some minimum time in covered jobs. (Usually 15 weeks or $500, sometimes in more than one fiscal quarter.)

3. The individual must have a continuing attachment to the labor force indicated by registration for work at an employment office (and sometimes be "actively seeking work" or show "willingness to accept suitable work").

4. Most states refuse benefits to those who terminate their employment under specified conditions.

The general purpose of these qualifications is to restrict benefits to those who become unemployed through no fault of their own. It is generally held that an employee who voluntarily leaves his job or is terminated through his own fault should take the consequences. The series of disqualifying reasons include discharge for misconduct or cause, dishonesty or criminal acts, voluntarily leaving without good cause, refusal of suitable work, participation or involvement in a labor dispute, pregnancy, customary layoffs of short and known duration, quitting to attend school or become self-employed, and fraudulent misrepresentation.

All of these disqualifications are subject to greatly different conditions under the state laws. The eligibility conditions relating to disqualification of strikers are those of greatest concern to us here, and those conditions are tabulated in Table A-9.

Not all states actually charge employers at the legal maximum rate, and most states reduce the rates charged employers who have good unemployment histories. Under the railroad program, as of 1966, the tax imposed on the carriers was 4.0 percent of a worker's earnings up to $400 a month, and was being collected at the maximum. The tax is imposed entirely on the employer in all states except the following, where the additional rates indicated are charged the employees: Alaska, 0.3 to 0.9 percent; California, New Jersey, and Rhode Island, one percent; and Puerto Rico, 0.5 percent. Employee contributions are usually earmarked for disability insurance.

The amount and duration of benefits is also included in Table A-10. The amount to be received depends on a formula involving some fraction of the high-quarter wage, and is usually designed to be one-half of the weekly wage rate for such a quarter. (A few states modify this to include allowances for dependents.) To be eligible, a worker must have worked a certain number of weeks or made a certain amount of wages during the base period, or both.

Benefits become available in all states except four after a one-week waiting period. In Connecticut, Delaware, Maryland, and Nevada (and under the railroad program) there is no waiting period. They then continue for the lengths of time specified in Table A-10. Under the railroad program, weekly benefits ranged (in 1970) up to $63.50, and were scheduled to be at least 60 percent of the claimant's regular daily rate of pay for his last railroad job during the base year up to the maximum. Benefits are available for 26 weeks, but workers with long service may receive additional benefits in extended periods if they exhaust their rights to normal benefits.

Use

More than any other welfare program, unemployment insurance use varies with the business cycle, and even a mild recession will create a large increase in benefits paid. During fiscal year 1971, benefits of more than $5 billion were paid out under the state plans, and almost $45 million additionally was dispensed under the railroad program. These amounts, for selected years since 1940, are shown in Table A-11, where also are found the monthly average benefits for recent years.

TABLE A-9. State Unemployment Insurance Laws Regulating Eligibility of Strikers

State	Duration of Disqualification		Disputes Excluded				Individuals Are Excluded if Neither They Nor Any of the Same Grade of Them Are		
	During Stoppage Due to Dispute	While Dispute in Active Progress	Other	Employer Non conformity with		Lockout	Partici- pating	Financing	Directly Interested
				Contract	Labor Law				
Alabama		X							
Alaska	X			X	X		X		X
Arizona			X	X	X		X	X	X
Arkansas			X				X		
California		X					X	X	X
Colorado			X			X	X	X	X
Connecticut			X			X			
Delaware	X								
District of Columbia		X					X		X
Florida	X						X	X	X
Georgia	X						X	X	X
Hawaii							X		X
Idaho			X				X	X	X
Illinois	X						X	X	X
Indiana	X						X	X	X
Iowa	X						X	X	X
Kansas	X						X	X	X
Kentucky		X				X	X		
Louisiana		X					X		X
Maine	X						X	X	X
Maryland	X					X		X	X

	1	2	3	4	5	6	7	8	9
Massachusetts	X								X
Michigan		X					X	X	X
Minnesota	X	X							
Mississippi	X					X	X	X	X
Missouri	X				X		X	X	X
Montana	X			X			X	X	X
Nebraska		X					X	X	X
Nevada			X			X		X	X
New Hampshire	X			X			X	X	X
New Jersey	X						X	X	X
New Mexico	X						X		X
New York		X							
North Carolina		X							
North Dakota	X		X		X		X		X
Ohio	X						X		
Oklahoma	X		X			X	X	X	X
Oregon	X	X			X		X	X	X
Pennsylvania	X						X		X
Puerto Rico							X	X	X
Rhode Island		X					X	X	X
South Carolina		X					X	X	X
South Dakota	X						X	X	X
Tennessee	X	X					X	X	X
Texas	X						X	X	X
Utah	X			X		X	X		X
Vermont	X						X	X	X
Virginia	X		X				X	X	X
Washington	X						X	X	X
West Virginia	X			X		X	X	X	X
Wisconsin	X						X	X	X
Wyoming	X						X		X

Source: U.S. Department of Labor.

Note: Various further restrictions are applied by some states in various categories.

TABLE A-10. *Unemployment Insurance Under State Plans
Financing and Benefits by State
April 1971*

State	Legal Maximum Tax Rate[a]	Taxable Wage Limit	Weekly Benefits[a]		Weeks of Benefits	
			Minimum	Maximum	Minimum	Maximum
Alabama	3.6%	$3,000	$12	$ 50	13	26
Alaska	4.0	7,200	23	85	14	28
Arizona	b	3,600	10	50	12	26
Arkansas	4.0	3,000	15	50	10	26
California	3.7	3,800	25	65	14	26
Colorado	3.6	3,000	14	77	10	26
Connecticut	2.7	3,600	20	123	22	26
Delaware	4.5	3,600	10	65	16	26
District of Columbia	2.7	3,000	9	73	17	34
Florida	4.5	3,000	10	47	10	26
Georgia	4.5	3,000	12	50	9	26
Hawaii	3.0	6,000	5	86	26	26
Idaho	5.1	3,600	17	59	10	26
Illinois	4.0	3,000	10	88	26	26
Indiana	3.2	3,000	10	52	12	26
Iowa	4.0	3,000	9	61	11	26
Kansas	2.7	3,000	15	60	10	26
Kentucky	4.2	3,000	12	56	15	26
Louisiana	2.7	3,000	10	55	12	28
Maine	3.7	3,000	10	57	30	26
Maryland	4.2	3,000	13	65	26	26
Massachusetts	4.1	3,600	18	104	30	30
Michigan	6.6	3,600	18	87	11	26
Minnesota	4.5	4,800	15	57	13	26
Mississippi	2.7	3,000	10	40	12	26
Missouri	4.1	3,000	3	57	26	26
Montana	3.1	3,000	13	42	13	26
Nebraska	2.7	3,000	12	48	17	26
Nevada	3.0	3,800	24	67	11	26
New Hampshire	4.3	3,000	13	60	26	26

TABLE A-10.—continued

State	Legal Maximum Tax Rate[a]	Taxable Wage Limit	Weekly Benefits[a]		Weeks of Benefits	
			Minimum	Maximum	Minimum	Maximum
New Jersey	4.2%	$3,600	$10	$ 72	12	26
New Mexico	3.6	3,000	12	58	18	30
New York	4.2	3,000	20	75	26	26
North Carolina	4.7	3,000	12	54	26	26
North Dakota	4.2	4,000	15	54	18	26
Ohio	4.7	3,000	16	66	20	26
Oklahoma	2.7	3,000	16	44	10	26
Oregon	2.7	3,600	20	55	11	26
Pennsylvania	4.0	3,600	11	60	18	30
Puerto Rico	3.1	3,000	7	46	20	20
Rhode Island	4.0	3,600	17	91	12	26
South Carolina	4.1	3,000	10	53	10	26
South Dakota	4.1	3,000	12	47	16	26
Tennessee	4.0	3,600	14	50	12	26
Texas	7.2	3,000	15	45	9	26
Utah	2.7	4,200	10	56	22	36
Vermont	4.4	3,600	15	61	26	26
Virginia	3.7	3,000	18	59	12	26
Washington	3.0	4,200	17	72	21	30
West Virginia	3.3	3,600	12	58	26	26
Wisconsin	b	3,600	11	72	14	34
Wyoming	b	3,600	10	56	24	26

Source: U.S. Department of Labor and Commerce Clearing House, *Unemployment Insurance Reporter*, 1B.

[a] See text for further details.

[b] Arizona, Wisconsin and Wyoming have no legal maximum rate, but had maximum charged rates of 2.7 percent, 4.4 percent, and 2.8 percent, respectively.

TABLE A-11. *Unemployment Compensation*
Benefits under State Plans
and Railroad Programs
Selected Fiscal Years, 1940-1971

Fiscal Year	Benefits Paid under State Plans	Average Monthly Payment per Recipient: State Plans	Benefits Paid Railroad Plan	Average Monthly Payment per Recipient: Railroad
	(000)		(000)	
1940	$ 482,511	n.a.	$ 14,810	n.a.
1945	71,208	n.a.	728	n.a.
1950	1,861,517	n.a.	113,769	n.a.
1955	1,759,873	n.a.	158,663	n.a.
1960	2,356,113	n.a.	215,201	n.a.
1961	3,908,190	n.a.	213,357	n.a.
1962	3,449,189	n.a.	163,249	n.a.
1963	2,955,247	n.a.	122,754	n.a.
1964	2,819,154	n.a.	92,588	n.a.
1965	2,519,514	n.a.	76,657	n.a.
1966	2,131,598	n.a.	52,355	n.a.
1967	1,971,566	$40.81	34,412	$73.85
1968	2,065,529	41.88	41,697	64.82
1969	2,030,599	45.00	40,841	88.50
1970	2,788,435	47.64	35,028	91.91
1971	5,172,886	51.84	44,957	74.44

Source: U.S. Department of Health, Education and Welfare, Social Security
Administration, *Social Welfare Expenditures Under Public Pro-*
grams in the United States, 1929-1966, Research Report No. 25,
Tables 1-6 and 1-7; and *Monthly Labor Review*, various issues.

No statistical use summaries are available covering participation in unemployment benefits by strikers or others involved in
labor disputes under the state plans. These data are available,
however, for strikers covered by the federal railroad program
and are shown in Table A-12. There it can be seen that since
January 1, 1953, when strikers became covered by this plan,
railroad companies have been forced to pay out more than $53
million to help finance strikes against themselves.

TABLE A-12. *Benefit Costs of Strikes in Railroad Industry
1953-1971*

Calendar Year	Benefits Paid		
	Strikers	Non-Strikers[a]	Total
1953	$ 596,300	$ 77,900 [b]	$ 674,200
1954	8,100	140,500 [b]	148,600
1955	4,342,100	1,715,000	6,057,100
1956	81,395	49,493	130,888
1957	870,262	2,582,123	3,452,385
1958	12,000	49,400	61,400
1959	1,190	7,800	8,990
1960	1,961,000	5,066,100	7,027,100
1961	122,143	1,043,874	1,166,017
1962	371,623	3,257,924	3,629,547
1963	2,566,280	1,373,400	3,939,680
1964	2,050,836	977,484	3,028,320
1965	510,780	926,942	1,437,722
1966	176,679	1,180,351	1,357,030
1967	930,530	1,176,547	2,107,077
1968	519,066	1,015,840	1,534,906
1969	308,090	663,640	971,730
1970	12,300	824,975	837,275
1971	4,626,600	11,569,435	16,196,035
Total	$20,067,274	$33,698,728	$53,766,002

Source: Figures compiled by Railroad Retirement Board and provided by
the National Railway Labor Conference.

[a] "Non-strikers" idled during labor disputes by refusing to cross picket lines.

[b] Figures of non-strikers in these years are incomplete.

Appendix B

UNION STRIKE ASSISTANCE DOCUMENTS

UAW Strike Assistance Program

TO ALL LOCAL UNIONS

Greetings: This Administrative Letter revises the Strike Assistance Program in accordance with the action of the International Executive Board on October 6, 1969, and in conformity with the changes adopted by the Special Constitutional Convention on November 8, 1969. The effective date of the changes will be November 10, 1969.

UAW STRIKE ASSISTANCE PROGRAM

1. Strike assistance shall be based on right in accordance with the rules and regulations approved by the International Executive Board.

2. The Strike Assistance Program shall be administered by the International Union, UAW, Strike Insurance Department in cooperation with the Local Union Community Services Committee.

ELIGIBILITY RULES

3. Strike assistance shall be available, UPON APPLICATION, to all members in good standing, who participate in the strike, under the rules established by the International Union.

4. Members must be in good standing BEFORE A STRIKE BEGINS to be entitled to strike assistance provided they meet the other qualifications. (This means that a member must be in good standing the day before a strike commences.)

5. A member in good standing is one who is not IN ARREARS IN DUES AS PROVIDED IN ARTICLE 16, SECTION 7 of the UAW CONSTITUTION.

6. Any member who owes a reinstatement fee, back dues, or a fine shall not be considered to be in good standing and is not entitled to strike assistance.

STRIKE PENALTY FOR DELINQUENT MEMBERS

7. A member who is or becomes delinquent in his dues and later acquires good standing membership by paying his back dues and reinstatement fee prior to a strike, shall be penalized two (2) weeks strike benefits for his delinquency.

PENALTY FOR DELINQUENT MEMBER WHO ESTABLISHED GOOD STANDING MEMBERSHIP

8. For each week during a strike a member waits to put himself in good standing, he loses an additional week strike benefits as a penalty for failure to become a member in good standing.

PROBATIONARY AND NEW HIRES

9. Probationary and new hires may become eligible for strike benefits only if they join the Union by paying the initiation fee and current month's dues PRIOR TO THE STRIKE TAKING PLACE. Failure to pay the initiation fee and the first month's dues will cause them to be ineligible for strike benefits for the entire period of the strike.

MUST BE ON ACTIVE PAYROLL

10. Only members of the Local Union on strike who were on the ACTIVE PAYROLL at the time the strike began, or those who are denied unemployment compensation as a result of the strike, shall be entitled to strike assistance. Members who are sick prior to a strike and are drawing benefits during the strike are not eligible to draw strike assistance.

MUST PARTICIPATE

11. You must PARTICIPATE in a strike activity assigned to you by your Local Union. Participation in the strike shall include services on the community services committee, picket line duty, educational classes, strike kitchen duty, soliciting committee, or lectures or other appropriate activities established by your Local Union.

MUST REGISTER

12. You must REGISTER and make application for strike benefits on the day assigned to you by your Local Union.

BENEFIT CHECK PAYMENT DAY

13. You must pick up your strike benefit check on the specific day assigned to you by your Local Union.

    NOTE!

    (It is physically impossible to register every member on the same day.—We do not have the facilities or manpower to issue the strike benefit checks on the same day. Therefore, it is necessary for you to cooperate with your Local Union by registering for strike benefits on the day assigned to you. It is also important that you cooperate by picking up your check on the day you are asked to be there.)

YOU ARE NOT ENTITLED TO STRIKE BENEFITS:

14. If you are unemployed.

15. If you are drawing sick and accident benefits.

16. If you are drawing workmen's compensation benefits.

17. If you earn $50.00 gross pay or more per week during the strike.

DEFINITION OF FAMILY STATUS

18. A single person is one without dependents.

    A couple means a member plus a dependent.

    A family means a member plus two or more dependents.

19. A person shall be considered a dependent provided that our member makes a substantial contribution to his maintenance and that he or she is commonly accepted as a dependent of our member.

20. A WOMAN MEMBER ON STRIKE SHALL RECEIVE STRIKE ASSISTANCE EQUAL TO THAT OF A SINGLE PERSON IF SHE HAS NO DEPENDENTS. IF SHE HAS ONE DEPENDENT, SHE WILL RECEIVE ASSISTANCE EQUAL TO THAT OF A COUPLE. IF SHE HAS TWO OR MORE DEPENDENTS, SHE WILL RECEIVE ASSIST- ANCE EQUAL TO THAT OF A FAMILY.

21. A man and wife, members of the same household, who are on strike, may apply for benefits as two single persons or jointly as a couple or as a family if they have dependents. If they apply as a family, only one member would make application.

22. Receipt of pensions, survivor benefits, unemployment compen- sation (in New York, Rhode Island and New Jersey), or vaca- tion pay shall not affect the eligibility of the member who is entitled to strike assistance, nor alter the dependency status of a member or his family.

DURATION OF ASSISTANCE

23. A member shall accumulate strike assistance credits beginning with the 8th day of the strike. He will be entitled to strike assistance Monday through Friday on a prorated daily basis.

24. Strike assistance shall be made available to the member be- ginning on the 15th day of the strike.

25. At the termination of a strike, an additional one week benefit will be made available to striking members.

26. Members who are not recalled to work will receive strike assistance until the day they return to work or draw unemployment compensation, if eligible for unemployment compensation benefits.

SCHEDULE OF BENEFITS

27. WEEKLY BENEFITS ARE AS FOLLOWS:

    SINGLE $30.00

    COUPLE $35.00

    FAMILY $40.00

28. A SINGLE PERSON WILL RECEIVE $6.00 PER DAY; COUPLE $7.00; AND A FAMILY $8.00 PER DAY FOR EACH DAY HE IS ON STRIKE, BEGINNING WITH THE 8TH DAY OF THE STRIKE, MONDAY THROUGH FRIDAY.

29. Strike assistance will remain at a constant level for the duration of the strike.

EMERGENCY FUNDS

30. Emergency strike funds will be made available upon a request of a Local Union up to $1.00 per week per participating member beginning the 3rd week through the 7th week; up to $2.00 per week per participating member from the 8th week through the 11th; and up to $3.00 per week per participating member from the 12th week to the termination of the strike.

31. This emergency fund can only be used to strike assistance to meet the emergency needs of our members and their families during the strike period, and only after the International Strike Insurance Department Representative, working in conjunction with the Local Union Community Services Committee, determines that all Local Community Agencies and services have been exhausted.

INSURANCE BENEFIT

32. The International Union, from its Strike Fund, will pay group life, transition, bridge and group medical-hospital insurance premiums for striking members who are entitled to strike assistance, in the event that the company refuses to make any provision for the continuance of coverage of these programs, thus jeopardizing the group life and medical-hospital program of our members.

STRIKE KITCHEN

33. The International Union will furnish each Local Union on strike with necessary monies to maintain a strike kitchen, beginning with the first day of an authorized strike.

OTHER USES OF INTERNATIONAL STRIKE FUNDS

34. Ordinary running expenses of the Local Union, including equipment purchases, are to be charged to the general fund of the Local Union.

35. The International Union will assume the cost of certain reasonable and necessary strike expenditures as authorized by the International Union Strike Insurance Department Representative.

36. Strike funds can only be spent in conformity with the policies of the International Union.

37. At the conclusion of a strike, all International Union strike funds, which have not been used in the conduct of the strike, must be returned to the International Union.

LOCAL UNION APPLICATION FOR STRIKE BENEFITS

38. Local Unions requiring assistance from the International Union must make their application for assistance to their Regional Director.

STRIKE RECORDS

39. All procedural records will be furnished by the International Union and must be used in the expenditure of all strike funds.

Fraternally,

/s/

Emil Mazey, Secretary-Treasurer
and Director, Strike Insurance Department

EM:ph
opeiu42

Source: "UAW Administrative Letter," Volume 21, Number 13, December 17, 1969. Copy of original in authors' possession.

Excerpts From OCAW Strike Manual

CHAPTER VII—WELFARE

A. HAVE THE RULES UNDERSTOOD EARLY.

1. SOME OF YOUR MEMBERS MAY EXPECT MIRACLES FROM THE WELFARE DEPARTMENT. Have it well understood early just what they can expect. Go over this subject with the members BEFORE THEY MAKE THE FINAL DECISION TO STRIKE.

2. THERE IS A LIMIT TO PAYMENTS. Both International defense fund and local welfare moneys are limited. Payments must be small and are paid only in cases of absolute need.

3. THERE ARE TWO POINTS to remember about welfare payments.

    a. No favors can be passed out.

    b. No one should get the idea that it is wrong to accept payments—that it is charity.

4. NO STRIKER'S FAMILY SHALL GO HUNGRY. That is a basic strike rule. Strike welfare is not a disgrace. Self-respecting union people accept welfare payments to help win their righteous battles.

5. PERSONAL FINANCES SHOULD BE PUT IN ORDER. Caution members to do this in advance of the strike. Thus, the need for some welfare payments can be eliminated.

B. ORGANIZE A WELFARE COMMITTEE.

1. THE WELFARE COMMITTEE must closely examine the needs of each applicant for benefit payments. No shirker should receive aid. False sob-stories should be exposed. But, of course, no deserving man should be in need. Every application should be handled as provided for in the form given in the Appendix of this manual.

2. REGULAR HOURS, REGULAR OFFICES should be maintained by the committee. Members should know just when and where they may make application. Interview office must be private.

3. COMMITTEE SHOULD HANDLE ALL REQUESTS. Don't let applicants get started pleading their cases before busy local officers and leaders. Let applications be heard ONLY by the committee. See that the committee treats all cases in a sympathetic manner and with due regard to the applicant's problems. Counselors should conduct the interview so that the applicant leaves in a favorable state of mind. The morale of the strike can be seriously disturbed by a person who goes out peddling a story of inconsiderate treatment.

C. INDIRECT ASSISTANCE.

1. CASH GRANTS ARE NOT the only or even the best means of assistance. *Mobilize the entire community behind the strike.* The welfare committee should see that these sources of help are fully checked:

   a. *Unemployment compensation benefits* (in cooperation with employment committee.)

   b. *Public Welfare agencies*, such as:

      Child Welfare Service (care of children who must be taken out of their homes.)

      Aid to Dependent Children (subsidies to homes so that children can be kept in homes.)

      County Welfare Departments.

      Aid to Blind.
      Aid to Crippled.
      Workmen's Compensation.
      Employment Bureaus.
      Vocational Rehabilitation.
      Old Age and Survivors Insurance (Social Security Board).
      Public Recreation Departments.
      Public Health Departments.
      Visiting Nurses.

   c. *Private welfare agencies. Large cities may have as many as 150 of these.*

      Hospitals, cancer clinics, tuberculosis associations, crippled children societies, hearing-aid-societies, family counseling agencies, child guidance clinics, nurseries, mental clinics, community centers, youth organizations, recreation leagues, Red Cross.

2. *PUBLIC WELFARE AGENCIES WILL BE SYMPATHETIC TO needs of strikers only to that degree in which the union is able to influence their thinking.* You will be competing with pressure put on by the employers. Here are some points to remember in arguing your case.

   a. *Persons who are in need because of unemployment, and are not receiving unemployment compensation, are the responsibility of public welfare agencies.* Responsibility of the government to promote the general welfare of the people is expressed in Federal and many state constitutions. *Public welfare is recognized as the right of the people in need and their worth and dignity as human beings are upheld by its principles.*

    b. A person's eligibility should be determined impersonally, in the light of legal requirements, available funds and fairness to others also in need. Impress on the community and the agencies these points:

> *An individual in need has a right to aid regardless of the cause of his need.*
>
> *Public agencies have a duty to remain neutral in labor disputes.*
>
> *Strikes are lawful acts which result when collective bargaining breaks down.*

3. PRIVATE WELFARE AGENCIES MAY BE PERSUADED TO make a liberal interpretation of their policies. *Salvation Army has said that they are ready to meet spiritual and material needs, solely on the basis of human need and regardless of group affiliation, race, creed, or color. Red Cross policy is that when there is suffering from any cause and fundamental needs are not being met, chapters may participate in extending relief to needy persons. Both of these organizations will be especially sympathetic to veterans and their families.*

4. CONTACT MERCHANTS, BANKS, ETC. *Ask these people to allow postponement of installments and other payments.* Ask them to extent new credit on such essentials as groceries.

Impress on the local business people that your strikers are the backbone of their business—that *their welfare, in the long run, defends on the welfare of the strikers.* Remind them that strikers will remember and appreciate, in better days to come, the good turn extended now.

Source: Oil, Chemical and Atomic Workers, *Strike Manual,* Chapter IV, pp. 22-25.

Index